The Eloquence of Silence

The Eloquence of Silence

Algerian Women in Question

Marnia Lazreg

Routledge New York · London

Published in 1994 by

Routledge
29 West 35 Street
New York, NY 10001

Published in Great Britain by

Routledge
11 New Fetter Lane
London EC4P 4EE

Library of Congress Cataloging-in-Publication Data

Lazreg, Marnia.
    The eloquence of silence : Algerian women in question / by Marnia
Lazreg.
      p. cm.
    Includes bibliographical references and index.
    ISBN 0-415-90730-6 (HB) — ISBN 0-415-90731-4 (PB)
     1. Women—Algeria—Social conditions. 2. Women in development—
Algeria. 3. Algeria—Social conditions. I. Title.
HQ1791.5.L39 1994
305.42'0965—dc20   94-6193
                                           CIP

British Library Cataloguing-in-Publication Data also available.

*To the memory of all the Algerian women
whose lives changed forever on July 3, 1830.*

To my mother and my sisters, Nadira and Mama.

Contents

Acknowledgments

This book survived a fire that engulfed my home when I taught in Amherst, destroying nearly half of the archival research I had done in Aix-en-Provence. It also survived three moves within three years, and two personal tragedies. I am very happy to finally share it with readers. It is clear to me that it could not have been completed without the support that my children, Ramsi and Reda, have given me over the years. Now aged fifteen and thirteen, they essentially grew up with it.

I am grateful to the Bunting Institute, Radcliffe College, and the Pembroke Center for Research and Teaching on Women, Brown University, for giving me fellowships in 1986 and 1985 that helped me to expand my knowledge of feminist theory and begin to take on the challenge of writing about Algerian women. A travel award made by the Mellon Foundation made it possible for me to experience the excitement of doing archival research on nineteenth-century Algeria that involved me personally as much as it concerned my subject matter. I will always remember the sense of awe and the feeling of discovery as I opened the first carton of files on the Arab Bureaus.

My heartfelt thanks go to the numerous women and men who selflessly gave of their time to answer my questions, helped me to get needed sources, or entrust me with their own copies of documents. The staff of the Bibliothèque Universitaire and the Bibiothèque Nationale in Algiers were particularly helpful and encouraging. It goes without saying that I alone am responsible for the interpretations presented in this work.

Last but not least, the memory of my father, my childhood recollections of the numerous women who filled it with their warmth, laughs, and humor, the thoughts of my mother and my older and younger sisters who bravely carved out their own space sustained my effort to salvage women from the doom and gloom of the discursive domination exercised against them in this country.

Note on Transcriptions

In order to ensure accuracy, I have retained the Algerian pronunciation of names of people as well as places; I have transcribed them in a way I feel is more faithful to the original pronunciation. I have kept French names of places where they are commonly used by Algerians, and adopted the Algerian names of places where they are also commonly used by Algerians. I have retained the French transcription of places, as it is familiar to Algerians as well as most people doing research on Algeria.

Introduction

In many ways this book is about understanding historical injustice. It is about the radical changes that affected Algerian women's lives as a result of the wars of colonization and decolonization as well as the establishment of an independent socialist state, all events over which women had little if any control. I initially wondered about the massive literature and works of art about Algerian women produced by colonial writers and artists, crushing women with their authoritative weight as they diagnosed them beyond the pale. I became puzzled when I realized that contemporary authors, some of whom claim feminism as their cover and source of intellectual legitimacy, had not broken away from the colonial mythification of women. I take this discursive form of violence as another instance of historical injustice.

It has always bothered me, as an intellectual, that writers could spin fantastic tales about women whom they know were unable to react to them primarily because they could not read what was written about them. The sense of entitlement that novelists and social scientists felt was undoubtedly a function of the lack of challenge from their subject matter. It is equally disturbing to hear contemporary young undergraduate and graduate students, who never gave thought to the complex dialectic of colonialism, revolution and gender, pass an irreversible judgment on Algerian women by declaring them "oppressed." With one word they erase a rich, difficult and painful history as well as women's struggles through it.

I decided to write a book that would avoid the assumption of an "oppressed" or "passive" subject and that tries instead to examine the interface between historical events and structures such as wars, economic, legal and educational policies, women and men. Although colonialism looms as perhaps the single most important factor in

1

women's lives between 1830 and 1962, it is by no means assumed to be the *cause* of gender inequality. It created the conditions of possibility of the ideologization of women by colonists and colonized alike and their structural silencing. It helped to unify native men's attitudes towards women as well as pave the way for the intrusion of religion in the political arena in contemporary Algeria.

A book about Algerian women raises questions about the existing feminist paradigmatic view of women we have become accustomed to calling "Third World," most specifically women in the Middle East, an area of study that is still confined to a residual categorical space. This book seeks to convey the complexity of women's lives, which so far has been flattened out by the assumption of unmitigated powerlessness. For example, in urban centers one may see a policewoman helping a veiled woman cross the street. The pediatric doctor on duty at Mustapha Hospital in Algiers may be a woman. The judge on a case involving a female suit brought against a state-owned business company is a woman. A young woman sues her father for appropriating an apartment that belongs to her. Examples such as these are as common as examples that illustrate women's vulnerabilities. Both must be accounted for. Herein lies the challenge of studying Algerian women. It will not do to dismiss what is positive as exceptional or class-bound, and uphold the negative as normative and reflective of a flawed culture.

Chapter 1 addresses theoretical/methodological issues inherent in the study of "other" women. It describes strategies used to write across cultures, avoiding the assumption of oppression, and approaching women's lives as expressions of meaningful projects of coping and transcending personal and social vicissitudes. Existentialism and genetic structuralism proved useful in providing me with a perspective that sees women's activities, no matter how mundane, as purposive, thus cautioning against their traditional dismissal as signs of powerlessness. Equally useful is the introduction of the temporal dimension in the analysis of the divergent conceptions and perceptions of cultural difference among colonists and natives.

Chapter 2 is an overview of what life was like immediately before the invasion of Algeria by France. Against the common wisdom held by defenders of the colonial venture, gender relations varied from region to region, and reflected the prevailing mode of production. Algerian society was part of merchant/peripheral capitalism playing a role in the economies of the Ottoman empire and European states such as France. Ottoman rule (even though it became increasingly loose by the end of the eighteenth century), domestic slavery (or the use of slaves for household labor), as well as the capture of Europeans in maritime skirmishes between Algerians and Europeans as a result of the collapse of Arabo-Berber rule in Spain in the sixteenth century combined to reinforce women's family vocation and their sense of place as members of extended kinship groups.

Chapter 3 explores the impact of the colonial war of conquest on women. The French venture radically changed women's (as well as men's) lives. It meant a change in name, as people's names had to be transcribed into Latin script; in identity, as individuals were given a new religious status as "Muslim natives" and women as "Fatmas"; in language, land tenure system, and the political system. To this historical injustice was added the discursive injustice of fictionalizing women's lives.

Chapter 4 specifically addresses natives' perceptions of the new colonial order and the identity changes imposed on women. Dancers and daughters of recalcitrant opponents of colonialism were transformed into prostitutes. The labeling of women as prostitutes, and the French demand for prostitution, betray the colonial gendered double standard. Although patronizing native women by asserting their alleged victimization, colonists used women's sexuality as a commodity.

Chapter 5 explores the contents of cultural nationalism as spearheaded by Ibn Badis and the 'Ulama movement. It is argued that the traditional reference to the movement as "reformist" is a misnomer. Ibn Badis's program was based on resistance to colonial encroachments on Algerian culture. Like colonial authorities, Ibn Badis perceived women as necessary to his goal of ridding Algerian culture of customs inimical to the *Quran* and habits acquired under the French. No reform was brought to the status of women.

Chapter 6 gives a glimpse of women's lived reality by describing the most common rituals and games that set them apart from both native men and French colonists. Women's activities were coherent and consistent, thus making it possible for the family to absorb as well as resist changes taking place outside and within it.

Chapter 7 examines the complex relationship between nationalism, colonialism and gender. Nationalism is seen as the other side of the colonial coin, making it the political phase of decolonization. The very different and specific ways in which women experienced colonialism made their participation in the decolonization movement logical and compelling. That both native male nationalists and French colonists misunderstood women's motives for taking part in the movement only underscores their lack of awareness of the gendered nature of colonialism and decolonization.

Chapter 8 attempts to unravel the ambivalent attitude of the Islamic socialist state towards women. This state formation adopted the sacrificial view of women formulated by the wartime F.L.N., while at the same time enabling women to benefit from some of its universalistic, gender-blind policies. The slow change to a capitalist economy has resulted in an abstract conception of women. Women emerge once again as the ideological pawns in the power politics that pit the F.L.N. against its religiose opposition. The 1984 Family Code, which restricts women's rights in matters of marriage, divorce and inheritance, illustrates the contradictions between the ideal of equality and the requirements of political expediency.

Chapter 9 addresses the various cultural changes and contradictions that have affected relations between women and men since 1962. Such contradictions help to understand the lag between economic change, family law, politics and everyday life.

Chapter 10 analyzes the emergence of academic feminism as well as a women's movement. Both events are marked by women's strong desire to search for an indigenous answer to structural problems. Women's appeals to legal rationality, constitutional rights, Algeria's revolutionary past and state intervention to protect them from institutional discrimination as well as the religious movement underscore both their strength and vulnerabilities.

Chapter 11 explores the contents of the religious movement's conception of the role of women in society. This movement is seen as an heir to the 'Ulama movement in its definition of the proper place for women. However, no matter how central the issue of female sexuality may appear, the religiose movement is not about women. It is about redefining secularism, and about power.

In putting this book together I was reminded of my frustration with the work of a respected student of Algerian society, Jacques Berque, who seemed to constantly backtrack and weave his thoughts in and out of apparently unrelated events and time periods, thus giving his work a fragmentary character. I realize now that he could not do otherwise. The study of Algerian women cannot be divorced from that of the complex and rich history of their country.

The nineteenth century, for example, was crucial in shaping gender relations within the native society and between natives and colonists. Yet this was a "long" century, both in the number of events that took place and in their differential impacts on women and men. It was the century of military warfare, land appropriation, the imposition of French as the official language, fictionalization of natives' lives and rebellions, among other things. Furthermore, these events were experienced differently and meant different things to the Algerians than they did to the new colonists.

The twentieth century is an equally rich and complex century that both consolidated French domination over women and men and put an end to it. It has been the century of the war of decolonization, the creation of a socialist state, the rise of religiosity in politics and the emergence of the women's movement. Any reference to Algerian women's present forces on the writer a foray into the past. I have attempted to give history its due, hoping that it will illuminate the present and help to define a different future.

I have used a variety of sources, primary (through archival research at Aix-en-Provence in 1987) and secondary, to give an initial account of women's lives which I hope will be perfected as time goes by. I have supplemented written sources with interviews and focus group discussions in Algiers and Mostaganem about the role played by religion in women's deportment since the independence of Algeria, with particular emphasis on the meaning of the *hijab*, the 1984 Family Code, the impact of the housing and water shortages on women, and the rise of the religiose movement. I spoke to social scientists from the University of Algiers, and from Wahran, especially the Centre de Documentation des Sciences Humaines in 1984. I supplemented these talks with a focus group comprised of sociology students in Algiers. I also held discussions with female and male lawyers to seek their opinions on the application of the Family Code. I attended weekly sessions of Family Court in the municipal district of Sidi M'hammad and later Belcourt in the summer of 1984 and fall of 1989. I interviewed women from the three main women's associations in Algiers. In addition, I interviewed five older women in their sixties and seventies from Algiers and Mostaganem in 1984 to ascertain whether some of the customs referred to in the colonial literature corresponded to or diverged from the customs with which they were familiar. Over the years I spoke to countless women and men throughout my travels in the country and occasionally served as a correspondent to young women and men seeking to discuss and understand their roles in a fast-changing society.

1

Decolonizing Feminism

> It has already formed its concepts; it is already certain of their truth; it will assign to them the role of constitutive schemata. It's sole purpose is to force the events, the persons, or the acts considered into prefabricated molds.
>
> Jean-Paul Sartre on institutional Marxism.[1]

Writing about women in Algeria has been the most challenging task I have undertaken so far. Not only did it concretize for me the difficulty of doing interdisciplinary research, and raise theoretical/ methodological issues, it has also led me to question the feasibility of writing and communicating across cultures about the subject of women. My project is not to entertain readers with one more exotic tale or shock them with another astounding revelation about womanhood in a faraway place. All I wish to do is communicate in intelligible terms another mode of being female. But this is more easily said than done.

Dealing with a subject with which people in this country are unfamiliar threatens to turn me into a social translator of sorts, a bona fide native anthropologist, writing for others about others. I have always resisted the quasiheroic stance assumed by experts on other cultures, and I have far too many questions about the validity of their knowledge claims to find comfort in mimicking them. My predicament takes on a more complex turn when it is realized that I am not writing "just" about another culture but about women from a culture with a history of distortion. Indeed, Algerian women and their culture have been mystified by more or less well-intentioned social scientists and feminists moved by something akin to missionary zeal.

Difference, whether cultural, ethnic or racial, has been a stumbling block for Western social science from its very inception. Nineteenth-century European ethnology and anthropology were established precisely to study different peoples and their institutions. However, regardless of the conceptual, theoretical, and methodological inadequacies and uncertainties in the works of many classical anthropologists and ethnologists, their interest in "difference" was a function of their desire to understand their own institutions better. This was the case with Durkheim's work on religion, Mauss on exchange and Malinowski on the Oedipus complex, to cite only a few. Although I do not wish to absolve Western anthropology of its Eurocentrism, it showed, at least in its heyday, some awareness of a common denominator between people of different cultures, a *human* bond. The notion of "cultural universals" or that of the "human mind," no matter how problematical, are expressions of such a common link between various peoples.

Contemporary American academic feminism has rejected, if not forgotten, this part of its intellectual heritage. Yet it has failed to do away with the evolutionary bias that characterizes social science in one form or another. In feminist scholarship (with a few exceptions) this bias is embedded in the objectification of "different" women as the unmediated "other," the embodiments of cultures presumed inferior and classified as "traditional" or "patriarchal." This would ordinarily be seen as a theoretical mishap were it not for the fact that academic feminists have generally denounced conventional social science as being biased against women both in its theory and its practice. They have specifically shown that it has reduced women to one dimension of their lives (for example, reproduction and house work) and failed to conceptualize their status in society as a historically evolving phenomenon. Hence, academic feminism has brought a breath of fresh air into the social science discourse on women, and has held the promise of a more evenhanded, more holistic practice. Surprise is in order when one sees that women in Algeria (or in any other part of the Middle East) are still dealt with largely in ways that academic feminists do not wish to be dealt with.[2]

Women in Algeria are subsumed under the less-than-neutral labels of "Muslim women," "Arab women" or "Middle Eastern women," giving them an identity that may not be theirs. Whether the so-called Muslim women are devout, or their societies are theocracies, are questions that the label glosses over.

The one-sidedness of the prevailing discourse on difference between women would appear intolerably grotesque if it were suggested, for example, that women in Europe and North America be studied as Christian women! Similarly the label "Middle Eastern women," when counterposed with the label "European women," reveals its unwarranted generality. The Middle East is a geographical area covering some twenty-one countries (if one counted members of the Arab League) that display a few similarities and as many differences. Yet a book on Moroccan women and another on Egyptian women were both subtitled "Women in the Arab World."[3]

This reductive tendency to present women as an instance of a religion, nation, ethnicity or race is carried over from American feminists' uneasy relations with minority women. African-, Chinese- and Mexican-American women as well as Puerto Rican women have denounced their exclusion from feminist scholarship and/or the distortions of their lived reality by "white," middle-class feminists. They have also noted that academic feminism reproduces the social categorizations and prejudices that are prevalent in the larger society.

Objecting to definitions that reduce women to their skin color, Rosario Morales emphasizes that she wants "to be whole," and reminds her readers that "we are all in the same boat."[4] Going one step further, Mitzuye Yamada inveighs against the burden placed upon individual Asian-American women to "represent" their racial group and speak "in ways that are not threatening to our audiences." In this sense they are made to reinforce the stereotype of the Asian woman.[5]

These relatively new voices express the underside of difference between women, and are a welcome reminder that feminism as an intellectual practice cannot merely rest on the consciousness of wrongs done to *some* women by men. It points to the necessity of developing a form of consciousness among feminists in North America (and in Europe) that transcends their sense of specialness and embraces what is human at the heart of womanhood across cultures and races. Decentering as well as deracializing one's self is a precondition for such a venture. However, it is a complex and difficult one, as it requires giving up a sense of entitlement for some and overcoming disability for others that is undoubtedly grounded in the racialization of one's self. It is remarkable that academic feminists do not tire of referring to themselves as "white" or "of color." Damning the Algerian revolution with a stroke of a pen (over exactly fourteen pages), Sheila Rowbotham, who refers to herself as a "white middle-class woman," sums a complex history as the battle between whites and nonwhites. Although she writes about them, she surprisingly asserts that "I do not know what it is like to be Vietnamese, or Cuban, or Algerian"— all women she classifies as "Black, yellow, and brown."[6] If her color is a barrier to understanding the special circumstances of these women, whence comes the authority that made her define their lives and characterize their roles in history? What gives legitimacy to her work on women whom she admits she does not understand? Is it the very color she uses as a shield to both empower herself to write and protect herself from criticism?

Third World women in the United States who have expressed their anger and disappointment at being objectified as the irrevocably unmediated other have also assumed that very otherness. They refer to themselves as "women of color," another linguistic sleight of hand ostensibly meant to supplant but that in fact merely recycles the old expression "colored women," the racist connotations of which need no elaboration. This expression has acquired common currency and is used by academic feminists apparently as a way of recognizing the existence of difference between women. The inability to examine the language in which difference is expressed renders ineffective objections to academic feminists' failures to address difference in adequate terms. The language of race belongs to the history of social segregation. To argue that minority and Third World women have adopted the term "women of color" as a liberating means to assert their difference and escape a homogenizing Anglo-American feminist discourse begs the question. By using this label they accept its referent and bow to the social group that gives it currency. As Pierre Bourdieu put it "the constitutive power which is granted to ordinary language lies not in the language itself but in the group which authorizes it and invests it with authority."[7] It is not "women of color" who have the authority to impose the language of race but the women who implicitly claim to have no color and need to be the standard for measuring difference. "Color" does not determine sex, but, like sex, it does become an opportunity for discrimination. Like sex, color ought to be questioned as a significant category in understanding human beings. Why select color and not hair texture, shape of eyes or length of nails to define women? Who is subsumed under the awkwardly expressed and marginally grammatical expression "women of color?" Does it include women who are pink, pasty or sallow-skinned?

This cumbersome term grounds difference among women in biology, thereby presenting academic feminism with one of its most telling contradictions. Feminists have been waging a battle against sociobiology, yet they find themselves reasoning along similar lines when faced with "different" women! The term has become widespread even among feminists who claim to pursue a Marxist or socialist tradition that should have sensitized them to the pitfalls of using race or color as a defining criterion of human beings. The captivating power of the label "women of color" *reinscribes*, with the complicity of its victims, the racialization of social relations that it purports to combat.

Michel Foucault's assertion that "knowledge is not made for understanding; it is made for cutting" illustrates the knowledge effect of this biological language.[8] If there is little knowledge to be gained by identifying difference with color, the process of "cutting," or establishing divisions among individual women, of measuring the distance that separates them from one another, is made easier. Knowledge as cutting is politically grounded and pervades feminist scholarship. The expression, "the personal is political," ought to be amended by substituting race, ethnicity or nationality for the personal.

There is, to a great extent, continuity in American feminists' treatment of difference between women, whether it originates within American society or outside of it. There is, however, an added feature to feminists' modes of representation of women from the Third World: they reflect the dynamics of global politics. The political attitudes of the powerful states are mirrored in feminists' attitudes towards women from economically marginal states in a world rent asunder by the collapse of Communism.

The political bias in representations of difference is best illustrated by feminists' search for the sensational and the uncouth. Mary Daly selected infibulation as the most important feature of African women as reported to her by Audre Lorde.[9] Local customs such as polygamy and/or veiling, wherever they take place, appear decontextualized and are posited as normative absolutes.

The search for the disreputable which reinforces the notion of difference as objectified otherness is often carried out with the help of Third World women themselves. Academic feminism has provided a forum for Third World women to express themselves and vent their anger at their societies. But the Western mode of feminist practice is no free gift, any more than anger is conducive to lucid inquiry. Individual Third World women are made to appear on the feminist stage as representatives of the millions of women in their own societies.

The dissenting voice that objects to the gynocentric language of difference unwittingly reinforces the prevailing representation of herself, if only because she acquiesces in the notion of difference as opposition, as polarity. The totalitarian character of the existing representation of difference appropriates differential items haphazardly, and incorporates them into a structure that becomes autonomous and stands for the lived reality of Third World women. An abstract anthropological subject deemed "oppressed" is thus created. Studying this constructed subject is not for the purpose of understanding her as such as it is to gather documentary evidence of her "oppression." Ironically, the language of liberation *reinscribes* relations of domination.

In assessing the issue of writing about Third World women, Gayatri C. Spivak points out that "First World women" and "Western-trained women" are complicitous in contributing to the continued "degradation" of Third World women whose "micrology" they interpret without having access to it.[10] Although essentially correct, this view obscures the fact that complicity is often a conscious act involving the interplay of social class position, psychological identification and material interests. To include all the "Western-trained" women in the plural "we," which also incorporates "First World" women, is to simplify the reality of the feminist encounter between Western and non-Western women. Some Third World women find comfort in acquiring a Western-style feminist identity that presumably dissolves their cultural selves and enables them to take their distance from those who resist looking at themselves through Western feminists' eyes. The problem for Third World women is that their writing is constrained by the existence of an imperious feminist script. Thus, instead of being emancipatory, writing for them is often alienating. Their satisfaction, if any, derives from the approval they receive from their Western counterparts, or the ire they draw from them if they attempt to rewrite the script.

Identity Politics and Feminist Practice

Asian-American feminists have pointed out that Third World feminists feel under pressure to choose between their feminism and their ethnicity or culture. This identification of feminist practice with Western culture has resulted in a contest between those who affirm their ethnicity or culture against "feminism" seen as a monolithic system of thought and behavior, and those who flaunt their feminism against their culture, implying that feminism stands above culture. Thus Third World female intellectuals find themselves either defending their culture against feminist misrepresentations or reveling in the description of practices deemed disreputable, but always sensational, in an attempt to reaffirm the primacy, validity and superiority of Western feminism.

A focus on the phenomenal manifestations of difference between women has also resulted in a crude politicization of race, ethnicity, color and/or nationality. Women speak as embodiments of these categories. It is only when a feminist's practice is racialized, ethnicized or nationalized that it somehow becomes worthy of interest. This form of identity feminism is sustained by the extension of standpoint theories to larger constituencies of women. Standpoint knowledge is in effect a *representation* of activity instead of the situated truth it purports to be.[11] By claiming standpoint as a foundation of knowledge, academic feminists have *produced* an activity that stands above and beyond a simple intervention of women's experience in constituted knowledge. When used by racialized women, standpoint knowledge yields an inverted double representation. They represent themselves in terms that already subsume and contain their representation.

The politicization of race, color, ethnicity and nationality is also the expression of a form of adaptation to the salience of racial thinking in the post-Civil Rights, post-Cold War era. The prevailing racialization of power relations in American society (which the corrective of affirmative action had already made palpable) is countered by the use of race/color, ethnicity and nationality as grounds and strategies of contention and resistance.

Among Third World academics this trend transcends the bounds of a simple awareness of ethnocentrism and cultural imperialism. It seeks to recenter existing knowledge, whether feminist or not. For example, Indian scholars have in the last few years focused on colonialism and postcolonialism to account for their own realities. Based on their understanding of the British colonial venture in India, they make generalizations that embrace other colonial situations which thus become ancillary props to buttress the Indian model.[12] The Indian experience, presented as normative, mediates our understanding of colonialism, a phenomenon as multiple and diverse in its expression as it was in its consequences. Such sanskritization of knowledge (feminist or otherwise) is perhaps a welcome change in centuries of Eurocentric knowledge, but it does not transform it. By focusing on India's colonial past, seen as constitutive of Indians' identity, it strikes a nostalgic note for a system of relations that needs to be overcome. In the same vein, the accommodation of African-American feminists to "white," middle-class feminism takes the form of an assertion of Black feminist epistemology grounded in the experience of slavery.[13]

Given this framework, is it possible to do scholarly work on women in the Third World that goes beyond documenting existing stereotypes? How does one put an end to the fundamental dismissal of what Third World women say when they speak a nonstereotypical language? How does one overcome the incipient ghettoization of knowledge about Third World women, who now figure in last chapters of anthologies in a space reserved for "women of color?"

Academic feminist scholarship on American women is generally critical without being denigrating, and therefore leaves hope for a better future for its subjects. American culture is not rejected wholesale, but presented as perfectible. In this respect, feminist critical practice takes on an air of normalcy that is missing in the scholarship on Third World women, especially those from North Africa and the Middle East. It appears as part of a reasonable project for greater equality. Conversely, the Third World feminist critique of gender difference acquires a maverick dimension. It is not carried out from within, with a full knowledge and understanding of the history and the dynamics of the institutions it rejects. It unfolds within an external

conceptual frame of reference and according to equally external standards. It may provide explanations but little understanding of gender
difference. In this sense, it reinforces the existing *"méconnaissance"*
of these societies and constitutes another instance of knowledge as
"cutting." Only this time, the cutters are also those who are generally
"cut out" of the fellowship of sisterhood.

Beyond the Religion Paradigm

I have explained in the past that there is continuity between the
body of literature produced by colonial scholars and contemporary
feminist studies of Algerian women.[14] Colonial critiques of native
women and men centered on Islam (as a religion and culture), which
also happens to play a predominant role in contemporary feminists'
scholarship. Visions of Islam constitute links in a long chain that ties
colonial and feminist practices over the past hundred years. They are
articulated in a paradigm I have referred to as the "religion paradigm," which continues to monopolize and constrain writers' and
their critics' thoughts (including my own) by compelling them to
address its parameters or submit to them. This paradigm has recently
been reinforced by the emergence of religiose movements throughout
North Africa and the Middle East, thereby giving credence to a self-
fulfilling prophecy.

The religion paradigm is steeped in a dual intellectual tradition,
orientalist and evolutionary, resulting in an ahistorical conception of
social relations and institutions. The orientalist tradition supports
the notion that Islam is an archaic and backward system of beliefs
that determines the behavior of the peoples who adhere to it. In the
popular culture Islam also conjures up a medley of images ranging
from the exotic splendor of the Arabian Nights, sequestered oda-
lisques, to circumcised virgins. Fancy and fact mix to create a notion
of massive difference. The language used to define women in North
Africa and the Middle East creates and sustains their irremediable
difference from other women. For example, a translation of French
feminist Juliette Minces's book *Women in the Arab World* (the original
title) bore the title *The House of Obedience* in an attempt to frame
the reader's judgment.

The veil has had an obsessive impact on many a writer. Frantz
Fanon, the revolutionary, wrote about "Algeria unveiled." Reaction
to the abusive imagery of the veil fails to escape its attraction. Fatima
Mernissi titled her first book, *Beyond the Veil*. In the spring of 1990
Condé Nast published an advertisement in the Sunday *New York Times*
portraying a blonde woman modeling a bathing suit. She stood up

waving a diaphanous white scarf above the heads of a group of veiled Moroccan women crouched at her feet. During the Gulf War the media were replete with contrasting images of veiled Saudi women and American women in combat gear. The persistence of the veil as a symbol that essentially stands for women illustrates researchers' as well as laypeople's inability to transcend the phenomenal expression of difference. Besides, veiling is close to masquerading, so that writing about women where veiling exists is a form of theater. Ironically, while the veil plays an inordinate role in representations of women in North Africa and the Middle East, it is seldom studied in terms of the reality that lies behind it. Women's strategic uses of the veil and what goes on under the veil remain a mystery.

Religion is perceived as the bedrock of the societies in which Islam is practiced. In an uncanny way, the feminist discourse on women mirrors that of the theologians. Writers invoke religion as the main cause (if not *the* cause) of gender inequality, just as it is made the source of underdevelopment in much of modernization theory. Two extreme interpretations of women have ensued. Women are seen either as embodiments of Islam, or as helpless victims forced to live by its tenets. Illustrating this second interpretation, a French-Algerian woman named an association she founded the "association of women living *under* Islamic law."

To break out of the totalitarianism of the religion paradigm requires a conception of religion as a process. It is misleading and simplistic to look upon Islam as a text that is learned and faithfully applied by all members of the society in which it is practiced. Emile Durkheim pointed out long ago that even a society of saints would produce its deviants. From a sociological perspective, religion may provide motivation for social action. It may then become secularized. Max Weber explained how this process took place in his controversial study, *The Protestant Ethic and the Spirit of Capitalism*. Religion may also be used as a mechanism of legitimation of inequality, or as a protest against it. Islam should not be analyzed differently from the ways in which other religions have been, without making it meaningless. If it were possible to isolate an independent variable that holds the key to all social ills (as is usually done in the case of Islam) we would undoubtedly have reached the utopia of a positive society that Auguste Comte, the founder of sociology, had in mind.

The point is neither to dismiss the role that Islam plays in women's and men's lives, nor to inflate it. More importantly, it is to study the historical conditions under which religion *becomes significant* in the production and reproduction of gender difference and inequality. The historicization of the relationship between gender and religion permits an appreciation of the *complexity* of the lives of women hitherto subsumed under the homogenizing and unitary concept of "Muslim." This approach further introduces a phenomenological dimension by relying on the lived experiences of women rather than textual injunctions and prescriptions made for them. It also helps to identify and explain lags that often develop between lived experience (in its social, political and economic forms) and religious dogma.

In the Algerian case, to place religion within a historical framework means introducing other equally powerful factors, such as colonialism, development policy, socialism, democratization and so on, that interact with religion in complex ways. Historicizing religion and gender is different from determining how each phenomenon appeared at various points in time. It sheds light on conclusions based on such a limited view of history. For example, one trend of thought maintains that where local customs survived the advent of Islam, women are freer.[15] Another trend points to the deleterious effects that the survival of pre-Islamic customs has had on women whose rights as spelled out in the *Quran* have been violated.[16] What matters is not so much that customs inimical to the Islamic spirit have survived, but through what process religion accommodates practices that appear to contradict its principles.

Thinking Differently About Women

I began this book ten years ago, when I became interested in feminist theory and the role it assigns "other" women. Unhappy with the culturalist conception that attributed to Islam a powerful causative significance, I initially inquired into the conditions under which religious norms did not affect women's behavior by looking at women's involvement in the war of decolonization which took place from 1954 to 1962. As I proceeded to study the social changes that had taken place among women since 1962, it became clear to me that to understand the present I had to understand the past, especially the colonial past which still haunts the present. Colonialism and its interface with the economy and religion overdetermine any study of Algerian women in complex ways that have yet to be understood. I am thus compelled to revisit two formidable realities, colonialism and Islam, that have defeated more than one scholar.

To write intelligibly about colonialism, for a formerly colonized person such as myself, is as difficult as it is to search one's childhood for possible clues to things that happen in adulthood. Besides, the cacophony of voices clamoring about colonial and "postcolonial" discourses has recently filled academic halls so pervasively that it has trivialized references to this most important event of the nineteenth century, and placed an additional burden on those seeking to come to terms with it. Finally, the intractability of the effects of colonial domination on natives' minds and behavior well after its institutional structures were dismantled makes its analysis always frustratingly tentative.

Apart from confronting all the issues pertaining to Third World women discussed above, writing about Algerian women must deal with the crucial problem of the audience it necessarily assumes. I am writing in English about a reality that is generally unfamiliar to an English-speaking audience. The problem is not only linguistic; it is also one of sharing with an audience a history and culture, a frame of mind, significant silences, and a multitude of things that are said but dispense with explanations—all that makes writing a fulfilling and emancipatory act. A solution to the assumption of an audience, without which I could not write this book, came to mind as I remembered a discussion I had in Algiers in 1988 with a young female sociology instructor who had given me her doctoral dissertation to read. In answering a question I had asked her about her lack of reference to the role played by family law during the colonial period, she asserted that "they had no such law then." I suddenly realized how misunderstood and remote was a past that was in fact quite recent for the generation of women who came of age after the colonial era. It is that generation that I have chosen to keep in mind as a fictitious audience that might become real should this book be translated some day. It is a different generation that does not share with its parents a memory of the colonial past, and is increasingly detached from the old agrarian and community-based value system. Through a combination of ill-devised school curricula and exposure to culturally hybrid media messages, it is very naive about its history and cultural roots.

The critical approach adopted in this book and its virtual audience make it an act of transgression. I assume no race, color, ethnicity or nationality as a legitimating ground for writing it. It has no identity politics and does not aim at being politically correct. Algerian women including myself have no privileged "standpoint" or perspective that makes them closer to a feminist truth than any other women. Like many women and men, they are caught up in an intricate historical web from which they are trying to disentangle themselves with the means available to them.

The Question of Method and Theory

Ideally, writing about women in Algeria should be so transparent as to simply reflect their reality unmediated, a sort of "degree zero" writing. Instead it is strenuous. I struggled to avoid being a social translator, just as I struggled to avoid speaking for others who, although very much like myself, might certainly feel differently from me. The most painful struggle was against the temptation to speak in the name of illiterate women who do not have access to the written word. Even if speech is respectful it still has the capacity to silence. I have chosen to let them "speak" by describing the games they played, the songs they sang, the customs they practiced.

Throughout their precolonial and much of their colonial history Algerian women wrote very little, if at all. Having no direct written testimony from women, I decided to have recourse to chronicles, monographs, travelers' accounts and essays written by Algerian men as well as by French men and women. The French colonial sources present a serious problem, as they vary in quality and commitment to colonial ideology. Nineteenth-century, self-serving, colonial accounts of native Algerians are a bizarre mix of curiosity, awe, prejudice, contempt and, at times, romanticism. They yield insight into the colonial psyche and thus help to appreciate the role Algerian women and men played in French colonists' self-understanding. My role in sifting through colonial writings was a delicate one. Having been born during World War II, I am familiar with some of the customs and practices referred to in the literature as well as the changes that have affected them. My personal knowledge, which I supplemented with interviews of women in their seventies, enabled me to have a referent point in determining whether an account was accurate. However, there are problematic practices with which I am not familiar. In this case, I recounted them only if they had been written about by more than two authors.

Given the ideological nature of colonial writings and the sparseness of information about how women lived immediately before the French invasion, I undertook archival research at Aix-en-Provence to examine records kept by the Arab Bureaus during the military phase of Algeria's occupation. I reckoned that these records, confined to reporting daily events that came to the attention of military officers, would be least tainted by personal prejudice. They were. However, my purpose was not to write the history of Algerian women in the nineteenth century, but to get a sense of the dislocations wrought upon them by a radical change in their society.

Studies of Algeria and its people began to take a more dispassionate, even if questionable, and at times objective outlook at the turn of this century, as colonial social science became institutionalized. However, studies of women remained, with a few exceptions, patronizing, one-sided and generally unable to comprehend their subjects' lives. The dearth of information by women in the nineteenth century and the first half of the twentieth century brings up the issue of silence in a multiple form. Silence as the absence of public voice is not synonymous with absence of talk or action. In fact, Algerian women acted throughout their history in ways that made their silence quite eloquent. Their silence was at times *circumstantial*, or the result of social, cultural or personal circumstances, such as trusting that the state would defend their rights and keeping quiet until these rights were grossly violated. At other times it was *structural*, or dictated by historically determined structures such as the colonial requirement that speech be expressed in French, thus disabling those who could not speak the language. *Strategic* silence was and still is a voluntary act of self-preservation when a woman feels it is better to keep quiet than to incur someone's wrath or disapproval.

To capture the richness and fullness of women's lives during the colonial era, and remove them from the crushing weight of colonial misapprehension, I introduced the *time* dimension in my analysis. Algerian women's lives were embedded in a different temporal order from French women, even though they lived during the same time. The time dimension enabled me to grasp the different meanings Algerian women attached to their activities, as well as the hostile or patronizing attitudes that French women exhibited towards those who did not share their time. Cultural temporalities set them apart, but often intersected with economic and political temporalities which brought them together as antagonists.[17]

Finally, accounting for women's lives under conditions of silence poses the question of intersubjectivity in all its starkness. Women's daily activities, the rituals they performed, the games they played, their joys and sorrows constitute the foundation on which families and their reproduction were and still are based. While the contents of these acts may be different, families in other human societies have similar foundations. Negative images of women are so widespread and powerful that they deprive their victims of subjectivity and agency and stand for their identity. The genetic structuralist view expressed by Lucien Goldmann provides a tentative answer to this massive problem that plagues the study of Algerian women. It is based on the principle that all human behavior is significant in the sense that "it can be translated into a conceptual language as an attempt to solve a practical problem."[18] If applied to women, this perspective makes it possible to study them as active agents in their lives instead of passive victims. It sensitizes the researcher to the signifying import of mundane activities, and restores individuality to women where it was annihilated by the unbridled empiricist bias at the heart of the prevailing academic feminist practice. Finally, it helps to problematize the written word when it substitutes itself for women's voices. This is no mean achievement within the Algerian context.

It might be argued that structuralism is structuralism. Calling it "genetic" only underscores its fundamental inability to accommodate the role played by the individual in shaping structures, if not changing them. Perhaps. But the problem is not to choose between structure and individual. Both must be taken into consideration if we are to understand women's (and men's) relation to society and to themselves. The foundation of genetic structuralism is unquestionably a necessary anthropological starting point. In addition, Goldmann's conception of the "transindividual subject" (just like Jean-Paul Sartre's "transcendental ego") constitutes another starting point for exploring the notion of intersubjectivity in the social sciences.[19] The transindividual subject is a construct that incorporates *and* sublates the determinations of social class and class consciousness, ideology and the social frameworks of knowledge. The transindividual subject is also a real subject keenly conscious of these determinations and the influence that the group has on her/his thoughts. More importantly, the transindividual subject is a *critical* subject engaged in a ruthless criticism of all partial worldviews including her/his own.

For Goldmann, this subject aims at reaching what he terms a "maximum class consciousness" that incorporates elements of the consciousness of other classes. This restrictive goal may be enlarged to embrace a multicultural, multisocial consciousness that is aware of social class as well as race and sex divisions. In a word, it must reach for a truly *world* vision, as distinguished from the Weberian "worldview." Such a world vision is predicated upon a decentering of the self that must shed its narrowly defined identity trappings. Presumably, it is more difficult for women and men whose identities are formed in powerful countries to shed these trappings, as they provide a reassuring sense of entitlement.[20] But the transindividual subject is a project-in-the-making and not a preformed mold which women (at least those doing research across cultures) ought to engage.

Writing about women in Algeria is akin to entering the Pascalian wager.[21] It involves taking the risk of sounding naive and utopian, and failing in the attempt to aim at a new form of humanism based on a reassertion of the primacy of the human over the cultural. However, it also brings with it the possibility of winning the wager. Entertaining the thought of research as a wager is accepting the fact that it is uncertain, and that all of us, identity feminists, humanists, hard-nosed scientists and others are part and parcel of the processes that made research on Algerian women fraught with uncertainty, and "expropriated [their] moral outrage."[22]

2

Women in Precolonial Algeria

Algerian Women in History

The advent of Islam divides precolonial Algeria into pre-Islamic and Islamic. Pre-Islamic Algeria is the favorite domain of colonial writers and more recently Kabyle-Berber oppositional intellectuals. They created a symbol of womanhood out of El Kahina (in Arabic, the "diviner" or "sorceress"), a Berber queen from the Djaraoua tribe of the Aurès Mountains, who unsuccessfully fought advancing Arab soldiers in the seventh century.[1] French writers saw in her an African Joan of Arc, and Arab chroniclers lauded her for her courage and her ultimate conversion to Islam. In general, Berbers see her as a symbol of the free woman in opposition to the stereotypical image of the "secluded" Arab woman. But their relation to her is complex, and may reflect a profound ambivalence towards women mediated by their hostility to their Arab compatriots. El Kahina is said to have "adopted" an Arab prisoner, Khaled, who may have tipped off advancing troops who defeated her. Her love for Khaled combined with her defeat to create a problem for Berber men, who explain it away as a mark of a fundamental Berber trust betrayed by a wily enemy. These notable markers in El Kahina's life are thus suppressed and her initial resistance to Arabs is emphasized, while at the same time her defeat is bemoaned as having dashed hopes for freedom and created an indomitable yearning for it. El Kahina's character and its various transformations may be read as a trope for the feminine condition.

In fact El Kahina has no name except the signifier of her gift of seeing into the future. There is no agreement on her real name or age. Her ethnic origins are equally contested. The North African historian Ibn Khaldun claimed her tribe had converted to Judaism. Some contemporary authors tried to prove her Jewish origins, just as others asserted her Graeco-Latin or Christian roots. Her geographical origins place her astride a divided space, Algeria and Tunisia. Claimed by three religions, remaining nameless, idealized by contemporary Berbers, she is the epitome of the appropriate woman whose constructed memory sustains struggles and politics that impact negatively on concrete women. Conversely, the various manipulations of her character point to a conception of women as beings with unstable identities who may be all religions at once, susceptible to molding to fit men's purposes. That contemporary women writers in Algeria hook their political dreams to El Kahina only underscores the symbolic abuse she has sustained.[2] Her humanity has yet to be given back to her.

Other notable but less controversial women marked the history of precolonial Algeria. A legendary figure, Djazya, whose feats were sung in long epic poems, reportedly played a key role in a battle between the Beni Hilal, an eleventh-century invading tribe and their Berber opponents, the Zenata.[3] At the dawn of the colonial era, Fatma N'Soumert, took part in an unsuccessful resistance to French troops in Kabylia in 1854. Charles-André Julien, a major French historian of colonial Algeria, devotes one sentence to her.[4]

The Algerian countryside and a number of cities are studded with white cupolas erected to honor female Sufi saints. Lalla ("lady") Maghnia, Lalla Sherifa and Lalla Kheira in Western Algeria, and Lalla Imma Tifellut in Eastern Algeria, are among the most notable female saints. Although revered by women, these saints are not expected to right wrongs or relieve personal ills in the same manner and to the same degree as male saints were. A woman visited a female saint's mausoleum as a way of partaking in the saint's grace (or *baraka*), an expression of sisterhood.

Of the nature of gender relations in precolonial Algeria there are only scattered references in French or English that one gleans from travelers' accounts (both native and foreign), diplomats, chroniclers and geographers. Foreigners' descriptions of Algerian customs are notorious for their distortions because of their unfamiliarity with the culture they observed and the general prejudices they harbored against Islam as well as the government of the Regency of Algiers, held responsible for attacks against European ships sailing the Mediterranean without the protection of a peace treaty. Contemporary reconstructions of life in precolonial Algeria (especially Algiers) suffer from a similar anti-Muslim bias compounded by an anti-Turkish prejudice. This is in keeping with a tradition in French colonial historiography that sought a justification for the invasion of Algeria in an assumed Turkish despotism. Finally, reconstructions of precolonial life often focus on Algiers, seen as epitomizing the rest of the country. Because it was the main political center, it is difficult to ignore life in Algiers. However, other cities such as Wahran, Bejaia or Qasantina were equally important.

Precolonial Algeria displayed a variety of modes of sociopolitical control and life-styles. Algiers was a thriving center of trade with European and Middle Eastern nations, and a base of privately and state-sponsored maritime warfare. A special language (made up of Spanish, Italian and Turkish) was used as a means of communication between foreigners who spoke no Arabic or Turkish and the native business community. Europeans captured on the high seas were held in Algiers until they were ransomed out by relatives. They usually worked as domestic servants or in various occupations, depending on their skills. Literature on or by these captives is abundant. However, little is known about the Algerian captives that European ship-owners bought and sold. As a French commentator put it: "In southern Europe, there were as many Muslim slaves as there were Christians in the Maghreb."[5] Europeans referred to Algerian ship activity that began in the sixteenth century as "piracy," thereby obscuring the fact that it initially was a response to the Spanish *reconquista* with its attendant expulsion of Muslims to North Africa, persecutions, pursuits of refugees to the shores of Algeria and attempts at seizing Algerian ports.

Although urban women did not go out without their veils, they were an integral part of Algerian life. In Algiers, they typically awaited the return of the ships from their forays into the Mediterranean, and greeted them from the terraces with the traditional ululations. Women used male European captives to help them to clean their homes, run errands, care for animals and carry their paraphernalia to the Turkish baths. Women did not veil themselves before these captives. The idea behind this practice, which remained in force later during the colonial era, was that no Muslim woman could be interested in a Christian captive. Some women believed that these men "could not see."[6] This attitude was testimony to Algerians' sense of superiority over Christian Europeans, and was noticed by travelers at the time.

Having a captive as a servant was not the monopoly of the rich. "From the royal palace to the most modest household, there are Christian slaves in domestic service" wrote a commentator.[7] Captives were also rented out by diplomats from the Algerian government for their domestic use.[8] Some of them fantasized about the women who employed them, claiming they had fleeting affairs with them. Theoretically sexual encounters were possible but, in fact, quite implausible given the extended nature of the Algerian family, which would have made affairs difficult to keep secret. A former captive, Thédenat, who became minister of finance of the Bey of Mascara in western Algeria in 1758, reported that he had free access to the Bey's household. He allegedly tried hard to ingratiate himself with his master's favorite wife, who wielded influence over her husband. The women for whom he worked were curious about this Christian male, whom they tried to convert to Islam.[9]

Thédenat claims to have seen a young woman caught in a romantic conversation with a captive miller.[10] Both were condemned to death, and subsequently reprieved. He also claims to have had an affair with a Black servant from the royal household.[11] Finally, he reports that the wife of a dignitary caught in an adulterous situation was hanged in the absence of her husband [an unlikely occurrence] while her lover was fined six hundred sequins [*sic*] and received four hundred lashes.[12] The inaccuracy of Thédenat's account can be deduced from his use of the sequin as the Algerian currency. All one can retain from his account is that extramarital affairs existed and did not go unpunished. The prohibition on having sex with European men extended to prostitutes. A violation of this law resulted in death by drowning. In addition, virtuous behavior for a woman was enforced in a city such as Algiers, where a woman caught in romantic company could have her name entered in a prostitution registry. The *Mezouar* or chief of police could delete her name for a fee.[13] It is unclear whether such moral code was enforced to keep women virtuous or to bring an additional revenue to the government.

Prostitutes were recruited among free women from Algiers, Black (usually slave) women who left their employers and women brought in from rural areas. Prostitution was legal, and kept under control. Initially meant to satisfy the needs of the celibate corps of *janissaries* (or Turkish troops that came to Algeria in the sixteenth century), it became less specialized and provided a source of state revenue, as fees were taxed. A request for a prostitute was usually processed through the chief of police, who would authorize the woman to make an appointment with her client. Prostitutes lived in private homes, and were classified according to their age as well as physical attributes.[14] Jewish women were not allowed to engage in prostitution, although a Dutch traveler claims to have visited a house filled with young Jewish prostitutes.[15]

Prostitutes who entertained Turks were exempted from taxes. They usually accompanied members of the military on weekend trips to their country homes, and sang for them in the numerous city cafés. It often happened that a prostitute would be patronized by a steady customer who would ultimately marry her. The practice of marrying a prostitute would persist in Algeria into the 1960s. This denotes a conception of prostitution that was different from that of the French. It was seen as a reproved act performed under duress. Therefore, helping the person who commits it was tantamount to bringing the person back to the faith. Perhaps the concept itself needs rethinking. In any case, while some of these women were able to find suitable husbands, others were sometimes abused by their clients. Among these at first were soldiers recruited from various parts of Turkey. They were often rough with the local urban populations, which tried to avoid them. An eighteenth-century French ambassador wrote that some of these soldiers beat prostitutes, and sometimes succeeded in making the chief of police order the prostitutes to reimburse to their clients the money spent on them.[16]

To prevent unwanted pregnancies, prostitutes used natural contraceptives prepared for them by female healers. Organized prostitution was prevalent in urban centers, primarily Algiers. Even there, according to a diplomat, social cohesion was such that "there are few bastards."[17] In small towns and rural areas family and community bonds made prostitution difficult.

While differences in wealth resulted in differences in status among women, life-styles in urban centers tended to be similar. The concept of social class, especially in its Western cultural connotation, may not be applicable to precolonial Algeria. Ethnic origin for the Turks, kinship and tribe, and clan among native Algerians formed the framework of one's identity. Poverty was not seen as an individual failing, and did not carry with it an insurmountable stigma. A military administrator, head of the Arab Bureau of Laghouat in southern Algeria in the 1860s was able to note that:

> Among the Arabs and even in the lower classes, one notices a decency, a natural dignity, and a sort of nobility in their facial expressions and actions worthy of the most aristocratic classes of our pseudocivilized Europeans. Nothing like this exists among the Middle classes of Europe.[18]

In other words, there was no culture of poverty. Likewise, there were no rigid class barriers that created specific class cultures, as happened in European societies.

Wealthy urban women displayed a surplus of gold jewelry, velvet, silk and satin clothes, and used the services of servants, both male and female. Nevertheless, their lives revolved around the same institutions as less wealthy women, namely the home, the extended family, the *hammam* (or public bath) and the wali's (or saint's) temple. Well-to-do women took an active part in rearing their children just like other women, and often did their own cooking. An observer noted that the "wife of the last but one Dey (or governor), Ali Khodja, prepared *couscous* herself" when her husband invited European dignitaries to dinner.[19] The institution of the *hammam* was, for women, the functional equivalent of the café for men. Here, women had their bodies cleaned, massaged, pampered, and sometimes healed while exchanging views and information about personal and social events. Visits to saints' mausoleums were occasions for congregating and exchanging tips about how to deal with marital or parenting problems, and about the degree of efficacy of the saints' grace. Friday visits to the dead were an occasion for all women to get reacquainted with friends, reflect upon their lives, shed cathartic tears and honor the memory of their loved ones.

Well-to-do women tended to be literate, and were taught to play musical instruments, especially the *'ud*. A whole tradition of refined living centered on women's artistic needlework, and culinary talents was developed, if not introduced, by the women who escaped the Spanish *reconquista*, and found refuge in Algiers and other urban centers.[20]

All women, rural as well as urban, prepared cosmetic products such as henna, soap, hair rinse (*ghassoul*), eye liner (*kuhul*), hair remover and perfume. Throughout the year women produced food, curing olives, preserving vegetables and fruit as well as meat. They also processed sheepskins for domestic use, made mattresses, comforters and pillows with wool, wove thin veils, blankets, men's coats and rugs. Although practiced in urban centers, weaving was primarily the monopoly of women in small rural towns. Before the end of *Ramadan* women also baked large quantities of cakes to exchange with friends, family and neighbors. The stereotypical image of women as unskilled, idle and bored that the French colonial literature propagated in the nineteenth century was a figment of the French imagination.

Girls generally attended school with boys until the age of nine, or were tutored at home. The Algerian traveller, Al Warthilani, wrote that his wife was "a blue-blood, independent, generous, distinguished, noble, and *literate*; she knew about one fourth of the *Quran* by heart, and litanies such as the *Wadh'ifa* of Sheikh Zarrug, and one part of Ibn 'Abi Zaid's *Risala*" (emphasis added).[21] Education was scholastic, based as it was on knowledge of the *Quran* and the Traditions, to which were added grammar, poetry, epistles and often elements of the history of Islam. Higher education was often pursued outside the country in one of the universities of the East, such as Al Azhar in

Cairo or Al Zitouna in Tunis. It is not clear how many women, if any, made it to such universities.

Educational institutions and opportunities were uneven, and varied from region to region. Al Warthilani bemoaned the fact that the Turkish rulers often seized the *medersa* (school[s]) as well as religious foundations which financed education. This, he wrote, "causes the disappearance of education and knowledge."[22] He also noted that in the eastern city of Qasantina the Turks discouraged teaching by religious foundations and seldom built schools. Al Warthilani also felt that the study of history was not emphasized, a fact he contrasted with the pre-Turkish past, when the university of the city of Bejaia boasted seven hundred women among its students.[23] One can surmise that under the Turkish government the education of women suffered as well. However, education was seen as a valuable attribute for women. In 1832, Léon Roches, a one-time convert to Islam, and former secretary to the Emir Abd-El-Kader, met Lalla Yamina, wife of the former Dey of Algiers, who impressed him with her education and independence of mind.[24] He wrote:

> It is generally believed [among the French] perhaps with some reason that the Muslim woman has no culture, and that she aspires to nothing but to please her husband and master, and give him children. As for me, since I have been in this Muslim land, I have been lucky to meet exceptions.[25]

Whether the women he met were truly exceptional or ordinary is not clear. His characterization may very well be a reflection of Roches' unacknowledged prejudice. The women Roches met were born and grew up during the precolonial era, generally seen by the French as having no literate women.

Al Warthilani noted that at least in two towns, Zemmora (Western Algeria) and Setif (Eastern Algeria), women went about unveiled just like rural women, and exhibited a great deal of freedom in their relations with men. In Zemmora he could not help but notice that women

> were ravishing with their black eyes, shapely breasts, and naked arms. They had to be the most beautiful women in the world. Even pious men could not remain untroubled by so much beauty. Husbands were proud of their wives, so it is no use preaching to them the requirements of Muslim law (that is, the veil).[26]

The same author also noticed libertine behavior among women in the city of Bejaia, where "innovative behavior [*bid'a*] has superseded traditional behavior [*sunna*] so that to follow *shari'a* appears innovative. . . . Women and men gather in saints' mausoleums at the end of *Ramadan* . . . to sing and dance, court, and cry of love."[27] Al Warthilani reports that on his pilgrimage to Mecca, women from the Beni Amer tribe traveled with his caravan.

> with their faces, arms and legs uncovered, thus displaying their charms for all to see. Furthermore, they tried to seduce the men who looked at them. I wanted to have them and their husbands observe [Muslim law]. This caused a severe fight . . . . We heard that some of these wicked women went even further. They claimed to hold divine powers when they were in fact slaves to Satan and their own insatiable desires. They offered themselves to men and warned that anyone who rebuked them inevitably met with disaster. A woman would tell a man: "If you don't take me, such and such disaster will befall you." Then, using some subterfuge, she appeared to make her curse materialize. And he who had felt ignorant, abused, cuckholded, defeated, betrayed, miserable, or simple-minded, actually believed that the libertine performed miracles.[28]

This report clearly indicates that relations between women and men varied from region to region, notwithstanding the normative *shari'a*. It is precisely these variations that will become blunted as the colonial era sets in.

Polygamy was practiced by the well-to-do but was not the norm even among them. The last but one Dey, Omar, was monogamous. Similarly, Dey Ahmed may also have been monogamous. He was criticized for having moved "his wife" with him to the Palace of El Jenina on the heights of Algiers instead of leaving her in the Qasbah palace and visiting her there once a week as was customary.[29]

In general, the life-styles of the rich served as a model for the less advantaged to emulate. This is evidenced in the widespread practice among urban women of borrowing gold jewelry from friends and neighbors to adorn themselves at wedding ceremonies. For a woman to appear in public without some gold jewelry was a sign of social failure. What was remarkable was women's willingness to part with expensive jewelry to help one another maintain decorum.

Women derived their social status from their fathers or husbands. In urban centers, ethnicity and wealth constituted the loci of status.

Turks held the apex of the social hierarchy. Offspring of Turkish-native Algerian marriages usually had wealth but few of the privileges that accrued to the Turks. Black women were to be found among servants and as legitimate wives, primarily of native Algerian men. They were brought from the Sudan or Niger by Tuareg merchants. Like Black men, they underwent training in Arabic and religion. Training centers were located in the Tafilalet (Morocco), M'zab (Algeria), and Fezzan (Libya). When freed, slaves joined a Black Corporation through which they secured jobs.[30] Black women as well as men often performed magico-religious functions, of which exorcism was a major component. Exorcism ceremonies were widespread in precolonial as well as colonial Algeria. They still exist in the M'zab region. In the eastern city of Qasantina exorcism may not have been the monopoly of Black women and men.

Gender Relations in Rural Algeria

Precolonial Algeria was the territory of the "great tribes," some nomadic, others quasinomadic and still others sedentary. Rural women did not wear the veil, and took part in agrarian activities. The well-to-do among them enjoyed life in what has been termed "large tents" meaning tents made of handwoven wool cloth, and usually filled with comfortable silk and wool cushions. Tents were not always signs of a nomadic life. Some families moved over a vast but well-marked territory to secure pasture for their cattle and sheep as the seasons changed. Others practiced a limited transhumance and had regular dwellings in addition to their tents. Life centered not only on the home, but also on the zawiya (the social and educational services provided by many mosques) and the market, usually held once a week in a neighboring village. Markets were held on different days in different villages, making it possible for people to travel from one place to the other, and come in contact with sellers and buyers from various communities. Unlike Algiers, status in rural areas was based on lineage, education and occupation. Those who claimed descent from the Prophet Muhammad were considered nobility or *shurfa*. Genealogy among the tribes was an important activity. Learned men (especially in religious matters) or 'Ulama, and those who held administrative positions for the Turkish government, the *Beylik*, enjoyed higher status than the tribesmen who lacked access to the centers of power, or could not stake any claim to noble ancestry. These tribes were often referred to as *R'iya* (plural of *Ra'i* or shepherd). Colonial historiography has traditionally represented these tribes as providing the bulk of the taxes exacted by the local functionaries of the Turkish government. In fact over the centuries the government was Algerian, as governors were drawn from individuals of Turkish ancestry born in Algeria. The implications of this status hierarchy for women were twofold. Women married within their extended family or tribe to preserve the purity of their lineage. However, when strategic interests came into play, women married outside the tribe to cement political alliances. Noble women had a strong sense of their pedigree, and frowned upon mismatched marriages. Legends are fraught with references to women who staunchly refused to marry outside their status group.[31]

Rural women wove rugs, blankets, clothes and pillow covers for their use and for the market. Like men, they took part in the network of commercial and cultural exchange that linked rural and urban Algeria. Caravans originating in the Sudan brought to Algeria, the Middle East and Europe gold powder and coins, leather and brass, and took back with them cooking oil, silks and brocades, among other items. The rounding of the Cape of Good Hope caused an irreversible decline in this trade, which shifted to a different route. Equally important was the news that the caravans brought with them from the countries they crisscrossed. In many ways, because political power was less centralized, rural areas enjoyed a freer exchange of goods and ideas than urban centers. Relations between women and men were also generally freer. This is exemplified in the poems that sung of love and romance. The beautiful scenery of the south, with its infinite horizons, cloudless skies and fiery sunsets often served as a backdrop to a poetic form that celebrated nature and women, one blending into the other. Women were sung of as "gazelles," symbols of grace and beauty, or "healers" of men sick with love.[32] Some of these poems were written but were withdrawn from the public immediately after the French invasion as a protection of one's patrimony lest it fell into the invaders' hand. The first such poem was released in 1929 in a modified form, one hundred years after the invasion.

The Nailiyat Case

South of Algiers, on the high plateau of the Sahara Atlas, lie the towns of Bou Saada, Djelfa, and Messaad, forming a triangle at the heart of the Ouled Nail mountain. The Ouled Nail tribe was founded in Bou Saada by a Sidi Nail, a Moroccan who emigrated to Algeria in the sixteenth century.[33] This tribe soon distinguished itself for the freedom its women enjoyed in sexual matters. While only women from the Ouled Nail acquired notoriety, women from neighboring communities of the Ouled Thou'aba, Ouled Sid Ahmed and Ouled Reggad exhibited similar freedom.[34]

Women would typically leave their rural milieu and settle temporarily in one of the nearby towns, where they entertained men with dances and songs. Often young women left with their mothers, grandmothers or aunts, who acted as their chaperons and kept house for them. If a Nailiya (a woman from the Ouled Nail tribe) became pregnant, she kept her child. A baby girl was particularly appreciated. Her aim was to find a suitable husband, and/or save enough money to help her parents out, and to return home where she usually bought a house with a garden.[35] Nailiyat (plural of Nailiya) were not rejected by their relatives and members of their community. After their stint in the town they could marry at home. However, further north their reputation was that of women "without shame." Indeed, to act "like a Nailiya" was an insult among northern women.

A Nailiya was not a prostitute in the sense that we know it today. She did not solicit. Dressed in a flowing satin dress, she usually sat on her porch; if a man caught her fancy, she invited him to her house to have a cup of mint tea, or at times ma hya (a liquor made out of anise). She did not ask for money, relying instead on the generosity of her client. Often, Nailiyat danced in public places at night, using their hands to enact the movements of birds. Their most famous dance was that of the "doves of Mecca," an interesting way of blending pleasure and religion.

During these performances, men watched until a dancer came close to one of them. At that point, the chosen man wetted one side of a gold coin with his saliva and stuck it to the dancer's forehead. After the fall of Algeria to the French, paper money replaced gold coins. The dancer would repeat her dance and approach other men who generally gave gold coins until the performance ended. A Nailiya often sought and had one suitor who visited her regularly before marrying her. Isabelle Eberhardt wrote a moving short story about a young woman from the Djebel Ammour area, who became a dancer while waiting for her suitor with whom she had eloped. The young man was killed before he could marry her.[36]

A notable feature of these performances was the demure deportment of the dancers. There was no orgiastic component to these public gatherings. The graceful movements of the dancers, their beauty, and the ritualistic character of the dances made the performances artistic events. The French traveler, Pierre Deloncle, noticed as late as 1926 that in Laghouat Nailiyat's "deportment is perfectly proper. Even when they enact the most precise love gestures, their faces remain absolutely serious."[37]

When the colonists discovered the Nailiyat they either branded them prostitutes, or waxed lyrical about their presumed ancient origins. To wit:

> From what old and forgotten Babylonian temple
> Have you emerged with such heavy eyelids
> And profiles of proud eagles?
> Majestic dancer with a smiling and solemn face
> Have you sprung from the dawn of times?
> Remote, with a sweep of your skirts,
> You conjure up all of ancient Orient."[38]

A popular notion among colonial travelers had it that Nailiyat engaged in what they perceived as prostitution as part of a rite of passage before marrying. Such an explanation did not take into consideration the fact that these women partook in the generally Islamic culture of their land. Nor did it consider the fluctuating economic conditions under which women and men in the area lived. A quasinomadic and pastoral tribe, the Ouled Nail was also subject to taxes by the Turkish government, payable in gold and silver. This may have constituted a particularly heavy burden in times of drought or other natural calamities.

Yet Nailiyat did not see themselves as prostitutes, and often objected to the degrading ways in which Frenchmen sought to deal with them. Thus, in 1853, Fromentin reported that a dancer interrupted her performance and left the room, "because one of our people allowed himself to be rude to the dancer."[39]

Frenchmen also remarked that Nailiyat danced fully clad. In 1883, a French writer, Masqueray, fell in love with one of the dancers he came to watch, and asked her to "take him." She coyly answered: "If God allowed me I would. But tonight, we are the daughters of *Sidi Abd-El-Kader El Ghilani El Baghdadi*.[40] This dancer in fact told off the Frenchmen by shielding herself behind her culture. Indeed, a daughter of saint El Djilani (misspelled in the quote) could not "take" a Christian man. The grace of her spiritual father (for the occasion only), a saint who lived and died in Baghdad but who had followers throughout North Africa, was meant to make her taboo for the Frenchman. Nailiyat's reluctance to consort with Frenchmen was confirmed by the Algerian male writer, Slimane Ben Brahim, a native of Bou Saada, the capital of the Ouled Nail country. He reported that Ledmia, a Nailiya famous for her beauty, and notorious for her rejection of Frenchmen, was once told that "these noble foreigners came from France expressly to see her." She replied: "May God damn their religion and the religion of their ancestors!" She ultimately yielded to her Algerian male friends and performed before the foreigners.[41] However, it must be noted that these men were presented to her as "noble," which means less objectionable than commoners, and as having come "expressly" to see her. According to the Algerian civility code she had to oblige her friends somehow.

As colonial expansion proceeded and Frenchmen's visits to Bou Saada became frequent, Nailiyat became a tourist attraction. Their performances changed to satisfy tourists' thirst for "oriental" dances. Thus belly dancing soon replaced the coy and theatrical hands performances. Similarly the body clad with satin dresses with long trails became more revealing under its cheap gauze and cotton made in the French city of Lyons. In the words of some observers:

> the royal and elegant clothes you admired on the old Bent Freha [an older Nailiya] are replaced with a rough and excessively short dress, cut out of a silk-like damask cloth with large gold embroideries. It is too stiff with its usual flounces floating ridiculously on the dancer's shoulders and over her black patent shoes.[42]

The town of Bou Saada was advertised in France's travel agencies as a main tourist attraction. Soon, the French *Syndicat d'Initiative* of Bou Saada (an office for the promotion of tourism) determined the contents of the Nailiyat's performances, insisting that they appear naked before their visitors. This enabled Frenchmen, frustrated by the veils that hid women from them in the north, to enjoy the spoils of colonial domination of women in the south. Colonial interference in Nailiyat's lives meant a loss of status of the dancers among their immediate community as well as the larger society. It may be that the derogatory expression "to act like a Nailiya," referring to women who have "no shame," reflects the transformation of these dancers into prostitutes. The old art form was found among older women only. In the 1880s Etienne Dinet (a Frenchman who converted to Islam) and his friend and coauthor, Slimane Ben Brahim, described one of these "old women" dancers in these terms: "under her make up you could see lines so terrible that it was truly amazing that a woman of such an advanced age was still able to exercise the occupation of love-making."[43] Naturally, it did not occur to the writers that this woman, Bent Freha, may have displayed signs of premature aging.

The transformation of Nailiyat into tourist commodities went hand in hand with their classification as prostitutes by the colonial administration. They were issued cards identifying them as such and restricting their freedom of movement. Loss of freedom was perhaps the most poignant dimension of the Nailiyat's new life. Etienne Dinet and Slimane Ben Brahim recount the story of Khadra, a card-bearing Nailiya, who had to bribe a native policeman working for the Arab Bureau of Bou Saada to spend a night outside the Café de la Joie where she performed. Rich clients engaged in similar briberies in order to prevent dancers they liked from leaving the café. Thus, Nailiya were literally prisoners either of the cafés where they performed or of the windowless rooms where they lived. Typically, the man whom Khadra loved, an impoverished tribesman, was killed by a rich client who wanted her for himself. Khadra's story dramatizes the plight of nineteenth-century southern Algerian women whose families were hard hit by a series of economic changes. Like many other tribal communities, the Ouled Nail had suffered from heavy taxation and land appropriation. Khadra's mother was able to retire into a comfortable marriage. However, by the time Khadra became of age, dancing was part of a prostitution act. Khadra had run away from an alcoholic husband whose achievement in life was to be the brother of the head of a religious order. She wound up at the Cafe de la Joie, constantly juggling the conflicting demands made upon her desirable body while her mind was elsewhere.

To entertain their new customers, Nailiyat developed a taste for beer and wine. Becoming a registered prostitute (or "cartées") in the European fashion meant that Nailiyat could no longer free themselves of the onus placed on their new activities. As professional prostitutes, they were subjected to periodic medical controls surprising their French doctors with their "cleanliness," and to scrutiny of their family background.[44]

The Case of the Azriyat

The practice of the Azriyat (plural of Azriya) in the eastern mountain of the Aurès resembled that of the Nailiyat because it was also based on women's sexual freedom. However, unlike their southern sisters, and perhaps because of their more inaccessible geographical location, the Azriyat were untouched by tourism.

Women who were orphaned, divorced, repudiated, widowed or unable to marry at the appointed age became dance performers and engaged in sexual activity with their patrons until they found a husband. This temporary practice cut across class lines and involved women from two specific tribal communities, the Ouled Abdi and Ouled Daoud. Azriyat traveled from village to village in the mountainous area during periods of economic slump. Typically, the Azriya lived alone and received her admirers in her home. If she lived with her family, she had to make sure that her patrons entered her room through a separate door. Like the Nailiya, the Azriya was accepted by her community. She usually kept the children born to her from her patrons, and was invited to baby showers as a way of ensuring that the newborn would be lucky.[45] This superstition may have been due to the belief that if a woman crosses, unscathed, into the world of sex out of wedlock she must be protected by some occult force. Indeed, even though being an Azriya was common and tolerated, it was also perceived as contrary to Islam's precepts. The conflict between the normative and the practical resulted in attributing to the practice a supranatural dimension.

The Azriya's social status derived from her transitional stage as being astride the sacred and the profane. Sexual activity in her case was dictated by economic necessity and other circumstances beyond her control such as widowhood, divorce, parental death, and so on. Being in a transitional state, she represented the struggle of good against evil. Her religiosity was not in doubt, and was expressed in her Quranic chants.[46] In addition, a successful Azriya would attempt to erase her past with a pilgrimage to Mecca, and pious behavior thereafter.[47]

It is sometimes argued that the Azriyat's practice was the vestige of some ancient hetaera ritual. It is perhaps more useful to place it within the context of life in the rough Aurès mountains, where gender relations exhibited distinguishing features. Women here constituted an important part of the labor force. They took part in harvests, shepherding, grinding grains and carrying ploughs on their heads during the annual communal ploughing. Normative rules of conduct often clashed with the rigors of life in the mountains. Communal life made sexual behavior more difficult to control. For example, some young women asserted their independence by eloping with a group of young men, and came back home with the ones they chose as their husbands.[48] Finally, during the spring festival, women were usually relieved of their conjugal obligations.[49]

During the nationalist struggle (1954 to 1962), the Azriya institution, just like that of the Nailiya, came under attack as one of the ills either caused or abetted by a morally corrupt colonial system. A number of Nailiyat joined the nationalist movement, refusing to entertain French men in particular. As for the Azriyat, their activity became more subdued as the Aurès mountains became one of the strongholds of the nationalist movement.

This quick glance at women's past at the inception of the colonial era demonstrates the variable nature of gender relations from urban to rural areas, northeast to south. Although women and men saw themselves as Muslims, their conduct was a function of their location in their family or tribal communities, and at times even their own individual needs. It is precisely this range of variability that will diminish as the colonial system of control becomes established. While both men's and women's lives were affected by colonialism, women experienced it in distinctive ways. A mantle of invisibility descended over Algerian women in the nineteenth century, spun not only by the ideological and contradictory colonial policies but also by natives' responses and reactions to them.

3

The Colonial War in Fact and Fancy

L'Algérie est un pays superbe où il n'y a que les Français de trop.
Théophile Gautier[1]

The question is to determine whether the Orient lends itself to interpretation, and permits it without being destroyed by it.
Eugène Fromentin[2]

Dehistoricizing Algerians

Fromentin's query points to the phenomenon of stripping Algerians of their lived history by subsuming them under the abstract concept of the "Orient," a concept with a French history. Although sympathetic to the natives, Fromentin had unwittingly posed the problem in colonial terms. The orientalization of Algeria meant its dehistoricization. The French fascination with the "Orient," spurred by Napoleon during his foray into Egypt in 1797, could not be satisfied. By moving the borders of the fictional "Orient" squarely to North Africa, the French imagination further contributed to its mystifying import. The French idea of the "Orient" became Algerians' new living space. From now on, Algerians will be figments of the French imagination.

Fromentin's query about the fate of Algeria had long been answered in practice. Algeria had already become a fantasy among military men, newly arrived colonists, travelers, novelists in search of inspiration and painters. To a greater or lesser extent, this motley crowd had "interpreted" Algeria and its people, women and men, before even landing on its shores. The Regency of Algiers had for years been feared by Europeans because of its corsairs. It was also known through the generally fanciful tales brought back to Europe by former captives. Priests were equally responsible for the exaggerated accounts of life in captivity which they needed to make in order to secure the ransoms necessary for the release of the women and men seized on the high seas and held in Algiers.[3]

The Regency of Algiers was shrouded in mystery, where tales of seraglios, gold, strange customs and cruelty excited and angered many a Frenchman. Algerians were known as "Turks," Arabs or

"Moors." They were perceived alternately as violent and untrustworthy ruffians, or as "bearded old men with a stately bearing, draped in clothes harking back to Antiquity, sporting a grave and wise look on their faces."[4]

Seventeenth-century French literature was fraught with plots involving devious "Turks" and scenes of kidnappings, as evidenced in the works of Tristan l'Ermite, Molière, Racine, Voltaire and Régnard (once a captive in Algiers). King Charles V, who led an unsuccessful attack against Algiers, may have contributed to French people's fascination with things "barbaresques." Algerians loomed in the French psyche as people out of time and place, unrelated figures moving in and out of fragmented sceneries having a dreamlike quality. Painters represented Algerians in Roman costume, or wearing feathers in their hair, and smoking peace pipes just like Native Americans.[5] The similarities between the fates of the two people were thus recognized, albeit the purpose of the paintings was less to draw sympathy to the Algerians than to highlight their presumably archaic form of existence. Vindictive irony was not alien to these paintings. Roman costumes were a reminder of Algeria's Roman past, which provided French archeologists as well as administrators with an added incentive to restore this land to what was assumed to be its European origins. Some of French painter Bonnart's plates bore irreverent legends. For example, "This tireless janissary fights night and day. He looks like a good devil in war as well as in love."[6]

Just as the people of Algeria were misrepresented physically, and used as props for costumes of a different time and place, the country itself was given a fanciful geography. A most commonly used map dating to 1745 was based on the sixteenth-century chronicles of an Arab traveler, Hassan Ben Mohammed, also known as Leo the African. It did not show Algeria's main river, the Chélif. It had all rivers run south to north, and placed towns inaccurately.[7] The lack of adequate information on the new colony was compounded by the fact that works written by Algerians on their country in Arabic were not translated by the French until the end of the nineteenth century. It is no wonder that the French imagined Algeria to be

> a big country, almost entirely covered with sand, and the ubiquitous palm trees. Sitting in the shade of these trees, men are found squatting to savor the pungent smoke of an enormous pipe. Nearby, a horse seems to bray triumphantly. In the distance, a strange-looking animal with an uneven back: the camel. Then come the lion and the hyena, a particu-

larly ferocious animal. On the shore, pirates are about to
kidnap a young woman . . . ."

The author of this account adds: "When I try to set the record
straight, I realize that I have convinced no one."[8]

When the invasion of Algeria was decided in July 1830, many French
people felt that it would open the door to the Orient, with its gold
and virgins-in-waiting.

> This perception was confirmed when in Staoueli [a village
> west of Algiers] a Turco-Arab camp fell in our hands. On the
> cushions piled up in the [tribal] chief's tent some convinced
> themselves they saw the imprint of a woman's body. From
> then on, there was not a military recruit who did not dream
> of treasures and odalisques.[9]

While more sober accounts of Algeria began to emerge in the 1840s,
they were still fixated on the "Orient," a symbol of the difference
between the colonizers and the colonized. In this sense, the conquest
of Algeria opened up a new space for French letters, arts and social
sciences. Some of the greatest figures in French literature were unable
to rise above the production of myths about difference. To grasp
the extent to which apparently sound minds could create images so
fantastically at odds with the lived reality of Algerians would probably
require psychoanalysis. The "discovery" of orientalized Algeria, a
mere twenty-four-hour boat journey from the port of Marseilles, was
for the French the functional equivalent of the discovery of Indians
by the Spanish conquistadors. The Spaniards engaged in a debate
among themselves over whether the newly colonized subjects were
to be treated as human beings (meaning children of Christian Adam).
Christianity was to "humanize" Indians. The French encounter with
nineteenth-century Algerians was unmediated. Not even Christianity,
which the colonizers attempted to spread among the natives, could
reform Algerians. It simply made it easier to apply French law to them.
Being Muslims or partaking in Muslim culture essentially meant that
they were irremediably beyond the pale. The issue was how best to
control them.

In the eyes of the French colonists, Algerians embodied absolute
difference. They looked different, dressed differently, had a different
value system, spoke and wrote a different language. Faced with such
a tangible difference, the French could either contain it by creating
special institutions to manage it, or neutralize it by applying to it
laws that destroyed its very foundations. Colonial authorities chose

to do both. While claiming to respect the natives' institutions, they constantly chipped away at them, and sought to subject them to legal norms that obeyed the political imperatives of the new colonial order.

Imagining Women: Virgins Without Souls

All Algerians from all regions were subjects of French imagination. While men lost their appeal to the French after the last tribal rebellions were finally quelled in the late nineteenth century, women never lost their appeal to the French imagination, whether in its literary, anthropological or political expression, until the end of the colonial era in 1962.

Through Algerian women, French male writers could satisfy their own desires to penetrate Algerian men's intimate life by having their wives and daughters as spoils of conquest. At the same time, Algerian women gave French men the opportunity to fantasize about the female sex in general. For, if one stripped the nineteenth- and twentieth-century discourse on Algerian women of its colonial trappings one would uncover French men's own prejudices against women in general. In addition, in Algerian women French authors found an inexhaustible subject to quench the public's thirst for what Fromentin called "the bizarre."[10] They wrote for a French audience about women who did not speak or read their language, and therefore could not agree or disagree with what was made of them. Algerian women were thus thoroughly objectified.

To French female writers, Algerian women provided the opportunity to bolster the colonizers' culture by presenting it as more liberating to women than the native culture was. The fact that French women had not yet received the franchise and lived under conditions that left a lot to be desired was not used as a basis for comparing the similarities between the two categories of women. French women, protofeminist or avowed feminists, generally wrote from a patronizing colonial perspective that equated native women's "emancipation" (a concept dear to colonial writers) with the adoption of French culture. The encounter between French women and Algerian women was thus mediated by the colonial factor which acted as an obstacle to a genuine understanding not only of Algerian women but also of French women's self-assessment.

The numerous novels and short stories that flooded the French market in the second half of the nineteenth century stand as a monument to French delirious fantasy stretched to the limit. It is beyond the scope of this book to do a comprehensive analysis of the colonial literary production of the nineteenth-century. Suffice it to say that

native women were portrayed as ignorant, simple-minded and manip-
ulative. They were always ready to fool a husband or a father to carry
on an affair with a Frenchman. On the simple, childlike characterization of women, poets were undoubtedly more eloquent than fiction
writers. To wit:

> Her colors are as harmonious as a poem
> She is a child, a Moor
> Who, with no more soul than a flower,
> Sings, wild and pretty.[11]

Jules Lemaitre, the author of this poem, truly captured the essence
of the colonial perception of native women as falling outside the space
of culture and history. Indeed, they are part of nature, just like birds
and flowers. This theme also echoed conceptions of women held by
chroniclers such as Clément Lambing, who wrote:

> The fair sex is not altogether fair here, at least in my opinion.
> No one can deny that Arab women have graceful figures and
> regular features, but they lack the essential requisite of
> beauty: a soul and individual expression. They all are exactly
> alike, and their faces express but two passions—love and
> hate; all nice shades of feelings they lack.[12]

The emphasis on "soul" may very well be an oblique reference to
Christianity, which stresses the existence of the soul as distinguished
from the body.

Islam, the religion of native women, was hardly perceived as being
on a par with Christianity, regardless of whether it too acknowledged
the existence of the soul. Being non-Christian, native women were
without religion. Nevertheless, one still wonders how a Frenchman
can write about the topic of native women's souls when he did not
speak their language, therefore being unable to communicate with
them, and had little if any access to them.

The racist implications of Lambing's statement are difficult to ignore. Native women are seen as "all alike." This imposed sameness,
the core of racial and ethnic prejudice, accounts for the tired clichés
found in novel after novel. The notion that native women were simple
characters unable to harbor more than one or two emotions fit neatly
with the conception of the Algerian male intellectuals who received
a French education at the turn of the twentieth century. "He passed
from superstition to the freest thinking. An intellectual and psychic
uprooting has prepared his virgin mind to ideas that sink in deeply."[13]

This allegedly makes for a personality all in contrasts. Many Algerians "resemble characters from Russian novels, subject to quick changes of mood, swinging from cries to laughter, enthusiasm to despondency."[14] It did not occur to the author to inquire into the nature of the education received by native men, as well as the colonial order that sustained it to explain these changes, if they in fact existed as reported. It seems as though "virgin" native men and soulless women could not overcome their simple nature.

The portrayal of native women as simple creatures was also evident in fictional works, where they appeared as indistinguishable from French female characters. As a French commentator put it: "They think, speak, feel like French women."[15] Lacking substance, they were made into mouthpieces of the colonial order. For instance, they looked on their culture as French women would, expressing horror, outrage, and often contempt. The only way for native women to escape their fate was to elope. However, their escapades with Frenchmen rarely led to marriage, if at all, purportedly because of the cultural obstacle. The theme of a Frenchman being loved by both a French woman and an Algerian woman, but marrying the Frenchwoman in the end was so commonplace that it sometimes needed some punch. Thus in reviewing a novel, *Les Borgia d'Afrique*, (a pun on the Bordjiya tribe of western Algeria) written by a Mme P. Coeur, Gustave Flaubert suggested that she give more life to her native character by creating "a scene pitting the Arab woman against the European woman."[16] In reality, the two societies, the natives' and the French, never opened up to each other. As a student of the Maghreb, Jacques Berque, put it: " ... the two groups united neither through love, nor through politics. There were no intermarriages, and no bastards!"[17] In fact, intermarriages existed but were extremely rare. Thus French colonists' imaginary ravings were a response to a need to erase in thought native women's and men's rejection of the new order in deeds.

By the turn of the century, pure fiction gave rise to a concern for realism. Authors like Lucienne Favre, for example, felt that reality was more powerful than fiction. She persuaded her Algerian maid, Fatma, to tell her story, which she wrote down for her.[18] However, if descriptions of native women became somewhat more accurate, their mode of presentation continued to be ideological.

The Flipside of Colonial Fantasy

The fictitious and poetic constructions of native women's and men's characters took place parallel to the military intervention throughout the nineteenth century, euphemistically called "pacification." While authors, women and men, were spinning yarns of impossible love, and fantasizing about native culture, colonial military authorities pursued the concrete agenda of breaking all resistance to French rule over Algeria. Native women suffered from military action as much as men did, but with a difference. As women they were subjected to more indignities than men. They were raped, forcibly held by military officers to satisfy their sexual desires, and often assaulted for the gold jewelry they wore. Such assaults took place on live as well as dead women's bodies.

The French colonial venture in Algeria was as savage as it was protracted. After the collapse of Emir Abd-El-Kader's resistance (1830 to 1844), it took another forty years of episodic rebellions before the country was finally subdued. The history of the captures of Algiers, Qasantina (or Constantine), Mostaganem and Laghouat, among others, is one of massacres of women, men and children. The first thirty years of colonial penetration were all the more brutal in that there were no international rules of warfare upheld. In the words of Général du Barail who took part in the capture of the southern city of Laghouat in 1852

> ... Streets and houses were filled with corpses of men, women, and children whom stray bullets did not spare. ....
> I saw two soldiers from the African batallion known as the "Zéphirs" pull a three-year-old, terror-stricken, poor little Moorish boy from his mother, who had just been disembow-eled with a bayonet.[19]

This little boy was "adopted" by the batallion, which he followed from campaign to campaign, "proud and happy."[20] Women, like men, suffered the pains of defeat. As du Barail pointed out:

> We struck down with the sword all those who resisted, and we sent those who surrendered to swell the miserable ranks of the men, women, and children of Laghouat. They were all prisoners at the mercy of their conquerors, with no convention protecting their lives or property.[21]

Yet, a report written by a Colonel Pélissier asserted that "women and children were respected."[22]

The story of these women, men and children has yet to be told from a noncolonial perspective. We do know that rapes were common and involved women of all ages.[23] Historian Charles-André Julien writes that

... During expeditions, native women who fell in the hands of soldiers could not escape their fate. The Zuaves (a special colonial military corps who took Zaatcha, an oasis south west of Biskra) raped women among piles of corpses. The Goum (a colonial cavalry corps) did not spare the women from the tribes they had already subdued. Canrobert [a miliary chief] came in time to save a "young and strikingly beautiful girl" over whom soldiers were having a fight. Her "clothes were torn" and she looked already "resigned to her fate." Unable to agree on who should keep her to himself, they gave her to the colonel who refused "to make a slave of an Arab girl" and surrendered her to a Qadi [Muslim judge] of the nearest village.[24]

General Lamoricière ordered his staff in the old and puritan city of Tlemcen to "proceed to recruit and set up a special feminine personnel which will bring excitement, if not health, to his men."[25] It was reported that some Spanish women were already making a brisk business selling alcohol and "thin bodies" to colonial troops.[26]

There was also evidence of some traffic in women among the captives. For example, when the Smala (the household and staff) of the Emir Abd-El-Kader was captured, a French administrator asked for and obtained the daughter of the Emir's secretary, Aisha bent El Hadj M'hammed El Kharroubi, from the Duke of Aumale who oversaw the capture.[27]

Women were more vulnerable than men to French troops and their occasional Algerian allies not only because they were women, but also because they were generally unarmed and often wore gold jewelry, an object in demand by the French. Colonial troops were known to have cut off women's ears and hands as a quick way of getting their earrings and bracelets when they seized Algiers. The practice of cutting off ears was often ordered by military chiefs such as General du Barail, who claims that his victims' ears were proof that his execution orders were carried out. A collection of these trophies was kept in the French city of Bordeaux by the family of Carayon Latour, a lieutenant of General Yusuf.[28]

There are few women's accounts of the colonial war years. The following is an excerpt from impressions expressed by an old woman from the city of Blida for the benefit of her grandchildren in 1906:

One day, a dog—may God burn him in his grave; yes, God should burn him just as he burned his Muslim brothers—climbed to the top of the minaret (of the mosque of Sidi

Belqacem, son of Ṣidi El Kebir) and called out: "Listen believers! God wants you to hear this for your own good. You are safe! The Roumi [the Frenchman] has retreated!" So we believed this announcement made by Ben Bahri. People went outside their home unarmed, happy and feeling safe. Unarmed! But the Roumi had surrounded and entered Blida. He sacked the city for two hours. With his sword he struck down women, and if one was nursing, he also killed her baby. As for me, I hid in a zgaou, a large wicker jar where we kept grain. God saved me from death. Oh my dear daughters you should have seen that day! Not a woman escaped except those to whom God gave a long life. Some sought refuge in between the beams of their ceilings. But soldiers pulled them down. Most of the men, like women, hid in the sewer. I remember that day well. It was a Friday and soldiers were given license to do as they pleased. My mother fled with a crowd to the mountain; my sister hid in a dirty water pipe.[29]

Women responded to the colonial invasion in different ways. A young woman is reported to have thrown herself into the Rummel canyon when it became clear that Qasantina, the city where she lived, was about to fall to the colonists. Inland, women encouraged men to resist the invading army, and helped treat the wounded. Some planned battles to avenge their relatives killed by the French army, as was the case of Mahbouba in Western Algeria.[30] Others participated as mounted fighters. Algerian lore was captured by the figure of Messaouda, a young woman reputed for her beauty, whose town *Ksar El Hiran* was attacked in 1842 by troops hostile to the Emir Abd-El-Kader, who attempted to rally the area against the French. As she saw her people losing ground, she ran out, untied her belt, and flung herself in front of the attackers, shouting: "Where are those who sing love for me? Where are our brothers? I would love them to be here. Let them come out and follow me if they don't want me to fall prey to the young Larbaa warriors."[31]

Addressing the role played by native women in the anticolonial struggle, a French woman wrote:

Arab women have helped their husbands so much in defending their motherland against us. If our soldiers cut their ears to steal their large solid gold or silver earrings they too brought some incredible refinement to the mutilation of their invaders.[32]

There was an isolated and less heroic tale of a widow who approached a French military administrator to signify her desire to convert to Christianity. She set off a diplomatic incident between the French military and the local religious authorities.[33] This incident was as spectacular as it was rare.

During the first thirty years of the colonial era women participated in a form of passive resistance. As a colonial writer noted: "Moorish women do not learn any housework skills; they refuse to work as domestic servants."[34] This refusal to cooperate with the new order was best illustrated by parents' reluctance to send their children to colonial schools. In Algiers, in 1845, a Madame Allix proposed to pay girls two francs a month and give them a free meal to entice them to her school. She managed to get thirteen girls, eleven of whom came from poor families.[35] When, in 1839, the French colonial government decided to train a small group of Algerian boys in a special school in Paris to serve as hostages to secure their fathers' cooperation with the colonial order, mothers began to dress their little boys as girls for fear they might be taken away from them.[36]

Socio-economic Impact of the New Colonial Order

The systematic policy of expropriation of land from Algerian landowners, combined with heavy taxation and money devaluation brought about long-ranging changes in the Algerian social fabric. Families found themselves penniless, and had to struggle to make ends meet. Women emerge as victims of a new world of frenzied business transactions which they did not understand. Since Islamic law guaranteed women the right to inheritance, they found themselves at the center of shady dealings between French lawyers, middlemen, money lenders and speculators of all stripes. Male relatives, equally lost in this motley crowd, often acted on behalf of wives and/ or sisters in order to help themselves. The head of an Arab Bureau wrote in 1853:

> It is widely known that there exists in Algeria a type of speculation which consists in buying up the property of natives, and above all those properties which are under expropriation, or which studies may lead one to presume will be necessary for the State. The speculators are aided in their search for these properties by Muslim *agents d'affaires* or *wakil*. . . . They bring before the *qadis* [Muslim judges] supposed proprietors, and above all women, thus obtaining powers of attorney so they can sell property, sometimes everything a family owns.

> Often, it is simply witnesses who come to say that such and such a woman, member of such and such family, declares [that her property may be sold]. In Médéa, a family lost in this fashion everything they owned, including their dwelling, to a European well known for this sort of acquisition.[37]

Women lost a main source of status and income with no possibility of recouping it, given the fact that colonial rule generally meant job scarcity and high unemployment among the native population.

The fact that Muslim courts allowed such transactions to take place should not come as a surprise. First, native courts were placed under colonial control; second, during situations of crises individuals (natives or French) seek to maximize their gains and cut their losses, or simply survive by all means necessary. Women were the weakest link in the chain of colonial domination. Even in cases where Muslim courts ruled in favor of women, colonial justice prevailed. For example, in a litigation over the administration of property placed in trust for her son, a widow, Khadidja Bent Uthman Khodja from Constantine, took her case to a special Muslim court, or *madjlis*, that gave her the custody of her son (and her property). However, the order was overturned by a French court in favor of her opponent, who sought to have access to the property.[38] This case dramatizes the situation of women, caught between the whims and demands, sometimes overlapping and sometimes contradictory, of Algerian and French men.

The new land policies, breaking up indivisible native property that held extended families, if not tribes, together, affected the strong kinship ties that characterized rural society.[39] Orphaned young women as well as women whose socially and economically weakened families were unable to cover over their unwanted pregnancies were driven to urban centers where they sometimes became prey to a new generation of pimps who inducted them in prostitution, as will be discussed in the next chapter. At times, prostitution was a temporary condition lasting until a woman found a husband. This was the case for ten women in the city of Constantine in 1851.[40]

The social disruptions caused by the new colonial order also compelled women to fend for themselves. Court records analyzed by Christelow indicate that, in the 1850s, a number of rural women went to cities seeking justice from husbands reluctant to grant divorce. There were also cases of orphaned women who left abusive husbands to seek redress from city *qadis* who were less likely to know the husbands, and therefore more likely to be impartial.[41] Finally, women were often left with no resources and had to request help from the colonial administration. In 1855, among the people receiving some form of aid from the social welfare office there were 128 old women and 1,107 women with children.[42]

The impact of land properties was compounded by that of famines that took place in the second half of the nineteenth century. A most telling description of the toll exacted by famine on women was provided by Hubertine Auclert, wife of a French colonial judge, and a feminist of sorts, who understood the chauvinism of her male compatriots and to some extent empathized with Algerian women. Auclert's description focuses on Kheira, a woman from the Beni Gharaba tribe that had lost 47,400 hectares of land out of 72,400 to expropriation by the colonial government, heavy taxes and the greed of corrupt administrators.

> Kheira's husband was among those who died of hunger, leaving her alone with a seven-month-old baby. Summoning her last strength, she harnessed her baby on her back and set out for the nearest town. On her way, she bumped into a Frenchman, who hit her with his cane: "Dirty *moukère!*" he exclaimed. "She is drunk on absinth." Kheira fell to the ground, and held up her baby to a Frenchman who was passing by, begging her to take it. She subsequently collapsed, and was taken to a jail, where she died that night. The doctor who examined her the following day declared that she had died of hunger.[43]

Famines exacerbated the plight of an increasingly impoverished rural population. Historian Charles-André Julien pointed out that:

> The rural *fellah* [farmer] was drawn into a vicious circle. If his crop was bad, he could not sow again without buying grains on credit from a European or a Jew at interest rates of forty percent over two months or 240 percent over one year. To pay back his debt, he had to resign himself to misery. If the crop was good, interest rates dropped sometimes to twenty or thirty percent in a single day.[44]

In addition to famines, three more calamities befell Algeria between 1866 and 1868, namely an invasion of grasshoppers that destroyed crops, an epidemic of cholera and an earthquake in the town of Blida.[45]

Charles-André Julien pointedly remarked that the 1868 famine was "particularly hard on women."[46] Auclert was able to capture the poignancy of women's situation. She wrote: "When you land in this paradise on earth that is Algiers . . . what strikes you immediately is the appalling sight of dirty rags piled up in the radiant light of the blue skies."[47] Upon close inspection, these turn out to be women, "sexless and ageless" creatures, walking barefoot and carrying their babies on their backs. They were the wives of the dispossessed tribesmen who, like Kheira, walked to the city in search of food. The city proved to be a disappointment to them as they were "harassed, brutalized, insulted in all languages by all the races that settled on their fathers' territory."[48] Many of these mothers kept their babies alive by feeding them blood drawn from incisions made in their veins![49] It is interesting to note that Auclert does not ask why it was that the colonial government did not attempt to provide food to the starving women and men.

The children left behind by the women who succumbed to hunger were taken over by Msgr. Lavigerie, an advocate of forced conversion of Algerians to Christianity, and baptized into the Catholic faith. They were systematically prevented from having contact with their surviving relatives.[50] Lavigerie claimed to have saved these children from Islam, a religion which, in his view, caused a number of ills, such as "laziness, divorce, polygamy, theft, agrarian communism, fanaticism, and even cannibalism."[51] He forcefully claimed that "they [the children] belong to me" because "I saved the life that is still theirs. Therefore, only force will pull them out of their shelters."[52] Yet, as Julien notes, colonists took a dim view of Lavigerie's proselytizing effort, for they were not willing to give land to these new Arabs even though they had become Christian.[53]

The issue of establishing orphanages for children was debated before the 1868 famine, and before Lavigerie set up his own institution in the Chélif Valley, in Western Algeria. A Muslim body of jurists, the *Conseil de Jurisprudence*, proposed the establishment of orphanages staffed by Muslims. The reaction of the Commandant of the Western town of Sidi-bel-Abbès to the proposal denoted less interest in the orphans than in the legitimacy of the colonial order. He argued that

> In the large population centers where reciprocal interests have brought natives and Europeans closer to one another, in the big cities of the Eastern province where the introduction of our methods has created less resistance among Arabs, an orphanage for young Muslim girls can stop many cases of precocious prostitution, and give the conquered people a lofty idea of our moral principles.[58]

Social Instability and Women's Identity

The nineteenth century was not only marked by a loss of economic security for women, it also ushered in an era of social instability. The relocation of tribes in order to ensure their control meant a forced uprooting of families. Women and men had to adjust to a new environment. Sometimes women witnessed, powerless, the exile of their husbands either to a distant province or to a faraway land. Auclert reports that a French administrator, on a visit of inspection to the tribe of the Ouled Mokrane, caught sight of a beautiful woman, Nedjma, wife of a Mr. Lakhdar, and fell in love with her. On the advice of his friend Chaya, a moneylender, the administrator framed Lakhdar, accusing him of an anti-French plot, and exiled him to Nouméa, Niger. Nedjma was thus appropriated along with Lakhdar's thoroughbred mare, Rihana.[55] Instances such as these underscore the increased vulnerability of women who could no longer rely on their male kin to protect them from male outsiders.

While women grappled with their disrupted lives, French administrators thought up plans to use them as a means of frenchifying Algeria. They proposed that "skillfully arranged marriages" between native women and French men "will succeed in fusing the two peoples."[56] It was also suggested "to send a large number of native children to special French high schools for several years in order to acculturate them."[57] A former head of the police in France, Baron Baude, proposed that "negresses [former Black female slaves] be brought in to become the colonists' wives," purportedly because "there are in fact very few women in Algeria"! Baude also felt that "the negress does not arouse in the white man the revulsion that the negro does in the white woman."[58] The point was to induce the eighty thousand or so French soldiers to remain in Algeria, thereby increasing the size of the population of colonists.[59] To add to this tale of demographic engineering, some colonists also advocated that the ninety thousand French homeless children be brought in from France to settle in Algeria.[56]

Camille Sabatier, a former judge in the city of Tizi Ouzou in the Grande Kabylie argued that "it is through women that we can get hold of the soul of a people."[61] In 1882, he prohibited women from this region to tattoo their faces as was common throughout rural Algeria. According to Sabatier, tattoos "were repugnant to French men." To make native women more attractive to his compatriots, Sabatier proposed that the Governor of Algeria issue a decree permitting the gallicization of Kabyle women's first names. This would facilitate "unions between the sons of our colonists, and the elite among young Kabyle women."[62] A believer in renaming as a way of performing a change of identity, Sabatier had already given Kabyle villages new names, a measure that the native population resisted. He ardently pursued a policy based on the "fertile wombs of Kabyle girls" who will ensure "the perpetuation of our race."[63] He chose the Grande Kabylie as his demographic laboratory not only because he had served there as a judge, and was familiar with it, but also because he belonged to a generation of French colonists who felt that the inhabitants of this region were "pure" Berbers and not Arabs, and could therefore be more suitable to frenchification. Not being an Arab meant for him not being committed to Islam. Naturally, the Kabyle population felt otherwise, even though it admittedly had its own prejudices against non-Berber coreligionists.

Sabatier's hope of perpetuating the colonial order through women was also shared by Auclert, who, despite her awareness of its excesses, saw it as a viable alternative. Thus she advocated that French women enter Algerian homes "on some pretext such as the census, and bring frenchification to their hearth. By entering tents and bolted houses they would introduce Muslim women to our life-style, and ways of thinking."[64] However, Auclert believed that her government was seriously interested in promoting the much touted "assimilation" of Algerians to French culture. In this, her "feminism" fell prey to her commitment to the colonial order, no matter how imperfect and problematic she knew it was.

Auclert's attitude was shared by other colonial women such as Madame Pierre Coeur who was in favor of converting women to Christianity, and gallicizing their names.[65] Unlike Coeur, Auclert understood that her society was male-dominated. She had a sense of her powerlessness as a French woman, to wit: "If French women had the right to vote, their African sisters would have long been delivered of the outrageous practice of polygamy, and the intolerable promiscuity they live under with their cospouses."[66] She nevertheless failed to understand that the ideological system that dominated Algerian women also dominated her. After French women received the franchise in 1947, they became French citizens whose entitlements included partaking in the spoils of the colonial system. They generally perceived their culture to be superior to that of the natives. They could feel sorry for Algerian women, but seldom questioned the role played by the colonial order in their suffering. They never bothered to find out whether polygamy or the chronic immiseration of native women wrought upon them by harsh colonial economic policies hurt them the most.

4

Exposing and Reconstructing Algerian Identity

This century is suddenly upside down and out of kilter . . . For
Algiers, gentlemen, my heart is mourning.[1]
Sheikh Abd-El-Kader on "The Entrance of the French into
Algiers."[1]

Algerians experienced a sense of disorientation, disarray and disorder at the occupation of their country by the French, well captured
by *guwal* (or minstrel) Sheikh Abd-El-Kader. It is thanks to *guwals*
that direct access to Algerians' perceptions of the impact of the new
colonial order on their lives is possible. They were men with a poetic
bent who, accompanied by one or two drummers, went from town
to town alternately speaking and singing about sociopolitical issues.
They often communicated with the public in metaphorical terms, and
articulated its concerns. Attributing their assessments and predic-
tions to Muslim saints at mythical meetings held to discuss Algerians'
fate, *guwals* identified colonial education, prostitution and gender
relations among colonists as the most important signs of a society
"out of kilter." Intertwined with these issues was religion, perceived
as the source of the essential difference between Algerians and colonists and the target of colonial policy.

Transforming Men into Women

From the Algerians' standpoint, the occupation of Algeria by Christian France was an irreverent act. Not only were mosques occupied
by colonial troops and turned into stables and arms depots, but lands
entrusted to mosques by individuals in keeping with Algerian law
were declared property of the French state. In addition, the consecrated formula which *imams* used during their Friday prayer was
changed to suit the interests of the new colonial order. The traditional
prayer invoked God's protection of the Turkish Sultan (the Caliph)
in Istanbul, the ultimate guardian of the Muslim faith. Upon the
occupation of Algiers, Général de Bourmont made the following

51

change: "Oh God strengthen whoever strengthens the Muslim religion."[2] In other words, for the Caliph they substituted the French *qua* Christian invader. In so doing, de Bourmont laid down the ideological foundation of the illegitimacy of French rule. Indeed, military occupation and conquest was one thing; tampering with Algerians' religious self-understanding was another. One minstrel mentions that: "They [the French] came to reveal the Muslims' essence (or "*ser*"). With this information, they will plan a campaign against us . . . . Then they will undertake the destruction of our beliefs."[3] According to Desparmet, who recorded these narratives, the Arabic word used to refer to the uncovering of Muslims' quintessence was *keshf* which means to reveal, to expose. The author's translation of "ser" as secret is grammatically correct but contextually incomplete. In colloquial Arabic "ser" means both secret and essence of something, especially charm. It refers to an intangible quality that accounts for the attractiveness of a person. In other words, this term indicates the specialness of the condition of being Muslim, which was about to be destroyed by becoming vulnerable to the scrutiny of outsiders. French colonization was equated with the appropriation of Algerian people, stripping them of the protective device of their beliefs, thus leaving them exposed to a number of ills brought upon them by the colonists. As is pointed out by the same narrator:

> They [the French] have placed immoral people [prostitutes] at the heart of our city, close to our families. They thus make a double profit: They make money off them, and ruin our values as well as our faith. They will soon exhibit before the public the daughters of Muslims on whose body they will mint money. What an odious business! We will see the Muslim woman sitting at the same table as a Jew, getting drunk under the quietly burning eyes of the true believers. When shall we see a Muslim government extinguish the fire that is consuming us?[4]

Algerians saw French tampering with their religious values as affecting not only their way of life but also their food. A narrative expressed in the future tense, although the reality it referred to was already occurring, warned that:

> They will flood our market with their impure products. The sugar they will sell us will be bleached through a process using bones of forbidden animals [such as pigs, and animals not killed according to the Muslim ritual]. They will mix lard

with their butter. The candles we light to our saints are made with pork [fat] and wax, and the soap they sell us is adulterated. We can no longer live in a state of purity; our prayers are no longer valid. Our body, soiled in more than one way, is but a mass of impurities.[5]

Hence a recommendation that the good Muslim should avoid contact with the outside world, now polluted by the French. The devout Muslim should rarely venture outside of his home. If he must, he should lower his hood over his face and walk with his eyes averted "just like a woman wrapped in her veil."[6] The recurring comparison with women denotes Algerian men's concern with losing all the trappings of masculinity and being rendered helpless, as they perceived women to be. A *guwal* put this point eloquently: "This race [the French] will get rid of all our exemplary heroes, shave our beards [a symbol of emasculation], and forbid us from carrying weapons. And so, it will make us look like women."[7] In addition, the French

will seek to abolish the study of the *Quran* in our schools to separate us from our religion. They will do their best to teach French to our children to turn them into renegades . . . . They will use every trick against the teaching of the holy Book. . . . How could I rally to a people intending to suppress the teaching of the Quran?[8]

The perceived emasculation of Algerian men was not accompanied by a promotion of the status of women. Colonial intervention meant a loss of status for men, now perceiving themselves as reduced to the social status of women, and an equally important loss of status for women, from decent (that is, Muslim) to immoral (used as prostitutes for Frenchmen's gain). To avoid this condition of ritual pollution and loss of status, some Algerians left their country and settled in Syria. Others lived in seclusion. One of these, saint Sidi Halou of Blida, a town south west of Algiers, is said to have kept to his home upon the arrival of the French, leaving it in a coffin on the day he died.[9] It stands to reason that if, among some men, the feeling of shielding one's self from the French meant refraining from interaction with them and their world, it would also signify for women an equal prohibition. The veil became women's refuge from the French denuding gaze. However, its form changed, becoming longer, and it acquired a new significance as a symbol of not only cultural difference but also protection from and resistance to colonial-*qua*-Christian domination. The idea of veiling one's self early, before the onset of puberty, and *voluntarily* became a sign of virtue among many Algerian girls growing up during the colonial era. Thus, *hijab* (protection) became the antidote to *keshf* (exposure). Calling a woman *"mekshoufa"* meant that she was physically exposed *and* morally bankrupt. This was a term of opprobrium that revealed Algerians' conception of colonial domination as physically and morally debasing.

However, men did not have to contend with veils. In due time more and more of them entered the French colonial world through education and/or business activity, while the great majority of women remained outside it. The vulnerability that Algerians felt before French power to peer into their innermost self—their "ser"—was dramatized by intellectuals' refusal to reveal or share their manuscripts with colonial intellectuals. Desparmet bemoaned the "secrecy with which natives surrounded their intimate feelings, and the care they took in hiding their handwritten collections of popular poems from us."[10]

The minstrel who bemoaned the transformations that had already begun to take place among the society of the colonized was both astute and prescient. He focused on the impending loss of memory of the heroic past, the inference being that this can occur thanks to a new, French-controlled education; the state of ritual impurity that causes religious practices to be illicit until a Muslim government is reestablished; a debasement of native women through forced prostitution; and the irruption on the public scene of the French couple, seen as an assault on the natives' sexual mores that did not approve of the public expression of sexuality or intimate relationships. The minstrel waxed eloquent in denouncing this last ill:

> Is it possible that these crude and shameless men [the French] have come to live among us with their blonde women coiffed like virgins with whom they walk, as couples, arm in arm?

These women were further described as "holding without blushing men's looks."[11]

The minstrel's vivid diagnosis of the new colonial order as signifying disorder for the natives will remain a major theme throughout the colonial era. After Algeria became independent, all three issues, education (especially language), religion and gender relations that subsumed the question of prostitution continued to haunt the Algerian government. It is as if the establishment of a colonial government and the cultural ideology it spawned have created an enduring memory of a collective trauma.

Transforming Women into Prostitutes

Prostitution was the first expression of the order of *keshf*, or exposure. As mentioned in Chapter 2, prostitution existed under the Turkish state, but it was both limited and regulated. It catered to the needs of the soldiers serving the state, and some dignitaries. Under French colonial rule, it became part of a system of social coercion that targeted families unwilling to collaborate with the new rulers, as well as a last resource for impoverished or desperate women.

One of the earliest impacts of colonists' control of Algerian women's sexuality was the emergence of sex-tourism, which turned dancers from the south, who were free to marry men of their choosing, into prostitutes. In addition, the radical socioeconomic changes that led to the uprooting and pauperization of the Algerian people up until the late 1870s were accompanied by a loosening of social bonds, making women who were left with no material support more vulnerable to coercion and induction into prostitution. Chapter 2 explained the process whereby dancers such as Nailiyat were turned into prostitutes according to the French model early in the colonial era.

The French interest in prostitution dates back to the invasion. Général de Bourmont issued a law on August 11, 1830, barely a month after he landed in Algiers, mandating a monthly medical visit for prostitutes.[12] Throughout the period of military rule, Arab Bureaus sporadically recorded the number of prostitutes that were brought to their attention. Commentaries that accompanied these records bemoaned the spread of prostitution, which they attributed to the immiseration of women. However, the socioeconomic changes that had affected them since the fall of Algeria were seldom linked to the French. Thus in 1850, an administrator of the Arab Bureau for the Algiers area wrote:

> Without counting the girls who are registered at the dispensary, there exists a large number of girls who indulge in prostitution in all classes of the population. This is one of the saddest consequences of the extreme poverty that we mentioned earlier. Such poverty is caused by some vices inherent in Islamic law, and the great ease with which *qadis* [Muslim judges] allow repudiation. For women who are essentially ignorant, lazy, and unskilled, there is no other means of subsistence than prostitution once their husbands have repudiated them, sometimes after a year or two of mar-

riage, with one or two young children who, according to Islamic law, must remain with the mother.[13]

In other words, prostitution was a natives' problem caused by their failing institutions and their flawed character. The solution to prostitution from this perspective lay in a reform of marriage and divorce law. Yet the colonial administration saw to it that native courts would no longer provide for needy divorced women, as they traditionally did, by cutting out a three-hundred-franc allowance earmarked for that effect. This was the case in the city of Constantine (in Arabic *Qasantina*) as early as 1849.[14]

However, demographic figures for the same year, 1850 (only twenty years after the invasion) indicate that other factors were at play that could explain prostitution; if indeed the activity referred to (which is not described) fits the French definition of prostitution, which rests on sex solicitation for money. For example, the number of deaths exceeded the number of births during the first fifty years of colonial rule. In Algiers, during the period of September to December 1850, there were 385 deaths and 221 births. More men (283) than women (250) died, leaving women to fend for themselves. The number of women charged with prostitution was 95. It is not clear what exactly these women did to be labeled prostitutes. The record indicates that 101 women were treated at the dispensary. Nine of them got married and two had their names crossed out from the register. It is possible that women with venereal diseases were classified prostitutes.[15] Divorces did outnumber marriages, but the number of women classified as prostitutes remained about the same. If prostitution was the result of divorce, the number of prostitutes would have kept pace with divorces. This example simply underscores the fact that in the absence of systematic data on prostitution beginning at least in 1830, no explanation is satisfactory that discounts the impact of the profound structural changes that affected the lives of women and men as a result of the French invasion.

Colonial discussions of prostitution leave the reader with the impression that women automatically turned to prostitution as a viable alternative to the conditions under which they lived. Yet there is evidence that women shied away not only from prostitution, but also from asking for public assistance. For instance, in 1849, in the city of Constantine, a mother with two children, from a "good family . . . could not bring herself to appeal to public welfare preferring to die with her children. Prompt help saved these unfortunate people from a horrible death."[16] Where a public assistance service, or *Maison d'asile* existed, individuals received two hundred grams of dates, 450 grams of bread, one cup of sour milk, eaten between 10 A.M. to 1 P.M., and five hundred grams of coarse couscous, seasoned with oil instead of the customary butter, consumed for dinner at 6 P.M. Upon patrons complaints, "we added a ration of coffee and tobacco, two trivial things which the poor in Algeria consider necessities of life, and of which it would be almost barbaric to deprive them." Patrons could not receive visitors without authorization from the Arab Bureau. In addition, they had to wear a metal identification plaque around their neck. The records do not indicate how many women stayed at these "houses," if any.[17]

In 1898, a document issued by the Governor General in Algiers noted that "prostitution in Algeria is widespread," and proposed to create special neighborhoods for prostitutes, segregated by race, because:

> The Arab man's, the native Israelite's, and the Arab woman's physiology, as well as tolerance of pederasty, and typically oriental ways of procreating and relating to one another are so different from the European man's that it is necessary to take appropriate measures to reduce promiscuity that caused all these ills.[18]

On June 15, 1944, the Prefect of Algiers ruled that women could register for prostitution at the age of eighteen but could not join a whorehouse before age twenty-one. However, "some women may be registered without their consent if issues of morals and public health demand it." Only two of the following offenses can lead to an automatic classification as a prostitute: "solicitation in a public place; patronizing a place of debauchery; keeping company with prostitutes, and male or female pimps; spreading a venereal disease."[19] Prostitutes were divided up into the *primaires* (or novices), and the *cartées* (or card-bearing professionals). The *primaires* could be paroled. Out of the eight hundred prostitutes in Algiers in 1937, two-hundred and fifty worked in whorehouses, while the others worked freely.

In France, a law passed on April 13, 1946 had prohibited the establishment of whorehouses, and punished pimps. Colonial administrators felt this law should not apply to Algeria, because "ethnic conditions are not exactly the same, and metropolitan French laws will not change the natives' ancestral customs."[20] In attempting to describe the colonial society's attitude towards this issue, a Frenchman wrote:

> it may be argued that Algerians are hot-blooded people who may cause disturbances should we open whorehouses. Yet,

there has to be a channel to the passions and vices of the men of this country. The security of our women and daughters depends on it."[21]

In fact, Article One of the 1946 law prohibiting the establishment of whorehouses was applied to France only. In addition, according to the April 24, 1948 law, files were to be kept on prostitutes, including their pictures, and sociobiographical information.[22]

The colonial view of prostitution was thus marked not only by a deliberate neglect of the ways in which colonialism contributed to a flourishing, if not encouraging, of this activity, but also by a constant desire to define prostitution as a sign of deficient moral standards among native people. Thus, "for the Muslim native, as a rule, prostitution is not truly a vice," whereas for Europeans it is "degrading and shameful." "Arabs do not frown upon it. They show towards it a kind of indifference that borders on sympathy." Algerians were seen as rejecting alcohol more strongly than prostitution.[23] The author of this statement, a doctor of public health, expresses apparent astonishment at southern women's pride in their activity, and explanation of it as a result of "*mektoub*" or fate. He failed to understand that by invoking *mektoub*, women wanted to convey the inevitability of their condition under the circumstances. The author adds that Nailiyat do not believe in venereal diseases because "after all very few Muslims have read Pasteur."[24] Yet the women he wrote about knew of syphilis, which they referred to as "*merd el Frendji*", literally the "French disease." Indeed, like tuberculosis, syphilis was, in natives' eyes, introduced by the French to their country.

It is noteworthy that Frenchmen who wrote about prostitution often invoked Nailiyat as examples of the alleged affinity between prostitution and native culture. As one commentator put it "natives cannot be said to have any sense of morality, since the south of Algeria is inhabited by tribes that indulge their women and girls in prostitution as a matter of custom."[25] In this, colonists revealed their bias against Algerian women, whose alleged oppression they never ceased to point out, but whose prostitution they deemed simply inevitable.

Precursors of Algerian nationalism, such as Emir Khaled denounced the colonial administration for tolerating, if not encouraging, prostitution:

The fallacy of protecting individual liberties has been used as a pretext for a complete relaxation of our mores. Prostitutes [literally public girls]—some of whom are ten years old—

move freely in our streets under the indifferent eye of policemen and vice squads.[25]

During the war of decolonization, nationalists charged that French
administrators also condoned the kidnapping of daughters of notable
Algerian men, who were then inducted in rural mobile bordellos (*bor-
dels mobiles de campagne*) for the enjoyment of French soldiers.[27] They
also pointed out that kidnapping was used to discipline fathers who
failed to cooperate with colonial authorities, or who resisted to putting
on a folkloring performance that included women for the benefit of
a passing colonial dignitary.[28] Kidnapping young women was sometimes a vindictive measure taken on behalf of Algerian collaborators
of the new colonial order whose desire for a woman was thwarted by
her parents.[29] If and when parents were able to trace their daughter's
whereabouts, they could buy her back.[30] Finally, nationalists revealed
that the colonial police frequent rounding up of natives for identification control often resulted in women being sent to whorehouses for
failing to produce a proof of their identity.

It goes without saying that native men were implicated in the prostitution of women. Women running away from an unhappy marriage,
seeking work or escaping the opprobrium of an unwanted pregnancy
migrated to nearby cities, only to find themselves in the hands of
unscrupulous men who lured them into whorehouses.

The French implicit promotion of prostitution and nationalists'
objections to it reveal the extent to which both groups understood
the crucial role played by women in maintaining cultural integrity.
The traffic in women was a daily reality that gave the colonial administration a powerful tool of social control of the indigenous society.

Colonial Education and Men's Consciousness

Just like prostitution, education was seen by both natives and colonists as altering the moral fabric of those who received it. Writing
about the first generation of French-educated Algerian intellectuals,
Augustin Berque pointed out that the 1900s in Algeria were "an
astounding period, empty, pretentious, wordy, lacking leadership,
generosity, energy, and ideals."[31] Through "unconscious mimicry,"
Algerian intellectuals were said to begin to physically look like
Frenchman, as Bretons and Basques were assumed to have done before them.[32] This alleged physical transformation was preceded by
an intellectual one. Algerian intellectuals liked to read Herbert Spen-
cer and Auguste Comte. Thus their desire to "frenchify, and de-Arabize
Islam" was reflected in their embrace of positivism.[33] Yet this desire

could be satisfied only if the colonial factor were to be erased. Augustin Berque noticed a loss of memory of the French invasion among Algerian intellectuals. He identified fathers as facilitators of this amnesia. He referred to an Algerian student whose "father had to abide by our rules, often playing a supportive role in our French Algeria."[34] This may be true of fathers who already had a stake in the colonial system as native administrators and well-to-do landowners eager to play a political role, no matter how limited at the time. Others allowed their sons to acquire a French education to help them to function better in the colonial society, most specifically to master the French language (a vital tool) and to learn professional skills. They sometimes sent their sons to both Quranic and French schools. They had a naive and instrumental conception of French education as somehow being value-free, and therefore incapable of affecting their sons' cultural identity. Yet conflicts did emerge in the minds and emotions of French-educated intellectuals which colonial writers such as Augustin Berque dismissively diagnosed as "infantilism."[35]

In many ways this generation of Algerian intellectuals lived a contradiction in terms. They were not embraced by the colonial society, which encouraged them to think, act and look French while at the same deriding them for their efforts. They were accepted neither by Algerian intellectuals schooled in the Algerian tradition (where Arabic was the medium of instruction), nor by the majority of Algerians who, in one way or another, escaped acculturation. Their intellectual and social isolation was compounded by the fact that they had no other model of society to offer their fellow Algerians but the French. The very topics they seized upon to express their ideas were either purely self-serving or hopelessly French-colonial. For instance, they agitated for the extension of political rights to the French-speaking Algerians like themselves, and the establishment of the draft, which they saw as the surest way of securing such rights. Their coolness toward religion was noted by colonial intellectuals such as de Foucauld, who wrote in 1912 that "this intellectual elite has more or less lost all faith in Islam." He also remarked upon the opportunistic character of this group, who "would keep the Muslim label in order to influence the masses."[36]

At the turn of the century, the French-educated Algerian intellectuals were estimated to number about one thousand to twelve hundred including twenty-five medical doctors, lawyers and professors, and two hundred teachers, all apparently men.[37] The small size of this group is a measure of the extent to which Algerian society, which by 1910 had reached four and a half million, fell largely outside the French project of frenchification through education. The secularist and reformist outlook of these French-educated Algerian men won them the label of "Young Turks," or "Young Algerians."[38] Some of them had become naturalized French, thereby separating themselves legally from the rest of their countrymen and women. As a rule, a naturalized Algerian would marry a Frenchwoman and live in a French neighborhood.

The significance of the rise of this group, even though it was very small, lay in its emergence at a time when French intervention in the legal system of the Algerian people was as frequent as it was haphazard. To Algerians concerned about the integrity of their culture, these French-centered men symbolized a future Algeria without its native values. They personified the colonized cultural dopes, unable as they were to see the limitations of the French ideological system of cultural assimilation.

It would be erroneous to imply that all the French-educated Algerian men embraced French colonial culture and ideals. Some acquired a French education while remaining attached to their own culture, and used their skills to bring changes in the lives of their compatriots. This was preeminently the case of Emir Khaled, a grandson of Emir Abd-El-Kader and a graduate of the French military school of Saint Cyr, who eloquently argued the case of the native population by skillfully documenting the blatant contradiction between the application of the French ideals of liberty, equality and fraternity to the French, and their denial to the natives. When addressing an international audience in July 1924, Emir Khaled typically opened his talk with a quote from the *Quran* as a way of asserting his cultural identity.[39] He advocated the study and development of Arabic and Islamic history. Perhaps Emir Khaled, a controversial figure at his time, pursued a historical mission in actively seeking social, political and economic equality for the Algerian people while retaining their identity as Muslims.[40]

But there were other, less famous Algerian men who nevertheless used their French education to engage in a similar course of action. For example, M'hamed Ben Rahal of Nedroma, a bilingual member of a regional aristocracy, mounted severe critiques of the colonial system of education, and ceaselessly advocated the extension of education to rural areas and the training of an Algerian corps of teachers.[41] Just like Emir Khaled, he was eager to preserve his Arabo-Islamic heritage. He remained a devout man who sent his daughters to school, and felt that science, political and educational institutions, economic organization, means of transport as well as commerce could be borrowed from the French. He argued that "Islam could keep pace with all phases of the evolution of civilization except in matters concerning dogma, morals, and the family."[42] Unfortunately, he did not explain how the requirements of "civilization" would affect all three aspects of Islam which, as listed, essentially sum up Islam. Nor did he explain why the family should fall outside the realm of "civilization." For including the family among the institutions to be revamped would have meant a redefinition of women's roles in the society of the colonized.

The role played by education in the lives of all Young Algerians, no matter their orientation, was reflected in their insistence on the extension of education to girls as well as boys. Indeed, Emir Khaled used French statistics to point out that, after ninety-four years of colonization:

> There are 1,200 schools serving 110,000 pupils for a population of 700,000. Natives' schools including gourbi schools (or rudimentary rural schools usually held in homes or tents) number 520 for 38,000 children out of a population of 5 million. The figure of 38,000 is in reality inflated given the fact that parents are compelled by their extreme poverty to put their children to work when they are six or eight as shepherds, shoeshiners, sorters in mines, helpers in wineries, etc.[43]

The number of Algerian boys attending schools would gradually rise to 225,289 by 1954, the year that marked the beginning of the war of decolonization. Although this is still a modest figure, it is higher than the figure of 81,448 for girls.[44] A striking aspect of the period 1880 to 1930 is the absence of women from the first generation of French-educated natives. The assumption is usually made that this was due to the fact that Algerians as a collectivity resisted or rejected the imposition of French education and culture, thus preventing their children, especially their daughters, from attending schools. While useful in understanding the survival of Algerian identity despite the severe colonial attacks launched against it, the concepts of resistance or rejection often lack explanatory power and may hinder rather than facilitate analysis. The Algerian social historian, Abdelkader Djeghloul, rightly pointed out that proponents of "rejection" "avoid analyzing the contradictions of the colonial educational policy as well as the diverse and complex reactions of the Algerian people."[45] In the first place, there were not enough schools built for Algerians at any time during the colonial era. In addition, and especially during the first hundred years, the French government was more interested in selective education for boys rather than girls.

Education Fit for Colonized Girls

While they were concerned about the creation of a group of French-educated Algerian men to serve as their links with the native population, colonial leaders evinced no such interest in women. This is partially due to the fact that as Frenchmen, colonists had yet to recognize the principle of equality between men and women in their own society, let alone in the society they had just subdued. In addition, French administrators came to Algeria initially as military men dealing with other men in arms. On both sides, the war of conquest had all the trappings of a men's affair, despite its consequences for women. Finally, like its predecessors in Latin America, the conquest of Algeria was meant, among other things, to reshape social relations on the colonial model deemed perfect. Thus, Algerian women were neither seen as legitimate interlocutors, nor perceived as necessary to building a new colonial order, ideological pronouncements to the contrary notwithstanding.

In this context, it is not surprising that the first attempts at educating native girls drew the ire of some colonists and the lukewarm support of others. Individual French women, some of whom were dubious characters acting as agents of colonization, worked more towards the rationalization of a budding teaching profession than to further the interests of native women. Space and money were some of the most important issues faced by teachers. For example, in 1852, in the city of Constantine, a school for girls occupied a ramshackle building that often closed for repairs. The principal, a Mme Aguire, reported a drop in enrollments primarily due to these problems. This must have been a small drop considering that the largest number of girls the school attracted was fifteen.[46]

In 1855, a Mlle Ursule Robin de Montmain, who held a teaching diploma from the University of Algiers, was authorized to open a school for girls in the town of Blida "at her own risks and expense." Mlle de Montmain produced a character reference to help her secure the authorization. She paid her original nine pupils two francs a month, gave them free supplies, a meal, and a veil. As the number of her pupils increased to forty she requested financial support from the War Minister, who granted it to her. Perhaps more so than Mme Aguire or Mlle de Montmain, Mme Allix, also known as Mme Luce, a teacher, attempted to interest the colonial authorities in financing an ambitious project for girls in Algiers. The school she directed had thirteen pupils whom she paid two francs a month to make sure they did not drop out. In requesting funds to increase enrollments to five hundred, she wrote to the War Minister:

> As you well know, Mr. Minister, in Africa as well as in Europe,
> women are the most powerful force. If you convert [*sic*] to
> our civilization 100,000 native girls of all classes and races
> in the Regency [that is, Algeria], they will, given the circum-
> stances, have the privilege of becoming the wives of the most
> notable men of their class, thereby guaranteeing for ever the
> subjection of this country to ours, and setting into motion
> the irreversible process of its future assimilation.[47]

She requested the sum of two hundred thousand francs to carry
out her mission, a figure that undoubtedly shocked her contemporaries, who were expected to work within a budget of about 3,600 francs
per school. Was Mme Allix-Luce in fact planning to arrange marriages
for Algerian women? This would fit with the general colonial project
of remaking Algeria's social fabric. Indeed, at the time, Msgr. Dupuch,
and Father Brumauld, founder of an orphanage on the heights of
Algiers, in Ben Aknoun, advocated marriages between one hundred
thousand orphaned girls and boys, after educating them in the spirit
of the new colonial order.

A colonial critic of Mme Allix-Luce's plan pointed out that her
school

> has always been controversial. Her reputation is doubtful
> among Europeans as well as natives who find her repulsive.
> Her school is attended by girls from the poorest families only
> because of the fifteen-centime stipend allocated to each one
> of them daily. "Never," said a native member of the General
> Council during its 1860 session, "would a self-respecting Mus-
> lim send his daughter to the school or choose his wife among
> her pupils."[48]

This critic, a M. Michel, Section Chief of the First Division of the
Civil Services at the General Government in Algiers, suggested that
an investigation of Mme Allix-Luce's school be made to determine
what becomes of the girls who graduate from it.

Mme Allix-Luce's grandiose plan for her "civilization" was apparently secondary to her desire to benefit from whatever subsidies the
French government allocated her school.[49] Although she called her
school "God's House," she had a less than charitable conception of
her pupils and their families. She wrote that:

> Misery and hunger are my real helpers. Algiers is full of poor
> and excruciatingly needy families, decimated by horrible pri-

vations. By offering these families a 2-franc bonus per month,
I silenced all their scruples. . . . Arabs are so tough, narrow-
minded, and mean with respect to monetary issues, that the
richest as well as the poorest among them avidly take advantage of my generosity.[50]

In fact, by her own admission, fifteen out of her seventeen pupils
were "horribly ragged."[51] No wonder Mme Allix-Luce's school was
characterized by her patron, Count Guyot, as "less a school than a
charitable organization."[52]

Although the July 14, 1850 decree established "Arab-French schools"
for boys as well as girls, the education of the latter was deemed
politically problematic. It might be argued that the education of all
Algerian children, regardless of sex, was seen by the colonial government as a political issue. Indeed, these schools fell under the jurisdiction of the War Ministry instead of the Ministry of Public Education,
which oversaw schools for French children.[53] However, the overall
nineteenth-century colonial education project was class- and gender-
based. The sons of notable Algerians were to be educated in special
school in France and in Algeria, to impress upon them and win them
over to the assumed superiority of French culture. Girls and boys of
commoners were to be taught French in Algeria (even if this required
teaching them some Arabic *and* the *Quran* as an enticement) as well
as respect and love for benevolent France. In addition, girls were
taught how to develop some of the skills usually fully or partially
acquired from their mothers and grandmothers, such as, for example,
sewing, knitting, weaving and embroidery. This tradition of including
weaving into the education that a native girl received in school continued into the 1940s. It was one of the reasons for which city mothers
often withdrew their daughters from school, for fear that the emphasis
on weaving, which required the use of relatively heavy metal tools,
and long hours spent sitting in the same position, might stunt their
growth. Schools for native girls were not meant to prepare their
students for careers or non-traditional marketable skills. Instead, they
reinforced their homebound vocation, thereby revealing the colonial
gender-bias in all its starkness. This is well exemplified by the evaluation of a "Muslim Girls School" in Algiers, made by a member of a
team of female inspectors. She wondered whether

it would not be more useful for Arab women to exercise their
memory by learning Quranic dogma, instead of French grammar, history or geography. What good is it for women whose
vocation is to spend their lives in their homes to know that

the world is divided into continents, or what is the difference between a sea, a lake, and a gulf? Alas, wouldn't such a sad science make them feel bitter about the obligation they feel to live only within their family. I worry that our laudable goal to make them happier might instead result in arousing in them desires and feelings that will make them stray from a resigned but honest life.

The solution proposed by the inspector was to "teach them a few notions of hygiene to help them to bring up their children."[54] She noted, however, that the girls sewed, embroidered and wove well and fast. She also did not fail to note that the two classrooms that composed the school were

> overcrowded, and air circulated with difficulty since there was no ventilation. . . . There is no room for writing lessons, and there are not enough desks. How could looms for weaving burnooses, or even equipment for doing embroidery be set up here? Despite the principal's good will and her commitment, it is impossible and basically unhygienic, to crowd sixty children in such a narrow space.[55]

However, the most insurmountable obstacle was neither space nor money. It was ideology. Colonial administrators simply did not believe in educating native girls. For example, in rejecting a request for a regular salary as the law required, made by a Mrs. Parent, principal of the Arab-French School for Girls of Constantine, administrators objected that the 1865 Law applied to principals of boys' schools only. The arguments invoked by administrators to convince policy-makers were remarkably similar to those made by their contemporary fiction writers: Algerian women's culture was allegedly an obstacle to learning, just as it was described as an obstacle to marrying Frenchmen in novels. Thus, in a letter addressed to the Director General of Civil Services in Algiers, a M. Michel, who had opposed Mme Allix-Luce's school, wrote on August 8, 1861:

> We must admit that in creating the Arab-French schools for girls parallel to schools for boys, the July 14, 1850 decree [sic] was ahead of felt needs, and overshot its mark. The education we want to give native girls will be for a long time to come incompatible with the role that native religious beliefs, mores, and domestic habits assign women in Arab society. It is purely utopian to believe that we will make

this society ready for reform by teaching urban native girls reading, writing, arithmetic, and sewing according to our methods. By bringing them up essentially as Europeans, we will make them unfit for Arab life; we are preparing concubines for European men instead of wives for native men.[56]

It is ironic that, in wanting to deny girls minimal education, colonial administrators cast themselves as defenders of the native men's domestic life. French women, in their own way, as was evident in the school evaluation quoted above, joined in this apparent "protection" of native life from the intrusion of education. Yet teaching native boys French and other subjects was not considered disruptive to their lives. Reporting on an award ceremony that took place in an Arab-French school for boys, a teacher wrote in 1852:

I sought to impress upon natives the usefulness of the French language, and the benefits of education for their children. I tried to dispel the many prejudices they still harbor against our teaching.

To make her point, this teacher staged a discussion between several members of a class on the merits of learning French. For example: Salem ben Kafsem says, in "*sabir*" language [a sort of patois spoken among the international community in Algiers before the French invasion]: "*Mi no tenir bisogno parlar avec les Francais, mi vouloir vivir avec les Mauros, per aqui l'Arabe basta.*" (But I do not need to communicate with the French, I want to live with Muslims only, and for this I only need to speak Arabic.) Ali ben Hammoud answers: "You speak like an ignorant child. There is no business where Muslims do not enter in contact with the French. They must deal with the French in all business transactions, even when they do commerce with natives only."[57] This example reveals a greater commitment on the part of colonial educators to attract Algerian boys to their schools by demonstrating to them the relevance of education to the real world.

Perhaps the implication of the debate over the education of girls was that natives ought to attend their own schools. However, most of these, called Quranic schools, traditionally attended by boys and girls, had been closed. In addition, the 1882 decree prohibited the remaining ones from opening during regular school hours to prevent competition with French schools, and subjected them to preliminary approval by a Prefect.[58]

A close look at the education received by Algerian girls, as reflected in yearly award ceremonies that included staged dialogues between students, reveal no essential contradiction with native life-style. Rather, it reveals the political goal that education pursued. Pupils were taught to love God and France. For example, during a ceremony held in Algiers at the Muslim Girls School on October 24, 1851, a skit written by a French "lady from Algiers" was acted by two Algerian girls, Aziza and Nefissa, who had come back from a trip to Amboise, France. It went as follows:

> Aziza: Nefissa, how sweet it is after being absent for days
> To come back to my mother and my country
> I feel so happy to be back!
>
> Nefissa: Ingrate! . . . How about France?
> Have you forgotten
> Beautiful France where so many friends
> Have adopted poor natives?
>
> Aziza: No, I know French people are our brothers [sic]
> I loved them.
> I proudly bring back to my friends memories of
> All that I saw, and marvelous stories.
> How rich the land is! Cities, rivers, mountains
> Flew before our eyes like a desert wind
> When steam* carried us through.
> Nothing in the stories we read is more frightening
> Than coming back to our shores
> On a flying dragon, howling, and spitting fire?
> And we were not really afraid.
> My story, I trust, will make my sisters
> Shudder and blanche with fear!
>
> Nefissa: Of your long trip
> Do you only wish to instill in them silly fears?
> Describe, dear Aziza, the silver river
> Rocking us softly and peacefully
> In the summer wind, when our souls
> Gently flew to Algiers shores.
> Oh! Protective France: Oh! Hospitable France!
> I bade you farewell with my tears.
> Noble land, where I felt free
> Under Christian skies to pray to our God:
> He made my wish come true, sisters:
> Today our first efforts have been justly rewarded . . .

---

*Perhaps a reference to a steam locomotive.

God bless you for the happiness you bring us!
And you, adoptive mother, who taught us
That we have a share of this world,
We will cherish you forever! . . .

Aziza: Thanks to the lofty examples you set for us
And your lessons, your humble child
Will nourish her mother with her handiwork.

Chorus

In this refuge open to our childhood
At the sight of our benefactors
Our hearts will sing our gratitude

Dear benefactors, we believe that God
Loves a prayer said by a good child.
Oh! But we will strive to do good
So that He will fulfill your wishes.

We beg the Prefect, our tender, and good Father,
Who cared so generously for us,
To hear our prayers
To make his children happy.

Our prayers go to you too beautiful and good ladies
Whose visit is beneficial to us,
Whose look enlightens our souls
And leaves behind something sweet.

This ceremony was attended by teachers and colonial officials, as
well as mothers who did not understand French. Awards given after
the skit covered topics such as study of the *Quran*, Arabic writing,
French grammar and dictation, arithmetic, memorization, reading,
geography, sewing and good behavior.[59] No history classes were held
during this period of time. The following year, 1852, the organizers
of the awards ceremony staged a dialogue between students arguing
the case of colonization, and timidly questioning the roles played by
fathers in the education of their daughters. The protagonists, Zoulikha
who had dropped out of school, Hanifa, Nefissa and Zohra, dressed,
like their one-hundred-and-one classmates, in traditional costumes,
represented "The Past and the Future":

Hanifa: I am so happy, dear Zoulikha, to press you against my heart!
After a six-year absence, I am so pleased to see that you are
still as good as you are pretty! So your father has agreed to

let you take part in our big party. You see, today we are
celebrating labor in this house.

Zoulikha: I am quite astonished, dear friend, to see myself amidst so
many charming sisters, and admire the beautiful things they
made with their industrious and delicate fingers. But you see,
my father loves me more than anything in the world. This is
why he could only remember our friendship. Today, I am sure
he can only think of the happiness I feel to see you again and
the pleasure I will experience from admiring your splendid
work.

Hanifa: . . . Shouldn't a father who loves his daughter so much forget
about this war from which my sister and I have suffered a
thousand times more than you? Should he not at least allow
you to come here and learn the art of making your leisure
useful and enjoyable?

Zoulikha: You are asking for the impossible. You are asking that my
father and I forget the unforgettable, the glory of power.

Hanifa: You are right, Zoulikha. It is difficult to forget that we have
been defeated. My father's death and the loss of my wealth
have more than once reminded me of the terrible events that
preceded our birth. Alas! I have often wept on our people's
graves. Today, I too remember. I have lost everything, I am
a poor orphan with this weak and young body. But I no longer
hate France because my father would not hate her.

Nefissa: How could he not like her if, alas, he could come back to life!
Instead of dying on the battlefield, our father could have lost
his life and fortune in a palace intrigue. What would have
been our fate after his torture? What did Deys have in store
for us when our fathers lost their favors? Yes, our father died
fighting. But could we have fallen in the hands of a more
generous winner? Instead of being subjected to infamy and
shame usually meted out to the weak and the vanquished, we
are as you see in a shelter. We have learned what your opulence
will never teach you: A sense of accomplishment we have
earned, an extreme pleasure derived from doing useful work
and exercising our hearts and minds to achieve the good.

Zoulikha: God: What have I just heard? You are orphaned and poor,
and you bless the hand that struck you! I live in the desert
with resentment in my heart where I still have a father to kiss
and enjoy the sight of his beautiful and ever so numerous
herds. Have you reneged on your God?

Hanifa: We are still faithful believers in God, dear Zoulikha, I already told you so. But can we continue to hate a generous winner such as ours, who does good instead of retaliating for our resistance? Can we speak of hatred, vengeance, and war when France takes care of us as her children? Thanks to a fatherly and intelligent administration, you may see for yourself the house in which we have found refuge from the miseries of the body and the soul.

Nefissa: These are good and proper thoughts. You must realize, Zoulikha, that France has always left the glory of command to those among our leaders who were willing to understand her mission. France respects our beliefs and customs. She even repairs our mosques, and protects your father's property as well as his person. We cannot afford to complain in the name of merciful God about a conqueror that showed us so much justice and gentleness.

Zoulikha: But then, if Christians are not the enemies of our God, and are not after us or our wealth, who are they? What do they want?

Hanifa: They are the soldiers of fate! They fight for justice! Their flag floats on our homes from Constantine to Oran, from the sea to the Sahara, because it was necessary that this strong and generous African land finally revealed the treasures we left hidden in her heart. Algeria had to be awakened to work and to wealth. To carry out such a task, just like giving birth to a baby, tears of blood had to be shed. Well, be fair, Zoulikha. When I say "be fair" I also have in mind all of our race, warriors, chiefs, and saints. Tell me now, whether Algeria's birth to light and to life has not cost France more than it did our tribes?

Zoulikha: Your question troubles and confuses me. Since I was born, I have known no occupation other than dreaming and making myself up in the mirror all day long. I can hardly understand the French sacred mission which, according to you, makes them our liberators and brothers. I am beginning to believe that my happiness is not so great. It means perhaps the absence of pain, but it is good enough for me. This may be why I am not as ready as you to forgive those who won over us at Sidi Ferruch and Staouelli [places where the French landed in July 1830].

Zohra: Why not, dear friend? Would it not be better to love us all than to hate us? If I had my way, all the little boys and girls

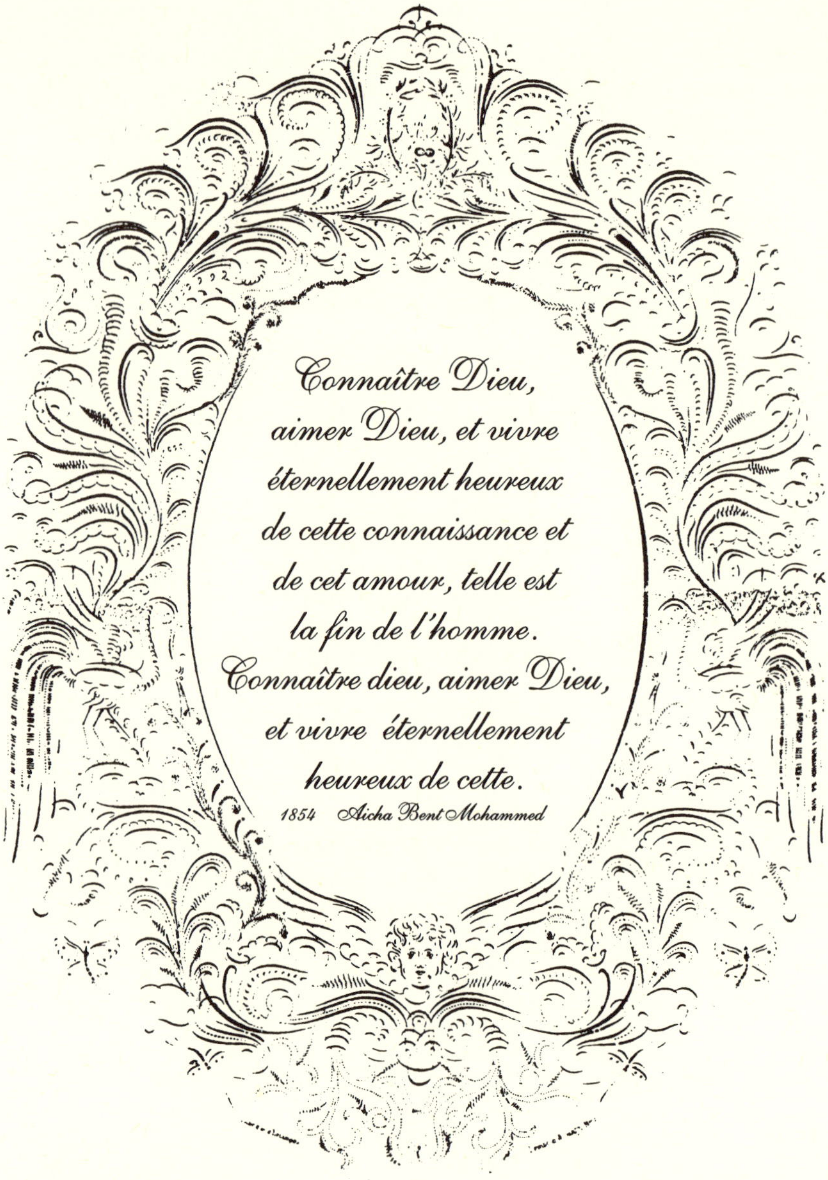
Connaître Dieu,
aimer Dieu, et vivre
éternellement heureux
de cette connaissance et
de cet amour, telle est
la fin de l'homme.
Connaître dieu, aimer Dieu,
et vivre éternellement
heureux de cette.
1854 Aicha Bent Mohammed

The ultimate purpose of man is to achieve eternal happiness through knowing and loving God.
(text repeated twice)
1854
Aicha Bent Mohammed

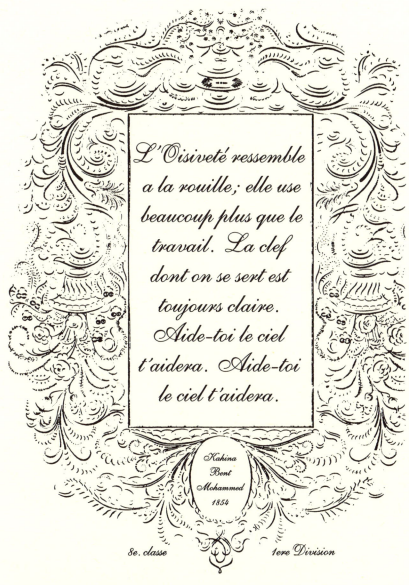

L'Oisiveté ressemble
a la rouille; elle use
beaucoup plus que le
travail. La clef
dont on se sert est
toujours claire.
Aide-toi le ciel
t'aidera. Aide-toi
le ciel t'aidera.

Kahina
Bent
Mohammed
1854

8e. classe   1ere Division

Inactivity is like rust; It wears you out more than work
A key that is often used is free of rust.
Help yourself, God will help you.
Help yourself, God will help you.
Kahina Bent Mohammed
8th class   1st Division

would go to school as I do. We would all learn to work, to make beautiful things. Work will make us good and virtuous. Soon, we will become attractive, love ourselves, and be happy as we are now in this pleasant house. Africa will then become truly the daughter of the sun, thanks to the splendid riches of its cities and country. But I am carrying on like a child. I feel, Zoulikha, that you need to hear other reasons to help you learn how to be happy by forgiving.

Hanifa: Dear Zoulikha, this beautiful and opulent existence of yours gives you but a foggy conception of yourself. At the end of each day, adorned with crimson and golden silks laid out for you by your black servant, you cannot tell whether you have truly lived. You spend your time admiring your pretty face in a mirror just like a dove does in the smooth and clear river whispering by your tent. As the sun sets, you are hardly aware that your life is one more day shorter. And you say this kind of happiness is good enough for you, poor friend! Do you know that *I* would not be happy with this existence at all? I need to feel happy with myself at the end of the day. I think I would not be able to sleep if I had not spent all my time, energy, and intelligence making progress in our work and acquiring greater wisdom. . . . I feel in my frail self what a generous nation might experience in her magnanimous soul: An indomitable desire to share my happiness with others. I am ready to take all risks to bring wealth to the hungry, science or art to those degraded by boredom and inactivity. Destiny must take a hand when a nation such as France is gripped by a divine desire to sacrifice everything for the happiness of her fellow human beings. France found herself in such a sacrificial mood when the Queen [*sic*] of Algeria witnessed an army, as formidable in combat as it was magnanimous in victory, land on her shores. Thus, I do not see our fathers' defeat as the conquest of the weak by the strong. I perceive it instead as the painful union of the past with the future. Zoulikha, *you* are the past with your wealth, boredom, ignorance, and ingrained prejudices. The future belongs to all these young girls, Nefissa's friends, who only want, like her, to be your sisters in wisdom and friendship.

Nefissa: [She outlines the work done by the French army in building roads, and bringing about security.]

Zoulikha: You are happy, my dear friends, because you have already caught a glimpse of magnificent horizons. Misfortune compelled you to experience work and the strenuous effort it requires, think noble thoughts, open your hearts to the good and the beautiful. You suffered in order to learn: I am suffering because I am ignorant. Whether we are rich or poor, we must pay this noble tribute to human nature. Farewell! I am going back to the mountain. I hope that France, ever so great and generous, will help us share with you her enlightenment and good deeds of which we are more ignorant. Schools like yours will hopefully be opened in the Kabylie, which we pledge to attend regularly. We will some day become, like you, French in our hearts. We will also become happy by developing our minds, and free by doing work with our own hands.[60]

The organizers of the ceremony pointedly mentioned that students recited this dialogue with "a perfect elocution and without accent."

A comparison of these staged discussions with those arranged between boys reveals that girls were subjected to greater and somewhat more abstract ideological indoctrination than boys. Although boys were taught to be "docile, submissive, and good subjects," these qualities were to be achieved through mastery of the French language (seen as an indispensable tool of communication), arithmetic, geography, history (which was not taught girls in the early schools) and religion. Knowledge of these subjects would lead to "independence, for he who does not know anything always needs others, and remains dependent on everybody." Boys pointed out in their staged discussions that knowledge of arithmetic would help their parents to "manage their businesses," and "keep their books themselves instead of relying on others, and risk being cheated." Acquisition of skills necessary for an independent, efficient life as subjects of France was the aim of education for these native boys, who numbered fifty percent more than girls, or 155. Whereas for girls work done by hand, especially sewing and needlework, would make them "sage," or good, by helping them to avoid boredom, and would occupy their minds. Boys were further exposed to stories with a moral to help build character, or to extoll the virtues of education. Thus, in one story, entitled "The School," children "see a young girl who works *and* sews in front of her house" [emphasis added] on their way to school. Their mother tells them:

Go to school, and educate yourselves. You will learn about the world and how vast it is with its rivers, and seas that rise into storms, and mountains so high that they hide behind clouds and their peaks are covered with unmeltable ice. You will learn accounting and arithmetic."

However, for good measure, and perhaps because tribal chiefs had been invited to the ceremony, the story adds: "But, children, you will learn what is even more valuable: How to understand God and love him; to be good and virtuous. For wisdom is more precious than science."[61]

Yet even the teaching of religion was deemed less damaging to boys than girls. As M. Michel put it:

> While bringing them [girls] up as Europeans you have kept them Muslim. You taught them ideas, customs, and ideals inimical to the domestic life of their compatriots. Yet *you have done nothing to open to them the European family.* Flawed in its conception, your institution can only have fatal consequences. (emphasis added)[62]

A remarkable feature of the girls' dialogues is the linkage established by their authors between the ideology of colonial legitimation and gender relations. Algeria's defeat is presented as the defeat of the girls' fathers, which daughters must forgive because it was ordained by God on account of France's mission to share the fruits of enlightenment with her new subjects. What is acknowledged indirectly is that young women were more affected by the defeat than their male counterparts, as they had lost not only their wealth but, admittedly, the security provided by their fathers. In addition, the memory of the defeat may be passed on to future generations by women, who must, therefore, be taught how to forget about it as a thing of the past. Finally, in order to legitimize orphaning girls, and seizing their fortunes, colonial teachers constructed the myth of the lazy, inactive girl, more interested in beautifying herself than doing something useful. Benevolent France, a recurring theme in schools for girls, would redeem native women by instilling in them the work ethic. What kind of work was this? Sewing, embroidery, weaving and so on, all activities that already existed among women. The pickings were slim, indeed. All exhortations to accept colonial domination remained hopelessly abstract. There is no mention of doing work for remuneration, or alleviating poverty. In short, girls were to do the bidding of France in a vacuum, a fact well perceived by M. Michel. The only concrete aspect of this education was to turn young girls into "dignified wives, and brave and honest mothers."[63]

The often-discussed parents' reluctance to send their daughters to these early colonial schools finds its main justification in this unabashed ideology. The education of girls was indeed a political affair that, somehow, was overshadowed by the equally political but more pragmatic education of boys. There is little evidence that girls were admitted to the "Arab High Schools" (or *Collèges Arabes*) created in the 1840s in Paris and Algeria's main urban centers. The purpose of these "collèges" according to the War Minister, Cubière, who wrote to King Louis Philippe in 1839 to interest him in the idea, was to provide "a special education for Arab children watched by honorable and pious men from their country, and taught by French professors according to guidelines and a program of study set by the Ministry of War." These high schools were designed to:

> impart useful knowledge in full recognition of the conditions prevalent in their country to which they will return. [They] will ensure the children's superiority over their compatriots in terms of scientific knowledge without changing their national character.[64]

While historians often maintain that, like the Arab-French schools, these high schools failed to achieve their goal, the fact remains that educators attempted to place and/or counsel students about career opportunities. Thus, four young men from Algiers were enrolled at the military academy of Saint Cyr, in France; thirteen from the city of Constantine went on to pursue careers as land surveyors, veterinarians, mounted customs officers, members of the cavalry and teachers.[65] It is true that the colonial prejudice against the education of girls was also leveled at boys. For example, a general commanding the division of the eastern city of Annaba (or Bône) bemoaned the fact that:

> the young graduates of the Imperial College quickly lose the benefit of their studies. They all aspire to become *caid* [a command position assigned natives in the colonial administration], or *sheikh*, thereby returning to the inactive Muslim life under the tent. They forget all they have learned.[66]

Muslim life-styles were seen as obstacles to becoming French for both boys and girls. Nevertheless, boys were trained for careers, but girls were not.

For a number of reasons, including settlers' hostility and the colonial administration's reluctance to provide necessary funding, the Arab-French Schools started to decline, beginning in the 1870s, before disappearing altogether. Until the 1950s the education of girls remained essentially the same in its general orientation as it was in the nineteenth century. The curriculum, however, no longer included the teaching of the Arabic language in grade schools, or the *Quran*. In addition, native girls' educational track was separate from their French counterparts. Schools for girls did not prepare them for the sixth grade entrance examination (or *examen de sixième*) which, if passed, enabled students to attend a *lycée*. The highest degree a girl could aspire to was the *certificat d'études primaires* at the end of the seventh grade. A native girl had to attend a school for French girls to be eligible for admission to a lycée. However, zoning requirements made it impossible for girls who lived in Algerian neighborhoods to attend French schools, thus ensuring a *de facto* segregation.

In other words, native cultural difference, acknowledged in the 1850s and accommodated in the curriculum through the teaching of Arabic and religion, was generally denied. In many colonial lycées, Arabic was taught as a second, foreign language after English. At the same time, the nineteenth-century bias against preparing native girls for occupations outside the home became institutionalized. The average native girl living in an urban Algerian neighborhood could not hope for a transformation of her life through education. It is hardly surprising that girls often dropped out of schools. Helping one's mother around the house or getting engaged took precedence over an education without a future.

Unlike girls, boys had options. If their parents objected to an all-French education, they could send them to one of the three *medersa* established for the purpose of training bilingual personnel primarily in the legal profession. In addition, promising boys were often encouraged to sit for the sixth grade entrance examination. Admittedly, opportunities were not equal among boys. However, while boys had to contend with issues of class, girls shouldered the burdens of class- and gender-bias within the same colonial framework.

This background sheds light on the absence of women among the first generation of French-educated Algerians. No women appeared among the Young Algerians. No women were found among the defenders or detractors of colonial culture or domination. No women articulated their grievances against colonial policies. No women voiced their opinions about their culture and institutions. This apparent silence was not self-imposed for some strategic reason. Rather, it was *structurally* induced. Women simply did not benefit equally with men from the educational opportunities available at the time, no matter how limited they were. Yet education is only one of the reasons that Ali Merad, an Algerian student of religious reformism, provides for the absence of a feminist movement in the 1930s. Merad does not explain why women had not, or whether they could have, acquired sufficient education to be able to voice their thoughts. Instead, he bemoaned the fact that Algeria had no indigenous Christian community that might have provided the necessary feminist ferment as, he felt, had been the case in Egypt at the time.[67] Merad is in agreement with colonists that native culture is inimical to change from within, a dubious notion at best. What he failed to realize was that, being largely bypassed by the nineteenth-century colonial educational policy, women were less prone to experiencing doubts about the validity of their culture as many of the French-educated men started to do. In this sense, women kept Algerian culture whole and cohesive, a tall burden and an invaluable achievement that has yet to be acknowledged.

To sum up, the minstrel's assessment of the impact of the newly established colonial order discussed at the beginning of this chapter was not without validity. It had the merit of raising the issue of acculturation through education, the debasement of women through prostitution, and the loss of memory of the past. It is primarily as a response to these problems that cultural nationalism will emerge, as will be seen in the next chapter.

5

Reform and Resistance

The exposure of natives analyzed in the previous chapter went hand in hand with colonial attempts, often timid and haphazard, at reforming their legal system, which included family law. This in turn triggered a reaction among some Algerian men eager to stave off the kind of acculturation that characterized the Young Algerians. Yet the French meddling with *shari'a* or Islamic Family Law was until the mid-fifties no more than a footnote to it. It was not until the war of decolonization began that French legislators attempted to remedy the most glaringly gender-unequal aspects of the law, as will be discussed below. In general, native culture did not hold any equivalent of the Indian sati or Chinese footbinding that would have provided the French with the opportunity for spectacular intervention to illustrate the struggle between "civilization" and barbarism. The veil gave colonists the stuff to imagine exotic tales, but did not otherwise bother them.

The sense of exposure felt by natives was exacerbated by social neglect and deepening economic inequities between colonizers and colonized. Between the two world wars a number of Algerian men began to address themselves to the problems from which their community suffered. They did not do so to claim more rights under the colonial system, as the Young Algerians did. Rather, they appealed to their compatriots to take stock of their lives in order to reorient them.

A Cultural Answer to Socioeconomic Problems

The men who undertook this task responded to a perceived gradual decline of natives' moral and social values, mediated by institutions such as religion, the family and education. They referred to themselves as the *'Ulama*, or scholars in religious matters. Unlike the acculturated Young Algerians, the *'Ulama*, also known as "reformists," had been schooled primary in Arabic, and had studied and traveled in the Middle East. They did not share with the Young Algerians the notion that the colonial order, when purged of its excesses, could be a model of society to emulate. Instead, they focused on the ills from which their society suffered, and proceeded to elaborate ways to remedy them within the framework of Islam. Unlike the Young Algerians whose audience was essentially French, the *'Ulama*'s audience was Algerian.

The most notable member of the *'Ulama* was Sheikh Abd-El-Hamid Ibn Badis (Ben Badis in Algerian Arabic), a native of the eastern city of Qasantina. Ibn Badis started his task of recentering his society at a time when not only Algeria but the whole Muslim world appeared to him to be in a state of disarray.[1] Indeed, the caliphate had just been abolished in Turkey, sending shock waves among Muslims all over the world. In addition, a purportedly "reformist" movement had already taken place in Egypt, under the leadership of Muhammad Abduh and his disciple Rashid Rida. Perhaps reflecting a sentiment common among his compatriots, Ibn Badis found Rida more inspiring than his master, and espoused many of his ideas about the role of Islam in everyday life. More specifically, he agreed with Rida's assessment that problems encountered by Muslim societies were primarily due to the adulturation of their values by Western thought.

Colonized Algerians found a great deal to be desired in Abduh's reformist ideas when he lectured them, during a visit to Algiers in 1903, about avoiding political resistance to France, and authorized them to eat meat from animals that had not been slaughtered according to Muslim rite and to wear French hats.[2] Abduh's apparent lack of awareness of the significance of the colonial factor in Algerian people's lives led the *'Ulama* to file a complaint with the religious authorities at Cairo's Al Azhar University, which came close to firing him.[3] This incident underscores the structural differences between Egypt, a nation that was ruled by the British through indigenous intermediaries, and Algeria, a settlement colony whose culture was at the colonists' mercy. This difference partially explains the nature of the debates that took place among "reformists," especially in matters concerning women. This does not mean that Egyptian theologians were more liberal than their Algerian counterparts on gender questions. It simply means that Abduh was freer to explore ways in which Islamic principles could accommodate the social values of British society. In contrast, Ibn Badis's project was to rescue native-*qua-*

Muslim values not only from explicit colonial encroachment, but also from Algerians' own actions. Thus Ibn Badis's task was one of self-preservation through inner regeneration. Such regeneration was based on a rediscovery of the *Quran*, as a source of ethics and guide to individual and social behavior, supplemented by the *Sunna* (tradition of Prophet Muhammad), and the exemplary lives of the *Salaf*, or the Prophet's companions. In Ibn Badis's view these guides of action had been all but ignored or distorted. The colonial system was perceived as having also abetted the social problems from which the colonized society suffered. These included prostitution, illiteracy especially among women, acculturation of young educated Algerian males, and most importantly, unhindered spread of popular Sufism, referred to by the French as "*maraboutisme*" (or the cult of saints). Popular Sufism (as distinct from ascetic original sufism) is a term I am using to refer to an array of practices that included affiliation with a Sufi order, participation in collective quasidance rituals held regularly by members, belief in the saintly status of past and present spiritual leaders of Sufi orders or men of great piety, as well as participation in yearly festivals in celebration of saints' birthdays. All such activities were open to women with the exception of group Sufi dances.

Ibn Badis and his contemporaries perceived their society as being in rapid decline, having lost its moral fiber, and perhaps even its identity. The method he chose to remedy his country's ills was to reread the *Quran* for his contemporaries in order to design a guide for regenerative action. He did so, however, in a pragmatic manner considered original that distinguishes him from traditional commentators of the *Quran* such as the Egyptian Rashid Rida, whose commentaries were dictated by the text rather than social reality.[4] Ibn Badis decided to choose specific passages from the *Quran* and use them as an interpretive framework for the problems posed by his society. In so doing, he meant to convey to his contemporaries the relevance of Quranic revelations to social, economic and political issues. He did not, however, offer new interpretations. Anything that strayed from the *Quran* was seen as a mistake that contributed to leading Algerians further on the path of distortion, and loss of identity. A similar procedure is used today among members of political groups advocating the establishment of an Islamic government.

This return to Algerians' cultural Islamic roots was perhaps dictated by the fact that the society offered to Algerians by the French as a "modern" model to emulate was also the one they blamed for their social problems, as well as the one responsible for the loss of their economic and political power. There was no alternative but to look to an idealized past. However, the class background of Ibn Badis may also account for his decontextualized, abstract and intellectualist approach to Algeria's problems. Although he diagnosed these problems adequately, he failed to see that many of the practices deemed un-Islamic were responses to concrete situations. The son of an aristocratic family that counted at least two of its members among the colonial administration, and grandson of a man who had been decorated by Napoleon III in 1864, he did not seem to grasp the economic dimension of his contemporaries' problems, especially women's.[5] Nor did he seem to grasp the role played in women's and men's lives of quasireligious rituals. For example, combatting the cult of saints, a practice that went against the spirit and the letter of the *Quran*, meant for women placing restrictions on an activity that took them out of their homes for ritual weekly visits to saints' mausoleums. It also meant castigating their affiliation with a number of Sufi orders that included women as their members. Although Ibn Badis did not target women specifically, there were as many women as men involved in the cult of saints, making his attacks on the practice also an attack on women.

In addition, his advocacy of education for women was not aimed at making women self-sufficient in terms of gaining marketable skills, thereby making their dependence on male relatives and prostitution less likely. Rather, it was meant to keep young Algerian men grounded in their culture by marrying suitable wives among their compatriots. This was best expressed by Ibn Badis's disciple, Sheikh Muhammad Al Bashir Al Ibrahimi, who exhorted men to:

> provide the young woman with a Muslim education stressing the power of the mind, the strength of virtue, and the noblest values. Thanks to this education she will compel these silly young men to return to their roots. Thus, fire will have been fought with fire.

This task was all the more important in that Ibn Badis's disciples argued that World War II had made Algerian men attractive to French women without husbands, thereby compounding the effects of acculturation. Thus:

> These (French women) search for desirable colonies of young men or men in the colonies. They are equipped with the most deadly weapons of the war! Make sure that our youth does not fall prey to this "colonialism" empowered as it is by its own "weakness" [that is, weaker sex].[6]

Ibn Badis's appeal for the education of women also stemmed from his insistence that Algerians as a social/ethnic group must be responsible for one another, a Quranic principle derived from the *sura* of the ant, which extolled the organic relationship between ants for the sake of the survival of the group.[7] This idea was later specified by his successor, Sheikh Muhammad Al Bashir Al Ibrahimi, by making the notion of the group synonymous with "motherland" (in Arabic *watan*, a term that does not connote a female component) which requires women's participation as wives and mothers. Thus, he wrote: "In fact, wife and children are the bonds that tie patriotic man to his motherland, and reinforce his faith."[8]

Given this background, Ibn Badis's ideas regarding women were not, and could not, be emancipatory in so far as parity with men or equality before the law were concerned. The "salvation" of Algerian society required the education of women—a project compatible with Ibn Badis's classical/purist conception of Sunni Islam—but not a change in their status which might jeopardize the integrity of the group. The needs of the "group," the "motherland," took precedence over women's needs. Yet the needs of the "motherland" were perceived as coextensive with men's needs.

Despite his lectures on social issues, ranging from the ethic of upholding contracts in business transactions to the consequences of avarice, Ibn Badis was more interested in political questions, to which he devoted more time. Perhaps his mission was a political one presented as a cultural reform. Even then, it is doubtful that political goals would obviate the searing issue of poverty among Algerians. Indeed, Ibn Badis was guilty of explaining poverty away as the result of the will of God.[9] At any rate, he encountered as much opposition from Algerians as he aroused interest. Indeed, the bulk of the population lived in rural areas and small towns where popular Sufism was widespread. The average individual had a strong identity as a Muslim who often performed five prayers a day, had some Sufi affiliation, belonged to a *zawiya*, and believed in saintly grace. French cultural influence generally eluded the majority of Algerians. In this, anthropologists such as Clifford Geertz were wrong in asserting that "scripturalism" enabled colonized Muslim people to preserve their identity.[10] In the Algerian case, the advocacy of some form of scripturalism as Ibn Badis proposed met with stiff resistance from not only heads of Sufi orders but also ordinary people. Indeed, the label Badisi, or a follower of Ibn Badis, was synonymous with unbeliever, so strong was the notion among the majority of Algerians that their popular Sufi beliefs were thoroughly Islamic. Neither the *'Ulama* nor the *Young Algerians* understood the fact that what passed for "popular Islam" enabled women and men to live their lives in relative autonomy, as if they were not colonized. Spiritual leaders, heads of *zwi* (plural of *zawiya*), provided counseling in family matters, and arbitration between individuals and groups. Yearly national gatherings to celebrate saints' birthdays enabled individuals to network and build community bonds. Finally, weekly individual and family visits to saints' mausoleums offered emotional relief, and helped women and men to cope with stress, illness and everyday cares.

To accuse spiritual leaders of *zwi* of ignorance of religious matters, corruption and social backwardness, as the *'Ulama* and Young Algerians did, was oftentimes accurate, but missed the point. They served much-needed psychological and social functions which neither the *'Ulama* nor the Young Algerians were able to provide. Indeed, women and men were able to seek refuge from colonial society as well as their domestic problems, and experience a sense of belonging in the rituals, values and solidarity provided by Sufism and belief in saints. They were able to give meaning to their daily existence and establish a sense of continuity with the precolonial past.

This lack of understanding of people's needs is best illustrated by Ibn Badis's treatment of the woman question. He did not extol the achievements of Algerian Sufi women who were considered saints, or those who distinguished themselves during the French invasion of their country as models to emulate. Instead, he exalted the deeds of women in the history of early Islam. Thus Umm Haram was depicted as an extremely devout woman who fought alongside her husband and died at his side during the holy war as Muslim troops were landing in Cyprus in 649.[11] Faith and sacrifice were the virtues demanded of women. Partisan of renovation of Sunni practices as expressed in the *Quran*, the Sunna and the Salaf (or the Prophet's companions), Ibn Badis did not share in or directly respond to the feminist ferment, meetings and debates that marked the 1920s and 1930s in Egypt, Turkey and France. A series of feminist congresses were held in Turkey, Iran and Algeria. However, although attended by Middle Eastern women, some of these congresses (such as those on mediterranean women) were primarily European women's affairs. Underscoring the absence of Algerian women at such gatherings, it was an Algerian man who made an appearance at the International Congress of Mediterranean Women in Constantine by presenting a report on Algerian women's situation.[12] Algeria had no feminist male writer as Iraq did with Jamal Sidqi, Egypt with Qasim Amin or Tunisia with Malek Haddad. It was as if the promotion of women's rights was tantamount to a denial of men's rights.

Yet articles on feminist activities taking place in the world were published regularly in the Algerian secular and pro-French paper, *La voix des humbles* (Poor People's Voice). Advocates of the promotion of women's rights found no audience for their ideas. They happened to be acculturated men, cut off from the rest of the native population by their life-styles and education. Theirs was not a feminist movement without women but rather, a monologue as well as an exercise in the expression of free opinion. They failed to produce a plan of action or a rationale for the advancement of women. A measure of their marginality was provided by their failure to arouse native public opinion's passion or ire as did, for example, the Tunisian feminist Tahar Haddad who advocated the promotion of women's rights on a par with men without necessarily departing from the tenets of Islam. Algerian reformists joined Tunisian theologians in condemning Mr. Haddad's ideas.[13]

Ibn Badis's group implicitly countered these echoes of feminism by publishing in their paper, *Al Shihab*, not only biographies of devout women of the heroic period of Islam, but also articles authored by the Egyptian theologian Rashid Rida, and initially published in the Cairo paper, *Al Manar*. These dealt with Rida's rebuttals of feminist arguments concerning the roles of women in Muslim societies.[14] Ibn Badis and his peers agreed with Rida that veiling was a religious duty protecting women from "depersonalization," that women could not have the same right to divorce as men without causing the "ruin of families," and that women could not inherit equally with men without contravening the spirit of the *Quran*. Polygamy was maintained as a right of men that could be opposed by women only by leaving their marriage in protest, thereby securing the right to divorce.[15] In addition, Ibn Badis accepted the opinion expressed by puritanical thinkers, such as Shekib Arslane, that dancing involving women and men should be proscribed, as it led to "bodies rubbing against each other, a first step towards fornication."[16]

Although they perceived themselves as moderate, Ibn Badis and his peers were all but moderate in matters dealing with women. It is surprising to note that as a practitioner of the exegesis of the *Quran*, Ibn Badis accepted Rida's interpretation of veiling, leaving his reading of the text on this issue silent. In this sense, the subject "woman" for him and his followers was less religious/doctrinal than social. He was caught between his desire to save Algerian Islam from customs that he felt threatened to turn it into a system of magical and superstitious practices buttressed by widespread illiteracy and ignorance, and the modernizing rhetoric of the French-educated Young Algerians. He opted for the path of least resistance, reinforcing women's customary roles while advocating that they be educated so that they improve their performance in these same roles. In other words, the burden of a revitalized native society was to be borne by women. This escape from the socioeconomic problems that women faced makes Ibn Badis's program appear quite ideological. Although the *sine qua non* of its success, women were not central to it. This use of women as ideological subjects did not allow for the creation of a social space that could have enabled them to enter debates over their status in their society as well as the impact of colonial rule on their lives. By defining socioeconomic problems affecting Algerians as problems caused by a lack of understanding and/or ignorance of religious texts, Ibn Badis and his followers subsumed the social under the religious. It is revealing in this respect that the golden age he held up to women and men took place not in precolonial Algeria but in Arabia, the cradle of Islam, during the early days of the Muslim empire. Women and men were relocated symbolically, hence foreclosing any discussion of their existential problems and an elaboration of adequate solutions to them.

A consequence of this transhistorical view of Algerians was a lack of specificity in the identification of the causes of social ills, as well as a failure to distinguish between problems inherent in the indigenous culture and those caused by colonial domination. In so doing, Ibn Badis and his followers added another layer of invisibility to women, and encouraged their silence. Indeed, women were caught between the self-serving pronouncements of the French colonists, the Young Algerians' perorations, and the allegedly rehabilitating exhortations of Ibn Badis's group. While men could transform women into ideological subjects, women had no counterideology to oppose and no public space left for them in which to express one. Theirs was a struggle of a different nature: survival. Ibn Badis is often perceived as having laid the groundwork for nationalism. He was credited with devising the motto: "Algeria is my country, Arabic my language, Islam my religion." Indeed; but the label "reformist" attached to his name is misleading as far as women are concerned. According to Ali Mérad, the concept of reform within the *'Ulama* context finds its justification in a verse in the *Quran*, which states that "I only wish to reform as much as I can," as well as a *hadith* that advocates "renewal" among Muslims every hundred years.[17]

Ibn Badis's undoubtedly heartfelt desire to upgrade his contemporaries' knowledge of their culture and instill in some of them pride in their identity did not extend to women as full-fledged members of their society, but as necessary props for men's salvation. Nevertheless, the *'Ulama* built schools for girls, although in smaller numbers than for boys. For example, by 1949, in the cities of Algiers, Qasantina, Wahran, and Laghouat, 138 schools for boys were opened, and eleven

for girls.[18] It is not enough to state, as Mérad did, that women remained, for Ibn Badis, "a delicate as well as thorny issue for which
Muslim opinion was not ready."[19] The point is to determine whether
Ibn Badis himself was ready to confront the woman question. He
clearly was not, just as he was unable to confront the issue of poverty.

Vagaries of Colonial Intervention in Natives' Family Law

It might be argued that the *'Ulama's* insistence on a return to pris-
tine religion was a response to colonial intervention in Algerians'
legal system, which was meant to absorb Algerians into French culture. Indeed, Ali Mérad pointed out that a precipitating factor was
the Jonnart Law of 1919, which spelled out naturalization terms for
Algerians living in territories under civil law.[20] This interpretation is
somewhat farfetched, since only certain categories of Algerians were
eligible for French citizenship. It is true, however, that naturalized
Algerians had to relinquish their personal status as Muslims, making
the *shari'a* inapplicable to them.[21] French legislators did subject Muslim courts to French courts, and gradually eroded and limited the
authority of Muslim judges in favor of French justices of the peace.[22]
This was a matter of concern for the *'Ulama*, which in March 1943
wrote a memorandum denouncing the poor training judges received,
their limited sphere of action and the anarchic structure of native
justice.[23]

However, prior to the advent of the *'Ulama* movement, French intervention in family law was motivated less by a desire for equity than
political expedience and control, often favoring the Berber ethnic
group over the Arab, the Ibadite M'zab religious community over all
others, and the northern region over the southern. The March 23,
1882 law obligated Muslim judges to register all Muslim marriages
with the colonial office of records within three days of the ceremony.
In addition, the April 2, 1936 law ordered Muslim judges to deliver
to spouses a marriage license within five days of the ceremony.[24]
Marriage and divorce being central to the Algerian family, proof of
either was not an issue among natives. These laws were passed to
make the administration of Algeria more efficient, and help in litigations among Algerians that were brought to French colonial courts.

The colonial authorities' use of French law as a tool of division of the
native population, albeit a risky one, was best illustrated by French
intervention in the Kabylie defined by colonists as entirely Berber,
and therefore, in their view, only mildly Muslim. After insisting that
custom law should be applied in this region, French authorities realized that there were no reliable native legal texts that could help

them to render justice according to custom. In addition, they soon found out that where custom interfered with the application of Islamic law, women bore the burden of the inequities that ensued. Ironically, French legislators felt compelled to uphold Islamic law in matters of divorce and inheritance, extricating it from its entanglements in local customs. For example, the local practice of having repudiated women pay their husbands a compensation greater than the value of their dowry was abolished by the May 19, 1931 decree.[25] Kabyle women had already been the focus of a 1902 decree setting their majority age at eighteen and making them eligible for the guardianship of their children. At times, French intervention was the result of a genuine misunderstanding of local customs. Thus, in 1930, confusing the native custom of child betrothal with actual marriage, French authorities ruled that "a declaration of engagement [understood in French terms as a promise of marriage] cannot be made before the age of fifteen unless an exemption is issued."[36] However, French legislators' interest in Kabyle women was unable to transcend the limits of their own male-centered view of women. Indeed, a 1944 ordinance stated that: "jurisprudence dictates that it is the husband's law that governs marriage" in cases of litigation arising between people from the Kabylie region who lived in other parts of Algeria where Kabyle custom law was not applicable. [27] French legislators' gendered view of women was not confined to the Kabylie. The August 12, 1936 decree set Sunni men's majority age at twenty-two and women's at twenty-five. However, married Sunni women became of age at twenty-two, thereby making marriage a rite of passage to legal competence.[28]

The most significant attempt at rationalizing Islamic law by codifying it was made in 1916 by Marcel Morand, dean of Algiers Law School. Code Morand became a document that was selectively used by Muslim and French judges, although it was never officially endorsed. Its purpose was "not to innovate" but to "formulate clearly and methodically the true principles of Muslim law."[29] Its author reviewed opinions by various classical Muslim legal scholars with a view to using those that seemed more equitable. It took place at a time when Middle Eastern countries such as Turkey and Egypt were giving some thought to reforms of family law. No doubt, this gave the code relevance and legitimacy. If looked at dispassionately, Code Morand could have been the product of concerned Algerian reformists. By and large, it did not tamper with the fundamentals of the *shari'a*. However, because it was initiated by colonial authorities who were already well engaged in the process of bringing the native justice system under control of French courts, it was perceived as one more intervention in natives' sense of cultural autonomy. Code Morand did away with provisions of Islamic law deemed inimical to the spirit of French law. For example, it overturned the prohibition on a Muslim woman marrying a non-Muslim man, and excluded different religious affiliations of spouses as well as apostasy from the grounds for disinheritance.[30] It is possible that these were seen as ominous changes, given that French-educated native men were slipping from their fathers' cultural grip. In addition, although mixed marriages involving native women and Frenchmen were few and far between, legalizing them within the *shari'a* may have seemed intolerable, since it brought Muslim women on a par with Muslim men, who were, and still are, allowed to marry non-Muslim women. Between 1948 and 1949, fifty-six mixed marriages were registered with the city of Algiers, fifteen of which were between an Algerian woman and a Frenchman.[31] Such marriages were more likely to take place in major urban centers than in small towns or rural areas, which remained generally untouched by them.

Reforming Islamic Law

It was not until 1957, three years after the struggle for decolonization began, that French legislators decided in earnest to reform Islamic law with a view to bringing it in line with French family law. This was the first time that colonial authorities finally concretized and acted upon their long-held conviction that Algerian women were "oppressed" by their culture and their men. The shift of emphasis from accommodating Islamic law to reforming it was motivated as much by a desire to rally women to the colonial aim of keeping Algeria French, as by the bureaucratic imperative of rationalizing the legal system by doing away with considerations of ethnic difference. The latter task was all the more important because colonists' opposition to an independent Algeria was gaining momentum. Thus, the July 11, 1957 law set majority age at twenty-one for both sexes, enabled women to become legal guardians of their children by default or if a deceased husband left no recommendation to this effect. Under the terms of the *shari'a*, a woman could become guardian only if her husband left instructions to this effect in his will. The law also created a Family Council in each case, comprised of six relatives from the mother's side and six from the father's side, a Muslim judge and a surrogate guardian. This clause was hailed by some commentators as a shift away from the male-centered foundation of Islamic law.[32] A February 4, 1959 ordinance and a September 17, 1959 decree prohibited early marriage, and made consent of spouses the sole requirement of marriages, thus diminishing the role of the family. A woman no longer required a guardian in order to marry, and most importantly, the right of a guardian to secure marriage for his ward without her consent was abolished. A woman's consent was to be given "verbally, in public, and in person."[33] Going against the prevailing custom, the law further spelled out that "unilateral promise of marriage, or the exchange of promises do not constitute marriage, or the obligation to contract marriage."[34] The law set marriage age at eighteen for men and fifteen for women. However, minors' consent was to be supported by their guardians in the presence of two witnesses before a Muslim judge or a city officer. To give legitimacy to their intervention, law-makers pointed out that they only meant to give Algerians a chance of benefiting from similar legal changes taking place in "neighboring Muslim countries" such as, perhaps, Tunisia.[35] In fact, the law was more daring in matters of divorce. It sought to limit men's abuse of repudiation by stipulating that it be formulated before a judge. A judge could oppose such a divorce. However, if he allowed it, the husband was liable for damages with interest. The law did not give women the right to oppose repudiation, but it did make it more difficult for men to use repudiation whimsically, therefore undermining an important foundation of their domestic power. As a rule, divorce was valid only if it was pronounced by a court. In a bizarre twist, the law was less liberal than the *shari'a* in outlining the conditions under which a woman could seek divorce. It cited overriding reasons such as "serious injuries or insults" leaving out grounds approved by Muslim jurists, such as impotence and other unobtrusive vices discovered by the wife.[36]

Unlike the Code Morand, the 1959 law went into application with various degrees of success. Divorces diminished, perhaps because of the fine attached to them. Nevertheless, repudiation continued to be practiced. But marriages before Muslim judges increased. In the past, a woman seldom appeared before a judge to express her consent. However, some couples (perhaps in an attempt to assert their nationalist views) dispensed with both Muslim judges and city officers. Admittedly, some women, especially in urban centers, took advantage of the law. Underscoring French legislators' politically motivated goal, the 1959 law did not apply to the religious sect of the M'zab, where fathers traditionally exercised their right to marry off their daughters without seeking their consent, and therefore, against their will. Keeping social peace in the southern M'zab territory took precedence over promoting women's rights.

Perhaps the timing of the law was the main impediment to its implementation. It was passed three years before the independence of Algeria, during the war which put people's loyalties to the test, and made their lives uncertain. Had it appeared at the turn of the century it would have made a greater impact on women's lives. By 1959 the battle lines were drawn between nationalists and colonists. The Front of National Liberation set up its own family courts wherever and whenever it could. The film, *The Battle of Algiers*, depicts a marriage ceremony attended by a F.L.N. judge who unites a young couple. Whether this event actually preceded the 1959 law, as the film (which recounts a 1956 to 57 war episode) implied, and how often F.L.N. courts were used, need to be ascertained. There is strong evidence that the F.L.N.'s intervention in family law was less reformist than purist at a time when women's participation in the war was recognized as both extraordinary and crucial. The F.L.N. did no more than limit dowry to five thousand francs (still an important sum then), and give its legal sanction to marriages between some guerrillas who fell in love with one another.

The main import of the 1959 law was felt primarily after Algeria became independent. It provided women who did not received satisfaction from Muslim judges ("Muslim" in the postcolonial context meant judges trained in the *shari'a*) to appeal to judges who were willing to refer to the 1959 law, which had not been repealed. The multiple interpretations of the *shari'a* and the selective applications of the 1959 law where the *shari'a* was deemed unclear or inconsistent with the law provided legislators with grounds to argue the need for a unified family law, pretty much as French legislators felt when they elaborated the Code Morand at the turn of the century. Their efforts resulted in the passage of the 1984 Family Code, which did away with many of the reforms of 1959, thereby institutionalizing inequality between women and men in family matters in violation of the Constitution, as will be shown in the next chapter.

Debating the Woman Question in Public

French intervention in family law, the emergence of native cultural integrity advocates, the creation of schools for girls by the *'Ulama*, as well as the rise of religious reformism in the Middle East, opened up a space among educated Algerians for a public discussion of the woman question. Native newspapers written in Arabic and French devoted columns to women, thereby providing a forum for young women and men to express their views on women's roles in society as well as issues affecting them. Editorials and debates began to appear in the mid-1940s in *Al Basair*, the new post-World War II name for *Al Shihab*, the Association of the *'Ulama*'s paper, which devoted a few articles denouncing excesses such as dowries set at prohibitive sums, and ostentatious weddings. It viewed with alarm declining age at marriage in rural areas. It also denounced the practice among Algerian men in urban centers of marrying late, often at thirty, thereby compelling women to wait longer to be married. Finally, the paper also reminded its readers that divorce by repudiation was misused. Issues related to veiling, mixed marriages, children and the role of women in society were taken up by the independent *Al Salam Review*, founded by a group of young male intellectuals.[37]

La République Algérienne, a paper issued by the *Manifeste du Peuple Algérien* (the Algerian People's Manifesto) a political association directed by Ferhat Abbas, who would become president of the Government in Exile created by the F.L.N., in the late 1950s, opened its column to letters from young women, and often printed interviews with feminists or notable women from the Middle East. Soraya Abul Nasr, an Egyptian feminist, emphasized the need for Algerian women to enter the professions as Egyptian women were doing and advocated the extension of political rights to all women.[38] In an interview, another Egyptian woman, Ceza Nabarawi, urged Algerian women to play a role in the liberation of their country. Asked what advice she would give her Algerian sisters, she replied: "Get an education, and give up the veil." Huda Sha'rawi, the well-known Egyptian feminist, was quoted as saying: "We are ready to help you. But we could not help those who have not begun to help themselves." It is unclear how she proposed to "help." Her statement, however, betrayed unfamiliarity with the double constraints (social and colonial) that weighed on Algerian women, whose experience she subsumed under her own. In this sense, Sha'rawi echoed Muhammad Abduh's lack of understanding of the specificity of the Algerian situation.[39]

In an interview, Mrs. Azzam Pasha, General Secretary of the Arab League, blamed "our fathers who confuse innocence with ignorance," and exhorted Algerian women to become "good citizens and mothers."[40] A Palestinian woman recounted her participation in the 1948 war, implicitly underscoring women's multiple roles, domestic and public.[41] In a veiled rejoinder, an Algerian woman living in Lyons, France, explained that she joined an Algerian youth organization to affirm her patriotism and "catch up" with Egyptian and Tunisian women.[42] These and many other interviews with women from Muslim societies held up for women the ideals of education, virtue and love for one's country in conformity with Ibn Badis's ideas. An article authored by a man, Mostefa Beshir, provided a searing critique of Algerian society:

> Will our brutalizing state of ignorance fostered by colonists become the hallmark of Algeria? ... Men have no natural right to use their wives and daughters as means to achieve their own ends, causing their womenfolk to miss out on their future.[43]

An editorial entitled "A shepherdess's message," and signed by a person whose sex cannot be determined since the first name is not spelled out, uses Joan of Arc's metaphor to hope for a better society:

> Even if this country that has fallen into anarchy is betrayed by its leaders and elites, a simple shepherdess could rise some day from the most remote corner of our native land to restore truth and chase away lies.[44]

Whatever the "truth" that the author had in mind, it appears that debates over women and their roles in society were managed and constrained. Information about foreign women focused primarily on the Middle East and occasionally on Muslim Asian countries to indicate that changes in women's status were taking place in cultures similar to that of the Algerians. This bespoke both a desire for a change in gender relations, and the direction that such a change should take. Indeed, French feminism was implicitly rejected as a topic of discussion and even more so as a source of inspiration. French women's interest in and activism on behalf of Algerian women was also rejected.

Thus, Marie Bugéja, daughter of a colonial administrator, wrote a book in 1921, reprinted in 1931, *Nos Sœurs Musulmanes* (Our Muslim Sisters) to "arouse a movement in favor of the neglected Algerian Muslim woman." She thought she "succeeded in doing so because I see many European women willing to participate in the renewal of this woman."[45] She recalled that when she embarked on her project she was told by her friends that she "will get nowhere, these women [Algerian] are stupid brutes."[46] Although she did not share her contemporaries' grossest prejudices against women, she nevertheless saw her mission as "humanitarian and patriotic." She felt rightly that her society was educating native boys and neglecting girls, which would amount to "taking one step forward and two backward" in terms of giving mothers control over their children. This would delay the assimilation of Algeria to France. For, in her own words, "my desire is that Algeria remain a possession of France."[47] The book was a series of anecdotes, observations and comments on the life-styles of Algerians and their interaction with colonists. Like Auclert, Bugéja often described injustices committed by her fellow Frenchmen against Algerians. Unlike Auclert, she recognized that structural changes had to be made to help women. Thus, she specifically opposed double standards and exceptional laws targeting Algerians, women and men. She also called for the construction of roads leading to villages, schools with large and airy classrooms, and "powerful means of propaganda" as, for example, infirmaries.[48] Paradoxically, Bugéja came closest to understanding Algerian culture because she did not dismiss it as an aberration while maintaining the superiority of her own culture. She blamed stereotypical images of women portrayed as "sexual animals or beasts of burden" on the male gender of French writers, and their lack of access to women.[49] She recognized, for example, that the *Quran* did not cause gender inequality.[50] However, when faced with behavior that, as a French woman, she deemed unlikely among Algerians, she expressed her disbelief, thereby betraying her prejudices. For example, when she saw, on a street in Algiers, an Algerian man helping a veiled woman get out of a carriage, she and a friend of hers stopped to observe the scene, wondering whether the couple was really Algerian.[51] Responding to a woman from the Kabylie who told her about her son, who had just been wounded in World War I, Bugéja answered: "Your son is under France's protection, and fighting under her flag. He is a brave man, doing his duty. You should be proud of him." The mother replied, in a typically polite Algerian manner: "It is true that my son likes your country, and I, his mother, like what he likes." Missing the point, Bugéja mused: "This ignorant and uncivilized woman knew from the depth of her village that France is loving and must be loved. Her son had told her so. How could she not believe a son?"[52] Love of France was to be the focus of the education she advocated for Algerian girls. Thus, by inscribing her activism in the larger colonial project of keeping Algeria French, she remained a French woman addressing a French public about native women. She may have influenced her French contemporaries in ways that are not clear. The editor of the second edition of her book, Edmond Esquirol, maintained that "many politicians, academics and journalists took from *Nos Sœurs Musulmanes* most of their information . . . [without] once citing the author to whom they owe everything."[53] Bugéja, also nicknamed "the Apostle," won the city of Paris' *Grand Concours Littéraire* (a literary prize) in 1930, in celebration of the one hundredth anniversary of the colonization of Algeria, for *Nos Sœurs Musulmanes* as well as *Visions d'Algérie*. There is some evidence, however, that her first book reached French-educated native women, some of whom paid her a visit after its publication.[54]

For a genuine debate between Algerian women and men (let alone between French and Algerian women) to happen a larger female audience of literate women was needed. But by 1951 there were only 6,696 girls in grade school,[55] making women's participation more symbolic than real. It is as if pressures for change in women's roles in society were bearing on Algerians from the outside world, but could not find support among the majority of women, who remained unaware of them or generally unable to act upon them. With the exception of Djamila Débèche, the first Algerian feminist, whose ideas will be presented in the next chapter, the women who were able to attend high school and college (numbering 1,014 and fifty-one respectively in 1954) remained silent on the eve of the revolution.[56] This silence was a reflection of women's structural marginalization by the colonists' society that perceived them as exceptional but did not embrace them, and the native society that admired their achievements with awe but was unable to empower them to speak on its behalf.

Instead, women's presence rather than their voice was given a space to fill in various native political associations, some of which were nationalist.[57] It is crucial to understand that this silence was the stilling of these women's French voices. The bulk of the women, who spoke little or no French and were also illiterate, could not be heard. They could, however, be seen. Thus, veiled women were seen marching in Algiers in a demonstration organized by Algerians for political rights in 1936, as was pointedly noted by Jacques Berque, historian of the Maghreb.[58] The thirties were a time of social unrest, marked by strikes in which Algerian workers took part as members of unions, even if in small numbers.[59] This might explain women's presence in the march.

In sum, the struggle between natives' cultural preservation reflex and the hit-and-run character of French intervention up until the war of decolonization centered on women as ideological subjects. By and large, French and native men mirrored one another's attitudes towards women's roles in society. Neither could transcend their male-centered view of women. Native men could not conceive of women as their equals, and perceived French attempts at reforming family law by rationalizing them as assaults on their cultural integrity, possibly their masculinity. Frenchmen used women to secure political gains, as they did with the M'zab region, and to achieve legal coherence by minimizing the differences between the *shari'a* and French family law. When they finally took their role of reformers seriously (in 1959), it was time for them to face up to the fact of Algerian independence (in 1962). Thus, they did too little too late. One positive result of the ideological use of women was that it opened up a space for discussing women, comparing them to other women in the Middle

East. However, discussions and debates over women fell short of native men's self-searching assessment of the part they played in the problems they denounced. Ultimately, discussions and debates remained academic, since no concrete solutions were worked out, except extolling the importance of education. This was a laudable but abstract goal, in the sense that education was not meant to significantly improve or change women's lives.

6

Women's Lived Reality in and Under Colonial Society

As women's roles in native society were the subject of newspaper articles in the francophone and arabophone press, and discussions among acculturated men, or religious leaders, women themselves remained generally unaffected by the attention accorded them.[1] As was pointed out in the previous chapter, the majority of women could neither read nor write Arabic and/or French, and therefore had no access to what was said about them. Furthermore, their material life circumstances—the stuff that makes change in gender relations possible—were not only left unaddressed, but also prevented them from being receptive to debates on women's roles. Indeed, women lived in relative isolation from both the colonial society and the world of native men. Their lives followed their own tempo albeit they intersected with those of French women and men at significant moments such as the two world wars, natural disasters, and the war of decolonization. In many ways they made their own history quietly, organized and furnished their world with activities and thoughts that gave it meaning. Their historical time was unique to them, yet it also cut across colonial historical time. They were in and out of the colonial social order that alternately silenced, and spoke for and against them. They asserted themselves with and against native men in ways that colonial writers generally misrecognized. A remarkable feature of Algerian women's lived reality that can be tapped through the study of change in family formation and relations, time, games, magical practices and tales is the degree to which it is at odds with prevailing conceptions of it grounded in social science practices. Women's silence registered by the colonial society gave rise to stereotypical views which are denied by the cacophony of voices that can be heard among native women's society. Similarly, native men's stereotypical conceptions of women are equally denied by women's everyday and ritualistic practices.

Women and the Family

The centrality of the family in women's lives was reinforced by its role as both a buffer against the colonial society and as the arena where the contradictions and inconsistencies of the colonized society played themselves out. Indeed, the socioeconomic changes that affected native Algerians impacted on their family structure and their perceptions of one another.

In the nineteenth century, changes in the land tenure system as well as the commodification of land affected the size of the family and the relationships between its members. One of the first acts of colonial sovereignty was to seize land placed in trust with mosques to be used for the good of the community of Muslims. Colonists put tribal/communal lands up for sale and often simply seized some of them, and established the principle that all land is alienable.[2] This last measure dealt a heavy blow to the social cohesion of the extended family and its relation to the tribe. Indeed, prior to the colonial intervention, the rights of individual family members to family-owned land were recognized, but custom made it difficult for them to sell the land of their forebears. In this, the Algerian/Muslim conception of land was fundamentally different from the European/French conception. Paul Charnay adequately analyzed the difference in these terms:

> Contrary to the spirit of the [French] Civil Code which perceived land in an impersonal manner, as an object that can be privately appropriated by a disembodied individual, Maghrebin property law always and implicitly aims at the survival of the human being.[3]

Heavy taxation combined with dislocations of families due to a protracted war of conquest compelled individuals to sell their inherited land, thereby weakening not only the group's social cohesion, but also its economic autonomy.

In their social consequences the new property laws had effects similar to those caused by the enclosures movement in Britain in the eighteenth century. Individuals were "freed" from the network of social relations that bound them to their kinship groups and to one another. However, while British peasants were ultimately integrated into the capitalist economy, propertyless Algerians remained marginal to colonial capitalism which required their dispossession. Paradoxically, this marginalization led to a reconstitution in a relatively new form of the family ties that had just been shattered. Indeed, as individuals found themselves thrust into a new economy that had little room for them, they used their immediate family as a resource to stay their course in the new social order. Hence the new family became smaller, including two generations, and sometimes conjugal. Due to voluntary and forced migrations, it also became relatively more mobile. In addition, its ties to the tribe and, therefore, to a plurality of families claiming common ancestry, gradually declined. A measure of such decline is provided by a study of court documents, which reveals that litigations involved families and rarely, if at all, tribes.[4]

For women, this meant that their male relatives, significant agents in protecting their matrimonial interests, were socially less reliable since they had shaken loose the bonds that tied them to their women and menfolk. Theoretically, this should have meant a greater "freedom" for women in relation to men. But the colonial framework within which these structural changes took place resulted in another apparent paradox. Women were compelled to fight male relatives who violated their property rights, *and* the colonial legal order that changed property laws. Furthermore, the new French property laws reactivated the property rights given women under the *shari'a*, but generally left it to male relatives to manage. Women became "free" to fight to keep their right to property. At a time when men often fought for the right to own as little as three square centimeters (the actual share of a patrimony claimed by a large number of relatives) in order to keep themselves anchored, women's action could only acquire a great significance.[5] Indeed, Charnay argues that "Women's influence was foremost among the reasons that caused the dismantling of family wealth from within."[6] This is no doubt an exaggeration, since women did no more than defend their rights trampled by both their male relatives and French courts.

As was pointed out in Chapter 3, in the second half of the nineteenth century there were numerous instances of brothers who sold their sisters' share to the family land without their knowledge, and evidently without sharing with them the proceeds from the sales. Similarly, some women fought French-controlled courts to retain inheritance given to them or their children by their fathers or husbands as *habous* meaning inalienable property.

Perhaps more significant signs of the structural changes affecting the family should be sought in the study of marriage contracts. For example, Jacques Berque noted that in Tunisia, beginning in the

1930s, urban women refrained from including a clause in their marriage contracts that prohibited their husbands from moving away from their familial neighborhood after marriage.[7] Indeed, the family being more mobile, as in Algeria, women could not insist on staying near their parent's home without losing a suitor. In the old days, parents (especially mothers) could insist that their daughters remain within their community after marriage.

In addition, parallel-cousin marriage, once a preferred type of marriage, lost its preeminence. Daughters as well as sons could be married to total strangers and sent to towns and cities distant from their homes. Pierre Bourdieu has adequately explained the fluctuations of parallel-cousin marriage among the Kabyle Berbers. He argued that the frequency of this type of marriage was a function of the volume of property held by the family, as well as, *inter alia*, the size of the family. Thus:

> Once the family property is divided and there is nothing to recall and maintain the genealogical relationship, the father's brother's daughter may be considered no closer in degree of kinship than any other patrilineal (or even matrilineal) cousin. On the other hand, a genealogically more distant cousin may be the practical equivalent of the *bent'amm* [paternal cousin] when the two cousins are part of a strongly united 'house' living under one elder and owning all its property in common.[8]

While family relationships among Kabyle Berbers may not be typical of Algeria, the practice of parallel-cousin marriage was affected throughout the country by the same property laws and the tribal dislocations that ensued, as well as by land sequestration carried out by colonial authorities. It is the colonial factor that Bourdieu fails to include in his analysis, and that prevents him from explaining how and why some families could maintain the custom, and others had to do away with it. At any rate, under circumstances where parents were unable to afford a dowry, parallel marriage was preferred.

In the absence of reliable studies of the impact of parallel-cousin marriage on women, one can only speculate. Once the material *raison d'être* of parallel-cousin marriage was severely undermined, its survival obeyed the logic of convenience. From the standpoint of a woman, marrying her cousin held some advantages. She knew him, as opposed to marrying a stranger, and she would expect to be treated as a member of the family instead of having to adjust and win the respect, if not love, of unrelated in-laws. Yet the family bond itself was often cause for avoiding parallel-cousin marriage. Indeed, daughters could not get the full dowry they would have received from a stranger. In addition, in case of unhappiness with the marriage, a woman could not easily use her customary right to leave her husband for a period of time until her differences with him were resolved. Nor could problems arising out of the marriage be aired freely since everything must be kept in the family, so to speak.

From the standpoint of the man, marrying his parallel cousin assured him of lower dowry, and reinforced his role in the family as a cousin and a husband. Most importantly, it fulfilled the symbolic function of preserving the "right" of precedence over other suitors given to him by custom. However, even this "right" could now be vacated by parents seeking better suitors for their daughters and eager to avoid parallel-cousin marriage. Parents used various strategies that effectively discouraged their kin. This could only be done once solidarity among kin had been seriously undermined by the deep economic changes that began in the nineteenth century. The waning of the parallel-cousin marriage meant that many young women would now marry some distance away from their relatives, and risk difficult adjustment to, if not mistreatment by, in-laws. The cliché of the punitive mother-in-law and jealous sisters-in-law who make life miserable for a young bride finds its roots in the changing family structure.

This change illustrates the separation of the ideal of *'ada*, or tradition, and *waqt*, or time, as in changing times. One lives in changing times which somehow must be made meaningful by anointing them with traditional rituals.[9] For example, in contemporary Algeria, young women attending universities date fellow male students without their parents' knowledge or approval. When their relationship becomes serious, the young men's relatives visit the girlfriends' parents to initiate engagement proceedings according to the age-old ritual. Thus, the new practice which defies the old tradition becomes legitimized by an appeal to the tradition.

Bourdieu perceptively distinguishes between rules and practices, explaining how practices seldom mean obedience to rules. Similarly, *'ada*, beginning in the colonial era, acted as a symbolic cover for changing practices. That at times parents insisted on obedience to *'ada* goes without saying. There may even have been some periods of time when *'ada* was preeminent. This, however, does not preclude the existence of slow but incremental change in directions that were at times beneficial, and at other times detrimental to women.

For example, a study of court documents covering the first half of this century indicates that boys and girls married at younger ages. In addition, the study also points out that *fathers* (usually perceived by the French as imposing their will on their daughters) often opposed the consummation of their daughters's marriage if they had not reached puberty.[10] Furthermore, many fathers requested divorce in the name of their unhappy daughters.[11] In addition, aware of the widespread disinheritance of girls by the combined forces of unscrupulous male relatives and a new legal system that offered women little protection, fathers sought ways of securing their daughters' economic futures. They typically created fictitious debts to their daughters, and left wills declaring some of their poperty *habous* (inalienable) as payment of the debts. Wise to this trick, French courts often opposed fathers' wills.[12]

Young women often defied not only marriage customs but also the family tradition of heeding the counsel and authority of male relatives in the choice of a spouse. For example, in the city of Bedjaia, a young girl of eleven petitioned the French court to have her formal marriage to an eight-year-old boy annulled. A young woman from Tlemcen declares to a French judge that she refuses the man chosen for her by her brother and agreed to by the *qadi* (Muslim judge) because she loves another man. Another woman from the M'zab unsuccessfully requested that her guardian be changed because he disapproved of her lover.[13]

At the same time that some women challenged the *'ada*, many experienced the rigidity of French courts, which often misunderstood the intentions of the *shari'a* or the cultural practices of Algerians, and ruled in ways that deterred families from seeking relief. Thus, a Muslim judge would invalidate a divorce by repudiation, which a French court would sustain on appeal.[14] There are also instances of women who appealed to French courts to help them to leave polygamous marriages but were either forced into them or charged damages for "defaulting on domestic chores and failing to carry out their conjugal duty."[15] Women who left their husbands for a plurality of reasons, including polygamy, were often returned by force by the police to their husbands. One such woman argued successfully that she could not be returned to her husband without losing face before her community unless he was compelled to secure the intervention of a notable man from the community.[16] In so doing this woman registered her contempt for the French court, which would have sent a police officer to return her to her husband. She also upheld a tradition of arbitration among native society which enabled her to argue that she *agreed* to return to her husband because of her respect for the notable arbitrator. This woman gave herself a way out. She would be able to leave her husband again after arguing that he did not respect the moral authority of the arbitrator. There was some irony in having a French court agree to uphold a native custom upon the request of a woman who had initially thought French justice would sustain her opposition to polygamy.

Women generally appealed to courts to seek freedom from their husbands for mistreatment, sexual incompetence and living arrangements that kept them with their in-laws and, more rarely, second wives. A husband's impotence is recognized by the *shari'a* as a ground for divorce. However, French courts sometimes accepted a man's sworn testimony that he was not impotent, thus invalidating a wife's competence in a private matter.[17] There is some evidence that French judges may have felt, as Charnay did, that "feminine contradictions are universal, and will not cease to astound me."[18] In other words, women's claims were not seen as legitimate, but as expressions of feminine wiles. In this, as in other family matters, the "French judge was perhaps unconsciously influenced by masculine superiority."[19]

Caught between two antithetical legal systems (the Muslim and the colonial) women often played one against the other in the hope of getting satisfaction. Sometimes, a woman would claim she was a concubine to her husband in order to obtain her freedom from a marriage that had not been registered with the court, as was the custom among rural people and the urban poor who could not afford the required fees, or those who refused to cooperate with the French administration.[20] The issue of unregistered marriages (or marriage *bel fatiha*), legitimate among Muslims but inexistent in the eyes of the French judge, hurt women throughout the colonial era. Indeed, a wife could not obtain pension benefits or alimony from a husband, especially if he worked in France, where he was often covered by social security.[21] The French reliance on written proof among natives who often concluded transactions verbally added another strain on women's lives, especially with regard to issues centering on child support, inheritance, and succession.[22] In general, a division of labor of sorts set in between Muslim and French courts. Muslim courts in urban centers found in favor of women in matters of repudiation, and were approached by native women and men to hear divorce and custody matters. Rural women and men typically appealed to French court for land issues. French courts were usually appealed to by women seeking payments of dowry and child support.[23]

A diffuse acculturation, strong and visible among segments of the population, such as the first generation of French-educated Algerians, spotty among others, who began to acquire French goods such as cars or bicycles, purely linguistic among still others, who began to incorporate Arabized French words in their speech, played a role in both the assertion of the *'ada* and its slow demise. Imagine a religious institution such as the *zawiya* using a French court in order to enforce its values on some of its members, when *it* fulfilled the functions of arbitration among natives who preferred to avoid courts.[24] Imagine also natives using French courts to enforce traditional customs among rural community members, such as the *tawsa* or free-exchange of labor for others.[25]

Acculturation is usually perceived as measurable in that individuals or groups can be observed to acquire the value and behavior patterns typical of the culture in which they were socialized. In the Algerian case, it must also be used to refer to intangible, nonmeasurable factors, such as perceptions of the French Other held by native women and men, and imperceptible changes in domestic life due to the use of French artifacts made out of plastic or aluminum such as pails, baking trays, cosmetics, barrettes and others that had displaced native crafts. All these items sound trivial, yet they play a significant role in anchoring individuals in a social space they identified as their own.

For the majority of Algerians who had been left out of the French school system, what might be termed "object acculturation" meant that their cultural identity was Arabo-Berber and Muslim but their daily activities were carried out with an increasingly larger number of instruments made by the French for French use. I am suggesting that this situation created an antinomy within Algerians who resisted acculturation, understood as the adoption of the French value system, but relied on a material culture alien to them. After the country became independent this antinomy disappeared, and a greater demand for such a material culture was made as socialist controls over imports stiffened. The new directed economy made it difficult for people, women and men, caught as they were in the web of rising expectations, to acquire from France or elsewhere material goods for which they hungered.

Acculturation in its various forms, some obvious, others subtle, had an unrecognized effect on family relations. I suspect that urban families who often avoided parallel-cousin marriage on grounds that it was genetically risky partook in the larger colonial opinion on this matter. Similarly, a new demand made by middle-class urban families that their daughters be housed separately from their in-laws may have been affected by the introduction of the couple as an alternative marriage type by the French.

This is not to say that Algerians imitated the colonists' life-styles. Rather, the profound changes in the economic conditions of Algerians laid the groundwork for social changes that *in form* resembled those in existence among the colonists. Thus, throughout the colonial era it was not unusual to see sons move out of their parents' home upon their marriage. While this may have been welcome by their wives, mothers (especially those that had borne only one or two sons) were left to live alone with their unwed daughter(s) after their husbands' death. The emergence of woman-headed households is difficult to pinpoint, but it is linked to a greater tolerance for male relatives shirking their duties as protectors of their womenfolk. This trend would accelerate in the postindependence era, which witnessed the emergence in large urban centers of homeless older women whose children (often sons) were reluctant to take them in for a variety of reasons, ranging from housing shortage to preserving conjugal peace.

Women's Speech and Time

It is difficult to envision the lives of women whose familiar landscape changed as radically as Algerian women's did. The severe ravages of the war of colonial conquest, compounded by the establishment of a new economic and political order, left women apparently silent. At least this is what one gathers from the relevant literature on the subject.

As was explained in the previous chapter, it is true that up until World War II women remained largely illiterate, unable to communicate through the written word, either in Arabic or French. However, under this structurally imposed silence a whole range of activities took place that required women's voices. Women's lives were filled with talk adapted to the gender and political status of their audience. Women's talk as well as silence are linked to the sexual division of labor. Women learned their communicative skills in the family—both the locus of their lives and a contested terrain.

It would be a mistake to consider the Algerian family as women's place only. Charnay did not mince his words on this topic: "Man, driven toward domestic life [by his struggle against colonialism] which disabled him, will directly and often closely manage the household."[26] In fact, men's presence in the family after their working hours made it (and to a great extent still does) a formal environment requiring women's adjustment of voice and speech demeanor. For example, women developed an elaborate body language based on eye contact and movement, supported by an occasional word here and there, with their female children and relatives meant to convey meanings they could not afford to spell out before their menfolk. In addition, women made liberal use of "equivocal language, and allusions" captured by the proverb "they [women] buy and sell men even when they [men] are sitting with them in the same room."[27] This proverb underscores women's linguistic skills in communicating with one another about and in the presence of men.

Women, especially in urban centers, were prone to using a precious form of language fraught with diminutive words.[28] Typically, women fell silent when men raised issues related to their handling of their domestic activities, or when they became angry. When interacting with one another, women talked about every aspect of their lives. A remarkable feature of their behavior was the ability to recount events in details that brought them alive. When interacting on occasion with colonists, women typically relied on body language (since most could not speak French), especially facial expressions meant to convey powerlessness and elicit compassion. Colonists often mistook these for either subservience or deceptive behavior to curry favor with them.

The division of labor, as reflected in gendered speech patterns and strategies, was only one aspect of women's *eloquence*. A second aspect was time. There is a sense in which women's time was different from native men's and colonists' time. Yet it also overlapped with both. Time, as a factor that partially accounts for women's voices and silence, acquires a special significance under colonial rule. Indeed, the measuring and marking of time used by women was based on the Muslim calender, which they kept dutifully. Native men shared this calender with their womenfolk. However, because they also lived in the world of business that was dominated by French time, measured by the Gregorian calender, they had the ability to be in and out of two temporal realities.

The gender difference in marking and accounting for time may explain the colonial notion that women were silent. In fact, their activities took place according to not only a different calender of holidays and rituals, but also social concerns. For instance, marriage negotiations and ceremonies, boy circumcision rituals, end of pilgrimage festivities, *Ramadan* nightly celebrations, seasonal food preservation, caring for the sick, among other things, involved women's participation to a greater extent than men.

As colonial rule proceeded, crises beyond women's control incorporated them into French and native men's time. Thus, World War I, the depression of 1920, the deflation of 1935, World War II and colonial wars in Madagascar and Vietnam brought women squarely into the society of colonists. Women lost husbands and sons in all of these wars, and were, thus, propelled into administrative offices seeking relief. Many women had no geographical notion of where Europe or Madagascar (which they pronounced "Madame Gasca") could be. Yet they understood that they were dangerous places to which the French sent their male relatives. Oftentimes, husbands and sons enlisted in the French army to put an end to chronic unemployment. When such decisions were made, women staged mock funerals attended by their friends and female relatives, before the departure of their loved ones to such faraway places. Rationing during World War II exacted a heavy toll on women who generally had to line up as early as 3 A.M. outside distribution centers to get their family rations. That women held a grudge against colonial rule need not be demonstrated. It is interesting to note, however, that writers such as Charnay were able to appreciate this fact. He felt it necessary to point out that women resented the colonial system.[29]

Retreating into women's time, the only time possible given the irrationality of French/native men's time, provided solace. This can be gauged by the often-hostile reaction of mothers to their sons' desire to marry French women. Such reaction could not be attributed to mothers' fear of their sons' acculturation only. It was also a reaction to the ripple, if not tear, that a French woman could cause to a native woman's time. Similarly, grandmothers' insistence that their French-educated granddaughters heed the age old 'ada had to do with the preservation of women's time, seen as a bulwark against colonial intrusion. Women's time was neither recognized nor understood by French women or men. It was dismissed under the catchall term of "backwardness." Whatever women said or did in their time was, therefore, of no consequence. They were perceived as "oppressed," the objects of men's will and having no agency.

Tales and Games

The oral tradition established by women through the manipulation of speech is exceptionally rich. Throughout the colonial era and before the advent of television, storytelling was the quasimonopoly of women. They told stories about colonial invasion, relationships between husbands and wives, parents and children, brothers and sisters, stepmothers and stepdaughters, about orphaned children, marital infidelity, unknowing incest and the anguish of living on the margin of power centers. All these themes were drawn from real life, and often rang true to those who heard them, although protagonists included fairies, jinns, ogres and ogresses. Generations of boys and girls were reared on these tales. As an Algerian writer who collected some of these tales from his eighty-year-old aunt Zouina put it: "During my childhood, I heard them [tales] many times shaking with excitement under my blankets, lying down between my sisters or my cousins."[30] Aunt Zouina spoke into a tape recorder, and ended her tales with the poetic Arab formula that most children have heard: "My tale ends here; I told you what was told me. My tale runs like a river; I told it to royalty."[31]

Tales varied from region to region but often used common characters such as that of *settut*. This was an old lady who took special pleasure in creating problems for younger women, and breaking up their marriages through lies, gossip and providing bad counsel. Another character is that of the ogress (in Arabic *ghula*) whose goal was to devour people. Typically she is defeated by a young and unassuming man, *hadiduan*, whose wits saved him from difficult situations.

It should not be assumed that men did not tell stories to their children. In fact there was a division of labor of sorts that characterized storytelling. Men, mostly fathers, often told stories not only to their children, but also to their wives, derived from the *One Thousand and One Nights*, or from early Islamic history. This was an important tool of socialization of the young into their culture, and was often the only instruction in history they received at times when illiteracy was widespread. Women's tales were centered on themes that appeared more familiar to women than the splendor of the *One Thousand and One Nights*, which, nevertheless, enchanted them.

If tales told by women wove bonds that tied them to their children and relatives, games and magical practices built a network of solidarity among women, whether they were related by blood or not. A favorite game among women was referred to as the *boqala*. This term designates a water pitcher made of clay with two handles, which was (and still is) used to divine the future. When used in the plural (e.g., *buaqal*) the term also refers to short poems transmitted orally from woman to woman and interpreted as omens.[32] The use of water as a means of foretelling the future lends itself to a number of theoretical explanations based on the ancient origins of this practice. The fact that this game, within the Algerian context, was exclusively female has given rise to interesting but farfetched explanations. For example, Martine Bertrand argues that women's "seclusion" made fetching water outside the home an extraordinarily appreciated activity that gave women a chance to learn about one another. Hence water came to symbolize information. In addition, this author invokes the *hammam* or Turkish bath, a place where women gather to wash themselves, receive a massage and chat, reinforcing the symbolism of water as information.[33] Linking the use of water in divination games such as the *boqala* to an alleged seclusion of women is too facile. If women were secluded how could they be allowed to fetch water? Rural women generally fetched water and they never wore the veil—the symbol of "seclusion." In addition, women also used astrology to divine the future; some of them would scrutinize the stars while reciting incantations in an effort to decipher an omen. Are we to say that "seclusion" led women to wish for the stars? Foretelling the future was a passion for women and men. Its intensity and degree of frequency (about which there is little information) may have to do with the sociopolitical framework within which women and men lived. It would be interesting to find out whether the use of the *boqala* changed under the colonial era.

At any rate the *boqala* was divinatory in a contrived manner. The game normally takes place at night, on a Wednesday, Friday or Sunday. It begins with the fumigation of an empty pitcher over a brasero sprinkled with incense and dried herbs. While the fumigation takes place, an incantation is recited, as, for example:

> We have subjected you to the scent of incense,
> Bring us news from cafés.
> We have subjected you to the scent of henna,
> Bring us news from Mezrana [e.g. Algiers]
> We have subjected you to the smoke from oil,
> Bring us news from all homes.
> We have subjected you to the smoke from a widow's clothes,
> Bring us news from men.
> We have subjected you to the smoke from burning wood shards,
> Bring us news from pilgrims [to Mecca].[34]

This formula, seen as having a magical power, sets the tone for the game. The pitcher is then filled with water, and an invocation poem is recited by the officiating woman. One version of this poem is as follows:

> In the name of God I start [e.g. the game].
> I say a prayer for the Prophet.
> I bless his Companions.
> I praise Ali.
> You may chat as you wish; your words are as solid as the air and the wind.
> As for me, my star shines and my candle is bright.
> Whatever the bricklayer builds collapses
> But, I am more successful.
> I called you, Oh my Lord and Savior,
> Deliver us from offense and humiliation, Oh Lord,
> Bu 'Alam El Jilali.[35]

Usually, after this invocation, assembled women are asked one by one to tie a knot in their belts or handkerchiefs and focus their attention on the person or the event they want to know about. A new poem is then recited, as the officiating woman and/or her two assistants (usually virgins) place the pitcher on her thumbs and order it to move left or right. The well-balanced pitcher is supposed to rotate in one direction, signalling a way of interpreting the poem that has just been recited.

What is remarkable about this game is that its "magical" quality is in fact contained in the poems improvised by women themselves. The rotating pitcher does no more than indicate to women how to interpret and anchor the meaning of their own poems, left purposely vague and metaphorical. In addition, the profane quality of the game (since Islam forbids divination) is cast in a religious framework by invoking God, his Prophet, his companions, and his son-in-law, Ali. As was pointed out in the analysis of the Nailiyat dance performance, religious themes are intricately linked to profane practices as a way of legitimizing them. Whether this is a practice that originated among women is not clear. However, it tends to occur in all occult or quasi-occult practices initiated by women. The invocation of the names of God and his Prophet is also supplemented by the invocation of the power and grace of Bu 'Alam El Jilali, a Sufi saint, known throughout the Middle East, whose name was Sidi Abd-El-Kader El Jilani. Women referred to him as the "flag-bearer" (Bu 'Alam), by which is meant the man who leads to success/victory. Thus women blend together the occult with their beliefs in Sufism.

A version of the *boqala* that takes place in the city of Mostaganem, but is usually associated with rural women, does away with the pitcher altogether. In this sense it should not be considered a *boqala*. I was introduced to it when I was thirteen years old. Its rules were similar to the ones cited by Martine Bertrand.[36] Typically, an unmarried (virgin) young woman prepares dry couscous with water gathered from seven fountains, and must refrain from speaking throughout the preparation. Fumigation includes not only incense and herbs, but also seven pieces of wool yarn taken from men's hats [*shwashi*], as well as a piece of alfa (esparto grass) taken from a basket. A poem/incantation is recited during fumigation. Late at night women go out on a terrace or roof, recite more poems, scatter the couscous in the air, and wait for a noise to disturb the portentous silence. If a train roars by, this signifies that the person in whose name the incantation was made will soon travel. The shadow of a passerby can help to specify the meaning of a poem.

A study of 175 poems reveals that seventy percent of them deal with love themes and the rest center on friendship, despair, solitude, gossip, regret of the past, religion and wishes.[37] Colonial domination never appears among the themes dealt with.[38] Indeed, the *boqala* was rooted in women's time that women protected from outside interference.

From 1974 to 1975, the Algerian national radio began to broadcast in French the game of the *boqala*, inviting women to contribute poems and to indicate for whom they "tied a knot." This weekly broadcast— every Wednesday from 9 to 10 P.M.—was successful in bringing together female and male listeners, who flooded the radio with poems written on postcards or phoned in. The objectives of the broadcast were not clear, and could be seen, as some commentators argued, as a way of stemming superstitious beliefs.[39] Perhaps this was a timid attempt on the part of the state radio to revalue women's contribution to popular culture at a time when a draft of a family code was in the works. It might also have been a way of socializing a new generation of young people into a family practice that had become redundant with the widespread use of television. Indeed, the broadcast emphasized the female origins of the game.

At any rate, the game, hosted by a female broadcaster, followed the established rules, but was sometimes given interpretations based on sociopolitical events instead of purely personal problems. For example, the following two verses of a *boqala* poem:

> I climbed on the roof to catch my dove. . . .
> And I rejoice in my enemy's misfortune
> As he did in mine.

was interpreted as meaning that the dove "symbolizes a personal concern such as a job, an engagement, a promotion, a material success, etc." The last verse was interpreted as:

> referring to our country. Yes, our people's struggle against
> colonial occupation, and our victory in becoming independent could be explored as a possible interpretation. This is
> all the more plausible that we are in the process of commemorating our struggle for national liberation.[40]

There is something appealing in a radio program that strives to incorporate women's oral literary activity into a larger political project. However, to result in changing attitudes towards women, this program needed to draw the necessary linkages between women's literary capacity, their social status and the meaning of the "struggle for national liberation." But the broadcast abruptly ended in 1975, despite its success. It seems as though an attempt at feminizing Algerian culture was dealt a deadly blow.

A major component of the *boqala* was its poetic form of expression, which women used as a seamless web from generation to generation. Indeed, some parts, especially openings, were the same, but the body of a poem often changed depending on the improvisational talent of a woman. Women also used their verbal skills in creating songs they sang at weddings, or that their daughters sang while balancing from swings. Finally, women also improvised eulogies for the dead in verse.

In parts of the country such as Western Algeria, entertainment on *Ramadan* nights often included women organizing skits, poking fun at one another and at male relatives whom they imitated in both clothing, voice and behavior. Whether women composed poems or put on acts, they derived pleasure from their activities.

Magical Practices

Perhaps one of the practices that most women shared directly or indirectly was (and, to some extent, still is) magic. By "magic," within the Algerian context, I mean the use of talismans and other objects for the purpose of influencing an individual's behavior, or causing harm to her/him. Colonial writers have documented magical practices in some regions of Algeria.[41] Apart from seeking to increase their luck, and/or protect themselves from envy that activates the "evil eye," women were in a constant search to control men's attitudes towards them. To make a husband "frash" meant to turn him into a doormat. To make a man "'ard" (or ground) meant to bend him to one's will and make him as powerless as the ground under one's feet. A cooperative husband was often seen by friends and relatives as a "mahkoom," or controlled man.

To achieve such an outcome a woman might use the services of a *taleb* (literally "student" or learned man) who prescribes a course of treatment that varies with individual cases but often includes surreptitiously soaking paper strips written with Arabic formulae in coffee, tea or soup, and feeding the concoction to her husband. What a husband ingests unknowingly can include cooked animal parts such as the praised hyena heart, so rare in Algeria. The principle at work here is that ingesting the organ of an animal perceived as embodying passivity will transfer this quality to the individual. Being less literate than men women did not engage in magical practices requiring the use of written materials. These were the monopoly of the *tolba* (plural of *taleb*).

However, causing men to be passionate lovers was sometimes the task of a woman who indulged in the occult. A common practice consisted of burning coriander grains, herbs and dried sperm, secured by a wife during intercourse, in a brasero filled with ambers at night. This was a way of igniting passion in a husband who had left his wife, or whose wife left him temporarily and hoped he would come for her. Men, too, secured the services of a *taleb*, albeit less often than women. Typically, an older man would seek to make sure that a younger wife became uninterested in men, or a spurned suitor might wish to prevent the object of his love from marrying. The expression "she is tied" refers to a young woman who cannot find a husband. She was "tied" maleficiently by her suitor (or his womenfolk) to him. In general, men were aware of women's magical practices, and occasionally complained of being "poisoned" by wives.[42]

The temptation is too great to interpret women's recourse to magic to influence men's behavior as a sign of their powerlessness. What must be considered is the fact that even happily married women were prone to using magic. In addition, oftentimes some men, especially in small towns, also tried to influence one another's behavior by wearing talismans under their shirts to make good impressions on superiors, or to maximize the chances of success of a business transaction. Perhaps it is the kind of behavior change sought that helps to understand whether individuals resorted to magic out of powerlessness or as part of an intricate web of values, norms and expectations. Where women felt powerless, as in battering, they sought all sorts of remedies to relieve this condition, including securing the soap with which a dead man's body was washed and giving it to a guilty husband to use for washing his hands. Thus, the batterers' hands will be unable to hit his wife since the soap will make them as dead as a dead man's. At any rate, magic was both an instrumental activity and a pastime.

Women usually helped one another by exchanging names of good "tolba" and fortune tellers. However, sisterhood was not always operative. Women engaged in magical practices against other women. This condition accounts for a widespread ritual, occurring at least once a year, aimed at undoing any suspected magical act against oneself even in the absence of a specific enemy who might have cause to undertake it. This ritual, named *f'sukh*, consists of burning a mineral called *fasukh* along with coriander and incense, and fumigating all rooms of one's house. It can also be supplemented by the *khfif* (literally lightweight), the practice of pouring molten lead into a brass mortar filled with cold water. The name "lightweight" may refer to the fact that the procedure results in making the client lose the weight of malevolent acts perpetrated against her. A woman who believes she is the target of someone's magical acts then stands with her legs spread apart over the mortar, which has been covered with a large sieve to make sure the shattering lead does not hurt her. The shapes that the cooled lead assumes are deciphered by the officiating woman, who interprets the nature of the magical doings against her client. The *khfif* was an entirely female activity performed on women as well as men who expressed interest in it.

Love and Masquerade

Tales, games and magical practices, when seen as problem-solving and adaptive strategies, acquire a particular significance in accounting for women's roles in colonial Algeria. They reveal women's sense of identity, and provide an inkling of their worldview. Women's lives were furnished with activities that responded more to their immediate, mundane concerns than with either religious dogma, or colonial ideology of "oppression." This is made amply evident in the practice of magic. It is also supported by instances of free love, as well as dressing like a man in order to circumvent the cultural prohibition on sexual activity before or outside marriage. A known but little-discussed practice is that of women dressing as men to meet their male friends at night, go out with them to public places or take short trips with them. In this way, a woman can slip out of her house at night without arousing suspicion among neighbors. The dress usually consists of the *jellaba*, a typical North African male coat with a hood. The hood is convenient to cover the head and partially hide the face. Naturally not all women dare to venture outside their homes dressed like men. However, some do. There is no study of this phenomenon that would shed light on its frequency and the social characteristics of the women who engage in it. Suffice it to say that two women I interviewed who admitted doing it were from lower-middle-class families, and were married. However, one of them revealed she went out dressed as a man to meet a young man she loved before she got married in the 1950s. She was able to slip out while her father and older brother were home. Her mother covered for her by saying that she had gone to visit an ailing grandmother. That some female complicity had to be present for this scheme to take place is evident and adds a romantic touch to it.

No matter how typical this kind of practice was, it does illustrate the gap between norms and actual behavior. It also points to the difficulty for a society such as Algeria, caught as it was between its own contradictions and colonial neglect, to regulate its members' sexuality according to its cultural ideals. It is no surprise to note that free love also existed, especially among women who had been divorced or widowed.[43] Their social status did not so much make them outcasts as it removed from them the fear that women usually had of losing their virginity, a fear that would have restrained their romantic behavior. The fear of being pregnant, equally real, could be allayed by the use of abortifacients, some of which caused women to become sterile.

Catharsis

Tales of princesses and ogresses, occult formulae and divinatory games combine with romantic escapades to create a picture of women living in a special sort of time. Existential problems often received otherworldly solutions. Yet at times, feelings of anger or pain were given outlets that hold psychoanalytic interests to our contemporaries. The practices of *jdib* and *zyara* are two cases in point. For example, whenever a woman felt that her problems were getting the better of her, she would organize a *jdib*. This is a gathering of a small number of friends and/or relatives, who form a circle around the woman while she shakes her head back and forth, letting her hair loose to the tune of an all-male band hired for the occasion. The woman's head movements become faster as the music becomes more intense, until she drops to the floor. After this point she is taken to her bed to rest. The band was traditionally comprised of Black men using drums and large castanets referred to as *qarqabu*. This practice was all but abandoned during the decolonization war as part of the F.L.N.'s ban on all expressions of festive life. It has been revived in the last few years, but the band is no longer Black, and is often comprised of women. Although it resembles exorcism, *jdib* did not involve any allusion to spirits. Yet the presence of Black musicians may reveal some close connection between the notion that a slave of old and a woman have in common some repressed anger. Whatever the explanation, these sessions had a cathartic effect on women, who usually felt better. This was an exclusively female practice, and men had to leave the house to allow the event to proceed.

Another social practice with a cathartic effect sometimes took place during the *zyara* or visit to the grave of a saint considered *hammi* or "hot." As a woman entered the mausoleum she began to wail, dropped her veil if she was wearing one, and often seemed to speak in tongues. A relative or a guardian of the mausoleum would try to restrain her. After a while, she calmed down, took a nap and awoke claiming to feel good. In 1955, I witnessed one of these quasitrances in Western

Algeria at the Sidi M'Hammad Ben 'Aouda mausoleum and was struck by the extent to which all those present—the woman, her three relatives, two other visitors and the guard—were pleased with the outcome. Indeed, this bore out the "hotness" of the saint. Again, interpreting this practice in narrow feminist terms would be inaccurate. Men also seek to be "worked through" or *takhadem* by the saint. In addition, not all women have this experience, and many go on several visits before they have it. Nevertheless, it was a practice that provided emotional release through belief in the efficacy of a saint's grace. Furthermore, this was another instance of women grounding themselves in their culture, and seeking solace in it. To what extent their existence took a different turn, as the war of decolonization began on November 1, 1954, will be analyzed in the next two chapters.

7

Nationalism, Decolonization and Gender

The decision made by Algerian nationalist leaders to achieve decolonization through military means, thereby waging a war against the French government, had a similar impact on women and men as did the French invasion of Algeria by French troops in 1830. There is a striking symmetry in the history of colonization and decolonization. Both events were brutal, marked by massive uprooting of the rural population for better control, and resulted in changing the social landscape of Algeria after all arms went silent.

Women found themselves once more flung into the world of warring men, caught between their own often-resentful feelings against a political order that kept them and their families at the bottom of the social hierarchy, their loyalty to male relatives actively involved in the war, and repressive colonial/military laws. This situation goes a long way in explaining the nature and extent of women's participation in the war of decolonization, which ranged from tacit acceptance to active commitment.

The prevailing feminist view, according to which Algerian women, like so many other women before them, were duped into joining the nationalist movement by unscrupulous men who later did not share with them the spoils of independence, must be rejected for its derogatory connotations that deprive women of will and agency, and its lack of understanding of the dynamics of Algerian nationalism.[1] To understand the relationship between gender and nationalism within the Algerian context, it is crucial to unravel its connecting links with colonialism. The concept of nationalism may very well be a misnomer when its aim is to achieve decolonization. Indeed, the other side of nationalism is colonialism, and all the grievances that native peoples had against it. When looked at from this perspective, women's participation in the Algerian war appears as a rational response to an otherwise irrational historical situation. Furthermore, this view preserves the meaning that women imparted to their action.

That women did not, as a group, share equally with men in the benefits that accrued from the independence of their country is a separate empirical question that must be analyzed as such. The women and men who engaged in the war against the French government risked losing their lives. Their actions were not always motivated by material gain. War movements, like other movements, acquire lives of their own that envelop their members with their own logic and rationale, often divorced from any consideration of what life might be like after the war ends. Women, just like men, found themselves part of a struggle that transcended their everyday lives and concerns. More than men, their participation in the war entailed greater personal sacrifices and dangers. Indeed, women risked loss of the protection and safety of their homes and families and the possibility of good marriage and family life, and faced the omnipresent danger of rape. They headed for an uncertain future, having radically upset the value system that had hitherto governed gender relations by stepping out of their usual home-centered social roles and into the world of urban and rural guerrilla warfare.

Patterns of Entry into the Movement for Decolonization

The actual number of women who participated in the movement of decolonization has yet to be assessed. The figure of 10,949 provided by Djamila Amrane, who studied the subject, refers to the women who were registered by the Ministry of War Veterans.[2] However, as Amrane is aware, this is an inaccurate figure, in that the Ministry's files do not contain an exhaustive list of the women who participated in the war. In addition, most of the existing lists were compiled using requests for certificates of participation in the war from the Ministry, made by women and men in order to get a pension, a job or a promotion. This statistical problem is due less to a gender bias than inadequate record-keeping. Men's participation in the war is just as badly recorded as women's. However, because men have asked for certification more often than women, they figure on the government's lists in greater numbers. Thus, the official records indicate that about 326,000 men took part in the war, either in military combat or civilian service. However, 48.90 percent of them were killed, leaving a total of 200,586 men. By comparison, 2.5 percent of the women registered had been killed.[3]

These statistics leave out women and men whose deaths were not reported, and women who did not apply for certification. To obtain certification, an individual must fill out a number of forms and provide, among other things, written testimony from supervisors or individuals who belonged to the same military outfit or civilian cell during the war. In other words, one must be literate, or rely on help to go through the motions of applying and, more importantly, one must have access to the relevant administrative offices. In this, women, especially in rural areas, were at a disadvantage, lacking the skills necessary to negotiate their way in and out of the maze of bureaucratic procedures. In addition, the men with whom rural women worked often moved to urban centers, leaving them without tangible proof that they had participated in the war. Finally, in cases where women worked in groups as food and refuge suppliers, only the leader was entitled to certification. It is unclear whether this restriction, which excluded from benefits women who took risks during the war, also applied to all-male cells. Nevertheless, these are factors that account for the underreporting of women's involvement in the war.

A distinction must be made between women who joined the struggle for decolonization as members of guerrilla cells operating in urban centers, those who left for the mountains where military battles took place, and those who lived in strategic rural areas and were drawn into the war by their very location without necessarily being members of the F.L.N. (National Liberation Front) or the A.L.N. (Army of National Liberation). Urban women comprised twenty percent of all women involved in the war, and generally chose to join the F.L.N. Rural women, especially those living in mountainous areas suitable for guerrilla action, had to give refuge to members of the A.L.N., either out of compassion or fear. They stood to lose the most as French military retaliation, and at times the F.L.N's, was swift and brutal. Their farms were often bombed by French planes, and on at least one spectacular occasion it happened that their male relatives and neighbors were killed by the F.L.N., as was the case in 1956 in Melouza hamlet, at the southern rim of the Kabylie, allegedly because they were members of a rival organization, the M.N.A. (or *Mouvement National Algérien*), accused of collaboration with the French.[4] This does not mean, however, that rural women did not consciously engage in anticolonial activities. On the contrary, 77.9 percent of the total female population that participated in the war was comprised of rural women.[5]

Unlike rural women, who were illiterate, urban women were generally drawn from the French-educated middle class, although other social classes were represented. Those who became famous because the media seized upon their plight were graduates of French *lycées*, or still attending one when they joined the F.L.N. This was the case of Djamila Bouhired, Djamila Boupacha, and Djamila Bouazza. Others were already employed as clerical workers, nurses or accountants for family businesses. Still others were unemployed young women waiting to get married, or were housewives.

How a woman entered the decolonization movement depended on her family circumstances, chance or direct recruitment by the F.L.N. For example, Djamila Bouhired had an older brother who was already a member of the F.L.N. Yet this did not make it easier for her to join. She was eager to do so, but was at first turned down by the head of one of the major urban guerrilla cells in Algiers, Yacef Saadi, because he "did not want mice in the movement."[6] A similar story is told by Zohra, whose two brothers used to discuss at night the war and its significance for Algerians. When she ventured to ask one of her brothers how she could join the movement, she was told that she was too young and that "this was not a woman's business." She felt "astounded by his mistake because this is also women's business. It is all Algerian people's business, women, men, and children."[7] Some young women, especially nurses, were directly approached by the F.L.N. to help them to take care of the wounded in the battlefield. Others were urged to take courses in first aid and join the guerrillas in the mountains, where their skills were needed.[8] At any rate, urban women would leave cities for the mountains when wanted, or when pursued by the police. There is also evidence that some women were recruited for their looks. For example, Fella Hadj Mahmoud, a young woman from Algiers, "was chosen by the organization [F.L.N.] because of her beauty and her European features," which enabled her to blend in with the French population and therefore go undisturbed by the police.[9] This quotation from a male reporter discounts *Fella*'s own decision to accept the invitation to join. She had been compelled to interrupt her high school education because her parents refused to let her go alone to Tunisia to attend high school, as was the practice among some families. Instead, her brother left, thus evading the trauma of living in a war-torn country. At the age of eighteen, being out of school and unmarried, she was free to devote herself to a task that seemed to give her life meaning.[10]

Some women joined the movement to follow a husband who had left for the mountains, as was the case of Naima, to take over from a father who had been arrested, as happened to Louiza Ighil Lahriz, or to do something about an injustice they experienced or witnessed. For example, Fatima B., who used to listen to her father explain to her "the meaning of the struggle for decolonization and the injustices on which French occupation rested," mentioned that:

all this talk would have remained very abstract to me because I was young. I would not have understood its meaning had I not witnessed a particularly horrible scene. It was in the summer of 1953 [sic]. I was at the home of one of our neighbors, who was pregnant, when French soldiers stormed the house. I was able to find a hiding place from which I saw everything that happened. They took the woman, cut her belly open, pulled out the foetus, and played with it as if it were a ball, exclaiming: "This is what we do to an Arab, a dirty Arab." I saw this with my own eyes before my fifteenth birthday.[11]

Reports of French soldiers, especially members of the French Legion, cutting up pregnant women's bellies were not uncommon during the war.

As the movie, *The Battle of Algiers*, accurately demonstrated, there were veiled women in urban centers who participated in the movement as weapon carriers and liaison agents. At times, a woman would team up with a man in carrying assignments, using her veil as a hiding device to get rid of a gun. Other women removed their veils in order to carry out assignments. However, a striking feature of urban guerrilla warfare was that it attracted generally educated women who were born in the 1930s and seldom wore the veil. This was the first generation of women who had attended French schools and/or a *medersa* (a Franco-Arab school where instruction was given in both French and Arabic), usually located in one of the three major cities of Algiers, Qasantina and Wahran. Many had already received a *Certificat d'Etudes Primaires*, the equivalent of an eighth-grade diploma, considered at the time an achievement for natives, and which crowned the end of a cycle of education beyond which most native children could not go. Attending a lycée meant sitting for a special sixth- or eighth-grade examination, theoretically open to natives but in practice made inaccessible because schools for natives did not prepare for it. Algerian children who happened to attend all-French schools were able to take the exam and thus attend a lycée. It is difficult to compare urban women guerrillas' background to men's with accuracy. Proportionately, it seems as though women had an educational edge. Ali-la-Pointe, the hero of the *Battle of Algiers*, for example, was illiterate. His counterpart, Hassiba Ben Bouali, was an educated woman.

In general, women who participated in the decolonization movement belonged to a cross section of the population. Some were daughters of businessmen, teachers, policemen, *muphtis* (or religious leaders), blacksmiths, hairdressers, farmers or unemployed men.[12] There were women of all ages, the youngest women being fourteen years old. The majority of women were twenty to fifty years old. They were, therefore, already married, and most had children. Interestingly, the number of women in the movement was proportional to the Algerian female population.[13]

The large proportion of rural women in the movement was a reflection not only of the limited urbanization of Algeria at the time, as Djamila Amrane points out, but also the fact that the major part of the war was fought in the countryside.[14] It must be emphasized that many a woman gave occasional help to fighters, and the majority of women empathized with them. Again, the *Battle of Algiers* made this point clear in a scene where men, disguised as women and running away from French paratroopers, burst into a home where a woman spontaneously embraced them and hid them in a well, thus saving their lives.

As could be deduced from the ways in which women entered the movement, their reasons for doing so ranged from wanting to redress perceived injustices committed by the colonial order, pursuing a family tradition of resistance or altruism, to giving meaning to one's life by playing a socially useful role and being part of an organization that requires that one rises above one's self. Illustrating this last point, a woman stated:

> I am happy that my life has meaning and a direction that I chose from the very beginning, which is that of the Algerian people's struggle against colonialism and oppression by foreigners. . . . I cannot express my happiness to be in the *maquis* better than by briefly taking stock of my positive experiences: First, I became aware of the superiority of our organization although I already knew that our struggle needed fighters and leaders. I understood that our army encompasses everything and assigns everybody the appropriate role and gives them the necessary responsibilities. . . . Secondly and equally importantly, I understood that the enormous apparatus that our leaders have rapidly set up rests on solid and proven foundations such as the confidence, devotion, participation and even heroism of our civilian population.[15]

Life as a Moudjahida

Women fighters, or *moudjahidat* (pronounced "moojaheedat"; plural of *moudjahida*), served in two capacities, military and civilian. The civilian arm of the F.L.N., or *Organisation Civile du F.L.N.*, included paramilitary activities such as throwing bombs at civilian targets or attacking policemen and individuals considered collaborators/traitors. It also included fund-raising, liaison work, provision of safe housing, food and medical supplies and purchase of weapons. Military functions involved being a member of the National Liberation Army (in French: "A.L.N.") which meant wearing a uniform and taking part in combat or auxiliary services such as nursing, communications, engineering, food preparation and so on.[16]

Women were heavily represented in civilian service as defined by the F.L.N., taking charge primarily of food supplies and an underground network of sanctuaries. Women also worked as liaisons and guides, collected funds from other women, obtained medical supplies, washed fighters' clothes and at times transported weapons from urban centers to rural areas. Paramilitary acts of destruction of civilian targets gave women notoriety, yet drew barely two percent (or sixty-five) of the women who joined the movement.[17] The bulk of women's work was less spectacular, perhaps even tedious, but equally dangerous. The number of women in the military arm of the F.L.N. represented about eleven percent, or 205 women. They were generally younger, unmarried women who could leave home without worrying about children. They worked primarily as nurses, for whom there was great demand, or took charge of food preparation. Very few women figured as soldiers engaged in combat.

French military reaction to women's involvement in the decolonization movement was brutal, yet has not been well documented. As Djamila Amrane notes: "It is impossible to assess violence committed against women during roundup operations in cities and rural areas. Many women were killed, raped, and sometimes even tortured in their own homes with portable electrical equipment."[18] One woman in five was either imprisoned or killed. Testimonies provided by surviving women reveal widespread torture and rape with a variety of objects, including glass bottles.[19] More than half the women registered by the Ministry of War Veterans who were killed were less than twenty-five-years-old, another evidence that the generation of women born in the 1930s bore the brunt of the war.[20]

It is clear that women's participation in the war was instrumental to its success. Yet, with a few exceptions, the nature of this participation fit in a "traditional" pattern of gender roles, where men held positions of responsibility and command, and women executed orders. In explaining the near-absence of women in combat, Djamila Amrane states that the F.L.N. "was not short of soldiers but weapons. This is why women being psychologically and physically unfit for combat were not hired as soldiers."[21] Contradicting this self-styled

Functions Performed By Women In The Decolonization Movement

Functions	Civilian Women	Military Women	Total
Sanctuary/Supplies	1,958 (63.30%)	6 (2.90%)	1,964
Liaison and Guide	677 (22.10%)	—	677
Fund-raising, Medical/Arms Supplies	286 (9.30%)	—	286
Nursing	56 (1.80%)	101 (48.30%)	157
Cooking/Laundry	—	991 (44.40%)	91
Urban Guerrilla	65 (2.10%)	—	65
Sewing	19 (0.60%)	1 (0.50)	20
Clerical	5 (0.20%)	3 (0.40%)	—
Political Commissar	—	2 (1.00%)	2
Armed Soldier	—	1 (0.50%)	1
Total	3,066	205	3,271

Source: Adapted from Djamila Amrane, "La femme algérienne et la guerre de libération nationale," in *Combattantes de la lutte armée*, monograph issued by *El Djazairiya*, p. 11.

statement, the review in which Amrane's essay appeared displayed pictures of women in uniform with their guns at the ready.[22]

Assuming that the F.L.N. intended to use its human resources rationally, it is still unclear why it was reluctant at first to arm nurses in combat zones so they could protect themselves. There is evidence that women requested weapons on numerous occasions before finally getting them.[23] In addition, there is no explanation provided by the F.L.N. for the near-absence of women (0.5 percent) in political positions inside the country, as well as in the Algerian Government in Exile established in Tunis, which remained an all-male institution until the end of the war. Yet there was ample evidence that women were able to run all-female groups in charge of sanctuaries, food supplies and so on. Furthermore, women's commitment to decolonization was no less intense than men's.

Fanon, Women and the Revolution

Frantz Fanon, the first analyst of women's participation in the movement, presented an interpretation that is close to the F.L.N.'s official position on this issue, yet is also very personal. Given his own participation in the revolution, a critical assessment of his ideas might yield an answer to the question concerning the F.L.N.'s ambivalence toward women. Fanon claims that "until 1955, the combat was waged exclusively by men," the implication being that women came in late.[24] Yet some women have asserted that they had been contacted by the F.L.N. in early 1955, barely a few months after the war started, in November 1954.[25] As it became more difficult for men to wage the war, according to Fanon, it was necessary to involve women. However, the

> women's entry into the war had to be harmonized with respect for the revolutionary nature of the war. In other words, the women had to show as much spirit of sacrifice as men . . . . A moral elevation and a strength of character that were altogether exceptional would therefore be required of the women . . . . The machine would have to be complicated; in other words its network would have to be extended without affecting its efficiency. The women could not be conceived of as a replacement product, but as an element capable of adequately meeting the new tasks.[26]

It is pointless to assess Fanon's ideas, expressed in 1959, against feminist ideals of the 1990s. But, because *he* chose to discuss the woman question in the Algerian revolution, his text must be analyzed as reflecting his feelings as both a male and a political activist. There is no denying that for Fanon, the entry of women into the revolution was a "complication" that could be overcome only if women were not only of the same moral caliber as men, but also "exceptional." They had to be like men and perform better than men. Why? Because of their body. Repeating what was at the time a standard notion among Algerian men and colonists, Fanon argues that women's "cloistered life" made their bodies feel less at ease moving about in the city streets. In addition, letting them into the movement might endanger their lives. Neither reason is compelling. Indeed, although veiled, women did go out to shop, to visit relatives in and out of the city or to see doctors. That there were some women who felt inadequate in French neighborhoods was not impossible. But the same could be said of men. As for the risk of being killed, it is well known that innocent women had been killed during reprisal attacks by French troops, a fact that radicalized many women, especially in mountainous areas, as historian Alistair Horne points out.[27]

Fanon is unaware of the implications of what he perceives as stages in the induction of women into the movement. For example, he asserts that married women were first sought, then wives of men who were already active in the movement, and later widowed or divorced women. Finally "volunteering unmarried girls" were accepted. He does not mention that the fear of rape and/or lack of trust might have accounted for the F.L.N.'s reluctance to let young women in. His explanation that unmarried women were avoided because they seldom ventured outside their home unaccompanied is contradicted by his report that these same women volunteered to join the movement.[28] Fanon's fascination with the Algerian woman's body is intriguing, as it goes beyond the parameters of the psychological analysis of the meaning of the veil and its removal for a body accustomed to it. Fanon waxes lyrical about the unveiled body. "The shoulders of the unveiled Algerian woman are thrust back with easy freedom. She walks with a graceful, measured stride, neither too fast nor too slow. Her legs are bare, and her hips are free."[29] This new body-in-the-world was the product of revolutionary learning. There is no room in his analysis for the woman whose body felt no inhibition as soon as the veil was removed, and who moved about with none of the inner conflict he describes. Considering the young age of the women who removed the veil, and the fact that in Algiers, the privileged site for urban guerrilla warfare, young women wore a wisp of a silk or cotton veil in a way that left their legs free and revealed part of their clothes and their hair, the emphasis on the body caught in the memory of the veil and struggling to adjust to freedom is overwrought. Furthermore, young women who attended high school, usually located in the European city, often folded their veils and put them in their bags as soon as they reached the European city, where they could blend with the crowd of French women. I interviewed a fifty-year-old woman in Algiers in 1970 who had decided to remove her veil. She felt relieved, free to do her shopping at the vegetable market without having to adjust her slipping veil. Her deportment was indistinguishable from that of other unveiled or European women. She recounted the surprise on the faces of the market men when she told them she was their old customer. Her daughter, married with children, wore the veil in her hometown in western Algeria, but took it off whenever she came to Algiers to visit her mother, where it was unlikely she would meet someone who knew her. These cases illustrate the relative ease with which women moved in and out of the veil, as actresses playing roles in different costumes.

While some of Fanon's remarks about the "dialectics of the body and the world" are important, his emphasis on women's "conflict" with their body transforms their participation in the war into a struggle over the veil. Here again, the mystique of the veil and a lack of intimate knowledge of the various ways in which women could move in and out of identities resulted in silencing their unique contribution to Algerian independence. Thus, unwittingly, Fanon's marvelling at the bodily transfigurations he observed stems from the same attitude as that voiced by his French contemporaries, namely a preconceived notion that women were oppressed, although he does not use the concept. However, unlike the colonists, he turns this oppression on its head by arguing that the Algerian woman *chose* "a form of existence limited in scope." In doing so she "was deepening her consciousness of struggle and preparing for combat."[30] It is difficult to see how, through what mechanism, an existence limited in scope could lead to revolutionary action.

Nevertheless, Fanon was right in pointing out that women's lives had been the object of a colonial mystifying discourse, presented as scientific, that could not account for their reality, since it was built to deny the very existence of that reality. There is, in Fanon's attempt at demystifying women's roles in society, another uncomfortable residue of prejudice he shared with his French contemporaries. He refers to women's existence prior to the war as "restricted but coherent." It was so because it was meant to be the

> fundamental strength of the occupied. All alone, the woman, by means of conscious techniques, presided over the setting up of the system. What was essential was that the occupier should constantly come up against a unified front. This accounts for the aspects of sclerosis that tradition must assume.[31]

This assertion encodes a familiar critique of Algerian society in the larger context of the legitimation of a revolution that decided to include women in its ranks. It says nothing of why the burden of resistance to the French should fall on women, and women only. Nor does it mention the role played by men in the perceived cultural "sclerosis." Most importantly, from the perspective adopted in this book, it does not explain why is it that what women do within a given cultural context is stricken by "sclerosis." Whose standards of women's lives and behavior are upheld when Algerian women's lives are characterized as "limited," "restricted," suffering from "sclerosis"? Are these a (Westernized) man's standards? Fanon's? At any rate, it is still unclear how these women were able to escape the impact of a "limited" existence and transform themselves into activists carrying out tasks "with exemplary constancy, self-mastery, and success."[32]

Ultimately, Fanon's piece on "Algeria Unveiled" does not shed light on the F.L.N.'s ambivalence toward women, except in blaming women's domestic life as a disabling factor which women, in time, were declared to have overcome successfully. Fanon's view adds a confounding element to this interpretation by also using the very domestic culture it criticizes as having prepared the way for women's entry into the war. For him, just as for the F.L.N. or the colonists, women's performance in the war will have remained a surprise and a puzzle. Missing is a historical analysis of the ways in which colonial domination affected women as women, and the meaning of the war as a momentous opportunity for women who decisively stepped into it. Nevertheless, Fanon was right, even if rhetorically so, to affirm that "revolutionary war is not a war of men".[33] One might add "only."

Sex and Revolution

Women's participation in the war of decolonization did not only bring up in all its starkness the F.L.N.'s ambivalence about women's roles in society as well as in the struggle against colonial rule. It also presented the F.L.N. with the challenge of the expression of sex and desire among its own ranks. The F.L.N's ambivalence towards women is illustrated by statements made by some of its leaders. Recounting her days in the *maquis*, a woman quoted a notable guerrilla leader, Colonel Amirouche, as saying that young women should devote themselves to the civilian population, to

> take care of its health and educational needs, and make it understand that we are constantly on its side . . . . He explained to us that women were best suited for tasks such as those requiring devotion, the purest part of the revolution. He also wanted to spare us the risks of battle: "at least unnecessary risks" as he said.[34]

It is spurious to try and second guess what Colonel Amirouche meant by purity in the revolution, and its association with women. Yet it is remarkable that he implied that the "civilian" duties assigned women were risk-free, when it was common practice among the French military not to distinguish between military and civilian members of the F.L.N. in the punishment they meted out to them. A position paper issued by the F.L.N. on August 2, 1956, known as the Soummam Platform, outlined women's roles as:

> a) providing moral support to fighters and resisters; taking care of intelligence, liaison, food supplies and sanctuary;
> c) helping families and children left behind by those at the front, in prison or in detention camps.[35]

These tasks are perceived as women's avocation. Assumed is a woman's nature that makes her suitable to roles of a moral and a social nature, even under conditions of danger. Thus, as the wartime publication of the F.L.N., *El Moudjahid* (literally the male fighter), stated in 1959: "Women's destiny at all times and in all societies has been to endure the worst and occasionally assume a sublime stance."[36] This quotation illustrates a deep-seated and widely held conception of women as creatures of sacrifice. On the one hand, it is recognized implicitly that women have and continue to suffer. On the other hand, such suffering is also seen as inevitable, a part of the feminine condition. Consequently, women could be, and were, asked to give more of themselves. Herein lies the apparent failure of the F.L.N. to transcend the sacrificial view of women, and replace it with a view that emphasizes control over one's life through action, as befits a woman revolutionary. Instead, women's involvement in the struggle for decolonization was presented as requiring some feminine qualities. Self-transformation through voluntary action for the national good was not brought up as an advantage for women in the movement. Rather, the abstract notion of "freedom," equated with entry in the war, was seen as the sum total of a presumed change in women's lives.

The entreaties the F.L.N. made to women in *El Moudjahid*, during the war, strike the contemporary reader as ideologically undeveloped and lacking in conviction. They betrayed unease and an inability to gauge the intellectual level of female audiences (no matter how limited in number) who were, at the least, literate in Arabic and/or French, and thus could read and interpret the paper which appeared in both languages. Indeed, the tone was often unwittingly condescending, and the level of discourse never rose above patriotic and/or moral admonishments. Furthermore, oftentimes the F.L.N. made pronouncements about women in response to French authorities' declarations on the same topic. Thus, the theme of "freedom" cropped up a number of times in *El Moudjahid* to counter the French critique that Algerian women lived under men's control. An article claims that "The Algerian woman does not need emancipation. She is already free because she takes part in the liberation of her country of which she is the soul, the heart, and the glory."[37] This heightens women's absence in the battle of words between men and *silences* their active participation in the war. Yet there were frequent articles by women in the pages of *El Moudjahid*, some of which recounted their activities in a column entitled: "Diary of a guerrilla."[38] However, these often poignant testimonials on how, why and where women joined the ranks of the movement are drowned out by the continuous F.L.N./

colonial government polemics about women's role in the decolonization process.

Paradoxically, the F.L.N.'s ambivalence about women's roles in the war did not prevent it from assessing women's contribution as "heroic." Two notable analysts of *El Moudjahid*, argue that it created a "myth" of the woman fighter which had little bearing on the actual military involvement of women.[39] These analysts are correct in pointing to the mythic import of an essentially ideological/political discourse on women (did the F.L.N. really mean what it said?). Nevertheless, they also fail to distinguish between the act of entering the decolonization movement and its concrete modalities. In so doing, they do not sufficiently appreciate the significance of women's participation in the war and what it meant for the French colonists. Indeed, washing clothes that belonged to guerrillas or transporting weapons for them were causes for arrest, if not torture. These may not have been "heroic" acts in and of themselves. But they were predicated upon surmounting a basic fear of French troops or police. As a woman mentioned: "Danger meant for me fear of being frisked while I was carrying weapons in a city."[40] It is not easy for outsiders to understand the role that fear plays in the life of individuals working underground. One confronts a mixed array of emotions, ranging from the fear of dying to the fear of getting caught, arrested, tortured, raped and so on. Women learned to control their fear, and marvelled at how it was superseded by a "calm that took hold of all of us and sharpened our senses remarkably when we were suddenly surrounded by the enemy, and were desperate to break through. And we usually did."[41] Perhaps it was heroic for young women who were generally used to a more or less sheltered life to find themselves propelled into a world of soldiers, agents, guns and bombs, where life was cheap and human suffering extensive.

Admittedly, the F.L.N. was in a tough spot, having to combat the powerful war and propaganda machines of the French government with more modest means. Its response to significant colonial intervention was generally tame. Indeed, the passage of the February 4, 1959 law amending the *shari'a* in matters of marriage and divorce, discussed in the previous chapter, was greeted in rhetorical and predictable terms. To wit: "So, some Frenchmen who are also Christian and Jews have deliberately dared tamper with the *Quran*, immutable in its essence, and impose with the sword the secular law of France on the Muslims of Algeria in their most sacred personal status."[42] The F.L.N.'s opposition to the law rested on religion, a factor that played little role, if any, in its customary pronouncements on women.[43]

The usually religion-neutral attitude adopted by the F.L.N. during the war was rooted in its opposition to the religious establishment, seen as a native arm of colonial domination of the Algerian people. The appeal to religion as a foundation of a critique of colonial intervention in family law documents further the ambivalence of the leadership of the F.L.N. about women's status, and its lack of a program for change that would include women. Women in the movement were already engaged in activities that would have normally been deemed in violation of religious principles as interpreted in Algeria. The F.L.N. was caught in a contradiction that was the hallmark of its rhetorical view of women, which had acquired a life of its own quite divorced from women's lived reality. As Chérifa Benabdessadok put it, the F.L.N.'s discourse

> shifted from a desire to narrate a lived reality to a discourse that does no more than contemplate a reflection of this reality sifted through unrecognizable lenses. This may be evidence of the evolution of a mythic discourse into a full-blown discourse of mystification.[44]

In other words, responses to colonial policies focusing on women, in this case the 1959 law, were consciously distorted by casting women's civil rights as a Quranic issue. The language of revolution that extolled the woman fighter who became "free" the moment she joined the movement gave way to the language of immutable gender inequality.

Assuming the F.L.N. was worried about losing popular support if the colonial government began to seriously redress its legal and social inequities, what did the F.L.N. do *in practice* whenever it could to give women and men an inkling of how they might live once their country became independent? As mentioned in chapter 5, there have been reports that, where the F.L.N. had a foothold, its leaders celebrated marriages, insisting that both bride and bridegroom be present to sign their marriage license. In doing so, the F.L.N. made sure that a bride consented to her marriage. However, there is evidence that the Justice Commissions sponsored by the F.L.N. were instructed to "rigorously" apply Quranic principles in matters of marriage and divorce.[45]

However, within the ranks of the F.L.N., expressions of desire at times went beyond what local leadership could tolerate. Thus, according to one report, "sometimes, a male and female soldier fall in love. When we think it is a serious relationship, we get them married. Sometimes, someone yields to temptation . . . . The order is then given to shoot the sinning temptress."[46] There is no telling whether this story is true as told. However, historian Alistair Horne mentions that: "Discipline was strict; as in many guerilla movements, illicit sexual relations were ruthlessly punishable by death."[47] There are no documented reports of evidence of common sexual abuse of women by F.L.N. troops. However, Horne claims that the political commissar of Wilaya 6 (or District 6, which covered the south of Algeria), a "wild and brutal figure" nicknamed Rouget (or Red Snapper) had "insatiable sexual appetites [that] drove him to claim a kind of *droit de seigneur* whereby the prettiest girls in the villages he passed through were earmarked for his pleasure. As most of the villages were Arab, this fanned a violent hatred between the two races [Berber and Arab], always latently smouldering."[48] Rouget was ultimately killed by Si Cherif, a military leader, who defected to the French in 1957. Horne's assumption that this act might have been ethnically motivated is debatable, since there is no research carried out on this subject that might reveal similar occurrences in other parts of Algeria. Women's vulnerability as women made their sexuality a special site for Frenchmen to express their anger and contempt for rebellious Algerians through rape, and more rarely for native men like Rouget to claim the spoils due the warrior. That Algerian leaders opposed acts such as Rouget's reinforces the prevailing view that relationships between women and men within the F.L.N., especially those in uniform, were generally civil. Women and men referred to one another as "brother" and "sister." As Horne, points out, "on the whole the F.L.N. woman was treated with respect never experienced before—either from her menfolk or from even the most liberal French emancipators."[49] What is meant by "emancipators" is unclear, but Horne is right in his assessment of women's commitment to the decolonization movement, his irreverence towards them notwithstanding: "All in all, the F.L.N. seemed to have far more to offer Muslim womanhood by way of an escape from thraldom than the French."[50] What Horne neglects to mention is that women had a lot to offer the F.L.N. to make its operations possible, especially as times got increasingly tougher for men.

French Reaction to Women's Militancy and Decolonization

The French government's war strategy was to take measures aimed at redressing some of the wrongs of which it was accused by the F.L.N., as for example lack of jobs and inadequate schools and social services. Some of these measures included women, but still as an ancillary category of people. Others, such as the 1959 family law, or the various *Centres Sociaux* directed by the well-known ethnographer,

Germaine Tillion, were meant to rally women to the side of the colonists.

A major effort made by the colonial government to improve Algerians' access to economic and educational opportunities is known as the *Plan de Constantine*, to be implemented within a five-year period between 1959 and 1963. This plan pointed out the "necessity to speed up schooling of young girls and to prepare them for access to a social life built on foundations different from those of their society." It also emphasized that "for right or wrong, women's influence on the evolution of Algeria and its future can be considerable."[51] Yet, after a long historical analysis of how the education of girls had been neglected by the colonial government, the plan cautioned that:

> the extent of underemployment among men is such that it does not allow us to give women systematic access to jobs in industry. There are, however, specifically feminine positions in commerce and administrative services such as social work and health that are suitable for Muslim girls. In addition, schools for home economics will be set up, especially in rural areas where grade schools will give a greater emphasis to the domestic aspect of social life. . . . What is needed is psychological action first in school, then through women's movements whose role is to teach women how to help one another in order to better discharge the social and family roles assigned to them.[52]

In other words, the French answer to women's status in the colonial society was that, essentially they should stay home where they can apply French methods of home management, or should work in limited numbers in feminine positions. This may very well be one of the reasons for which women preferred to join guerrillas in the *maquis*. The special emphasis the colonial government placed on women's "social" vocation led to the creation of sociomedical centers under military control in some parts of Algeria, such as El Asnam, as a way of co-opting women by catering to their health needs. Finally, the *Loi Cadre* of 1957 gave Algerian women the right to vote without restriction. All these measures were taken within the context of a psychological warfare declared by the French against the F.L.N.; thus their ideological nature was clear to native women and men in the decolonization movement.

Perhaps the most spectacular example of the colonial appropriation of women's voices, and the silencing of those among them who had begun to take women revolutionaries (such as Djamila Bouhired, or

Hassiba Ben Bouali) as role models by not donning the veil, was the event of May 16, 1958. On that day a demonstration was organized by rebellious French generals in Algiers to show their determination to keep Algeria French. To give the government of France evidence that Algerians were in agreement with them, the generals had a few thousand native men bused in from nearby villages, along with a few women who were solemnly unveiled by French women. After this momentous act, "all together sang the *Marseillaise* and the military *Chant des Africains*.⁵³ Rounding up Algerians and bringing them to demonstrations of loyalty to France was not in itself an unusual act during the colonial era. But to unveil women at a well-choreographed ceremony added to the event a symbolic dimension that dramatized the one constant feature of the Algerian occupation by France: its obsession with women. Little is known about the handful of women who were unveiled publicly by French women, their circumstances or the conditions under which they were brought in. According to Horne, who devotes one paragraph to this event, they were "acquiescent Muslim women."⁵⁴ The F.L.N. stated they were "the all-around maids of the General Government [the colonial government] as well as boarders of whorehouses."⁵⁵ Fanon referred to them as "Servants on the threat of being fired, poor women dragged from their homes, prostitutes."⁵⁶

Fanon adequately explains that the immediate response of many women "who had long since dropped the veil once again donned the *haik* [Algerian word for veil], thus affirming that it was not true that woman liberated herself at the invitation of France and of General de Gaulle."⁵⁷ The forced unveiling of a few women meant increased emphasis on reveiling and veiling, thus causing what Fanon termed a "turning back, a regression."⁵⁸ However, he also saw a positive, unintended consequence to the French interference with the veil, in that veiling henceforth lost its "exclusively" traditional character, and became an instrument for political action. In fact, prior to May 16, 1958, the veil had already been used as a strategic device, under which and out of which women and men alike carried out paramilitary assignments.

In reality the event of May 16, 1958 did lasting harm to Algerian women. It brought into the limelight the politicization of women's bodies and their symbolic appropriation by colonial authorities. It brought home to Algerian women their vulnerability, at a time when many of them thought they were making history and imposing themselves on men's consciousness as more than mere sex symbols. Their sexed body was suddenly laid bare before a crowd of vociferous colonists who, in an orgy of chants and cries of "Long Live French Algeria," claimed victory over all Algerian *women*. Much has been said, and rightly so, about the generals' manipulation of the veil as a political symbol separating the colonizers from the colonized, or its meaning as native *men's* last bastion of resistance to the French, guaranteeing a safe haven of personal power in an otherwise dominated society. Little has been written about its meaning for *women*.

Beyond its obvious political meaning, the public unveiling of women was the expression of French colonial men's deep-seated erotic obsession *and* French women's frustration with native women. Fanon, as a psychiatrist, was able to tap the complexity of the psychic impact that Algerian women had on both colonial men and women. In the colonial male's psyche, the veiled woman represented mystery, hidden beauty, but also an object of possession by aggression due to the frustration stemming from being seen by her but not seeing her. In the European man's dreams "the rape of the Algerian woman is always preceded by a rending of the veil. We here witness a double deflowering. Likewise, the woman's conduct is never one of consent or acceptance, but of abject humility."[59] Aggressiveness also appears in colonial men's disparaging remarks about women's appearance when they finally saw a woman unveiled as doctors did.

Colonial women experienced similar problems with Algerian women. If they did not dream of possessing them erotically, they perceived them as symbolically obliterating their own existence as (French) women. The veil made colonial women uncomfortable, as did every task that Algerian women performed, from rearing children to cooking and taking care of their homes. It is not by accident that schools for Algerian girls emphasized home economics, which meant the ways in which French women felt a home should be managed. The veil, for the colonial woman, was the perfect alibi for rejecting the Algerian woman's culture and denigrating her. But it was also a constant reminder of her powerlessness in erasing the existence of a different way of being woman. She often overcame her handicap by turning it into an advantage. *She* is superior to these veiled women, who hide their beauty instead of displaying it as she does. In any case, they must be deceitful to their men, while she is is truthful to hers.

The problem experienced by the colonial woman does not end with the veil. When in the presence of an unveiled woman, she at first exults in what she perceives as the triumph of her culture over that of the colonized. Unveiled women used to be asked questions such as "how have you succeeded in breaking through?" or "you see, if it were not for us, you would be wearing the veil just like your mother."[60] Soon, when faced with an Algerian woman who reflects back to her

her own image in a different body, the French woman feels as uncomfortable as she did with the veil. As Fanon put it:

> Not only is the satisfaction of supervising the evolution and correcting the mistakes of the unveiled woman withdrawn from the European woman, but she feels herself challenged on the level of feminine charm, of elegance, and even sees a competitor in this novice metamorphosed into a professional, a neophyte transformed into a propagandist.

Her response is then "to make common cause with the Algerian man who had fiercely flung the unveiled woman into the camp of evil and depravation."[61] In other words, with or without the veil, Algerian women could not be accepted as full-fledged individuals or as equals.

Impact of the Revolution on Gender Relations

Women's entry in the decolonization movement was revolutionary in the sense that it upset patterns of gender relations as we have known them since at least the second half of the nineteenth century. Yet there is an unrecognized continuity in women's participation in the political/military life of their country. Chapter 2 pointed out women's resistance to invading French troops. Chapter 6 noted that Ibn Badis and his disciples selected biographies of women who fought alongside men during the heroic period of Islamic history, and presented them to women as role models to emulate. Thus, in the 1950s, women were rekindling a tradition that had been established before them. This does not mean that their contribution to the independence of their country was less significant. Rather, their militancy was not *ex nihilo*. It built upon a tradition, and was sustained not only by the memory of the brutality of the first forty years of colonial rule, but also by their own marginalization by a social order that used them as the cornerstone of a merciless ideological warfare.

As pointed out in the previous chapter, women had as many grudges as men against the colonial order, if not more. Entering the war against the colonizer was an opportunity to even the score, regardless of whether it was perceived in this clear a fashion. It was also a chance to take charge of one's life, and finally break in deeds and not in words the structural and discursive silence imposed upon them for more than a century. The 'Ulama, colonial administrators and writers, F.L.N. leaders and intellectuals, including Fanon, all held conceptions of women that were at odds with women's lived and felt reality. The surprise registered by the F.L.N. as well as colonial authorities at women's performance in the war was a function of the degree to which the silencing of women had been equated with their physical absence from the world of men. Yet women were in that same world, although not of it. They were in it as the concealed, invisible other, witnessing it and living through it according to their own tempo.

Women's participation in the war impacted on their lives in more than one way. First, women forged bonds with one another that transcended the usual episodic solidarity that characterized their relations during peacetime. The experience of jail and torture was a significant component of this bonding, which cut across class, ethnicity and geographical origin. Second, taking charge of educational and paramedical tasks, among others, in rural areas gave urban women a sense of responsibility and purposive action, as well as a perspective on their own lives. Third, carrying out risky missions some distance from home gave the women who undertook them confidence in themselves and a sense of partaking in history in the making. Fourth, for the majority of the women who were drawn into the maelstrom of the war indirectly, because their husbands, sons or daughters had been arrested, the war meant taking charge of a farm or business left behind, and/or searching for missing relatives from jail to jail, and from detention camp to detention camp. This was well illustrated by the film *Le Vent des Aurès*, portraying the life of a woman in search of a missing relative. Fifth, the women who joined the *maquis* rubbed shoulders with men who were complete strangers to them, and whom they often had to protect when they were wounded. The masculine mystique of strength and omnipotence was thus broken, showing men to be as vulnerable as women in adversity. Last but not least, the very act of entering the war was an expression of will. Young women met fathers head on and told them they were leaving home to join the struggle. As attested by many women, as well as historians such as Horne, women often returned to their revolutionary activities after they were tortured and released from jail.[62] Women were respected for their courage and bravery, and for dying for what they believed in. Perhaps the most notable impact of women's participation in the war was the impression they made on the collective consciousness of Algerians, males and females. The number of parents who named their newborn daughters Djamila after the three famous women urban guerrillas became legion. The publicity given by the colonial press to women's involvement in the war helped to propel them into public life. Attempts made after independence to erase the memory of women's entry into the Algerian psyche, as will be discussed in the next chapter, are a function of the severity with which it was affected.

Nationalism and Feminism

It has become commonplace at feminist meetings to cite Algerian women's participation in the war as having been for nought. The implication being that had women abstained from the war, or created a feminist movement as an alternative to joining the F.L.N., they would have fared better. Looking at the past from the vantage point of the present is easier than reexperiencing it as it was lived. It is difficult to imagine a feminist movement, by which is meant a movement focused on the promotion of women's rights exclusively, emerging during the war. Who would have been its leaders? Who would have been its adversaries? French men? French women? Algerian men? All of these?

Apart from a history of manipulation of women by colonial authorities that made any feminist activity suspect in the eyes of Algerians, native associations were only tolerated and often subjected to harassment, if not banned. An Algerian feminist association that would have inevitably questioned the active complicity of the colonial order in women's exclusion from high school education, training, health care, housing, jobs and so on would have found it difficult to survive. Only an association bent on criticizing Algerian culture and men, and blaming both for all the problems women experienced would have been welcomed by the colonial society.

As it happened, there were women's associations in Algeria prior to the war, which some Algerian women joined. The *Union Franco-Musulmane des Femmes d'Algérie*, established by French women in 1937, was essentially a colonial political association that drew half of its membership of thirty-six from well-to-do Algerian women. The Communist *Union des Femmes d'Algérie* attracted very few women and was disbanded in 1955. The *Association des Femmes Musulmanes*, sponsored by a liberal Algerian party, *Mouvement pour le Triomphe des Libertés Democratiques* (or M. T. L. D.), was established in 1947 and disbanded just as the war began on November 1, 1954. This was an all-Algerian association which aimed at helping the families of the men arrested for political activity, and raising women's political consciousness.[63]

That throughout the war women did not voice "feminist" concerns as we understand them today, namely opposition to the veil, reform of family law and so on, should come as no surprise. Women, like men, felt that their basic political and economic rights were denied by the colonial order. Unlike men, their ability to express their discontent and act upon it was constrained by their transformation into ideological pawns in the battle between the colonizers and the colonized. The failure of the F.L.N. to become more responsive to women's needs in concrete rather than abstract ways, was due to at least two reasons. First, women were absent from its leadership, especially among the intellectuals responsible for drafting position papers and advising on policy. Second, the F.L.N. was the only organization opposing the French, all others having merged with it or been destroyed by it. This meant that no differences of opinion or strategy could be expressed while the war was still in progress. Thus, at the Women's Democratic Federation meeting held in Vienna in June, 1958, an Algerian woman declared that "for the moment, the question facing the Algerian woman is not the right to work or to improve her standard of living but to put an end to this horrible war."[64] It was true that, in a country ravaged by a savage war, women's right to work was not a priority. However, one of the causes of the war was precisely the denial of the right to work for both women and men. This could have been made clear at the risk of having to repeat history. But many of the women who joined the F.L.N. strongly believed that their participation had somehow permanently transformed their country's value system. "We knew that Algerian women would take part in the rebuilding of our country" said one woman.[65] "We thought we would earn our rights. We thought they would *naturally* be recognized later" echoed another (emphasis added).[66]

When all is said and done, the participation of women in the war of decolonization was not in vain, as will be shown in the next chapter. The judgment summarily passed on Algerian women by British feminist Sheila Rowbotham only reinforces the notion that revolutions against hunger, unemployment, poverty and political discrimination are necessarily revolutions in structures of consciousness. Her assertion that "Algerian women await liberation" is meaningless, just as is her statement that she *does not* know "what it is like to be Vietnamese, or Cuban, or Algerian."[67] Indeed, how *does* she know that these women need liberation or that the Algerian revolution has failed, as she claims. The Algerian revolution accomplished the task it set for itself: remove the French from Algeria.

What Rowbotham fails to recognize is that a colonized man is just a man whose basic right to food, shelter, clothing and happiness are not recognized. Fighting for those rights does not make him a perfect human being. For him to understand the meaning of modes of suffering and inequality other than those inflicted upon him by colonial might requires attaining a form of consciousness that is willing to rise above its own victimization and implicate itself in that of others. The history of revolutions in other parts of the world has not provided concrete examples of how such consciousness might be reached. Consciousness of difference between women and men as an instance of *social* inequality, instead of the expression of biological difference ordained by a divine force, is not the automatic outcome of militancy in a decolonization movement. It is the product of a historical struggle marked by setbacks as well as successes, depending on the conjuncture as will be shown in the next chapter.

8

State, Socialism, Development and Women

Decolonization disturbed capitalism but did not overcome it.
La Charte d'Alger, 1964, p. 56

When Algeria's independence from France was declared on July 3, 1962, one hundred and thirty-two years after the establishment of a colonial system of domination, it seemed as if it caught Algerian leaders by surprise. The ideological nature of the various policy declarations they made from 1954 to 1962 was revealed to the Algerian public in all its starkness, as a power struggle between factions of the F.L.N. ensued while the French were withdrawing. The lack of a political and economic program tailored to the historically-specific Algerian situation was evident as a new state was formed on the ruins of the colonial government structures. This had momentous consequences for women. Indeed, not being organized as a political faction or as members of one, they could rely only on leaders' memories of their contribution to independence for the promotion of their rights and the recognition of their needs.

Ben Bella's Feminizing Government

For a brief period, from 1962 to 1965, it seemed that Algerian socialism, as practiced by the first government of independent Algeria, would actively pursue the gains made by women in encroaching on the collective conscience of their countrymen. The first president, Ahmed Ben Bella, was wont to threaten men who harassed women on the streets with forced labor in the Algerian desert. The frequent references to women he made in his speeches angered the common man. Housewives reported that men at the market often alluded to these speeches, promising that "their time will soon come too."[1]

The most important political text issued by the Ben Bella government was the *Charte d'Alger* (or the Charter of Algiers), which contained an analysis of the socioeconomic and political problems of Algeria just after its independence, and recommendations about how to resolve them. Most importantly, it identified socialism as the mode of production in Algeria. Socialism was defined essentially in economic/managerial terms. For example, the charter emphasized that "socialism cannot be defined solely in terms of the nationalization of the means of production. It can also and primarily be defined in terms of worker's self-management, the only solution to the double contradiction of private property, and the separation between management and labor."[2] During the transition from capitalism to socialism, the F.L.N. party was, among other things, to "abolish the exploitation of man by man." The text does not spell out the concrete ways by which to realize this generic ideal, except by emphasizing that workers' self-management is a key to the "beginning of the era of freedom."[3]

There is much in the charter that a formerly colonized person might agree with. Inspired by Yugoslav socialism, and written primarily by two Algerian socialist intellectuals, Mohammed Harbi and Hocine Zahouane, it used concepts that had acquired common currency among European socialists, thus repeating their mistakes and distorting the Algeria-specific problems even as it adequately identified them. For example, the people, women and men, are referred to as the "masses." This undifferentiated concept makes it difficult to understand how it relates to the reality of social classes. Similarly, the use of generic "man" prevents the identification of a gender-specific form of inequality or "exploitation." This may explain why a special section of the charter was devoted to women, to address their status as a special group. The analysis of women's roles in society is remarkable for its neglect of the function played by women's assumed "inferiority," in both colonial capitalism and Algerian socialism as presented in the charter.

The charter points out that:

> For centuries the Algerian woman was maintained in an inferior condition justified by retrograde conceptions and erroneous interpretations of Islam. Colonialism aggravated such a situation by triggering among us a natural reaction of self-defense that isolated women from the rest of society. The war of liberation enabled the Algerian woman to assert herself by carrying out responsibilities *side by side with man*, and taking part in the struggle. (emphasis added)[4]

The theme of the war having given birth to women is revisited by the charter, which was unwilling to discursively allow women's participation in the war to be the product of their own activity. It appears that it was the proximity with men that gave women's action value and legitimacy, not their action itself, or the reasons that led them to engage in it. The charter quotes from the *Tripoli Program*, an F.L.N. policy statement, to point out that the past weighs heavily on the present. It also emphasizes that equality between women and men must become real. However, the recommendations are general, and expressed in the conditional tense.

> The Algerian woman should be able to participate effectively in politics and the building of socialism by joining the ranks of the party and national organizations and acceding to positions of responsibility. She should be able to put her energy in the service of the country by taking part in its economic life, thereby genuinely promoting herself through work.[5]

This conditional statement in effect indicates that women's roles, being shaped by a negative history, will not change immediately. Indeed, the party's action, limited to "giving women positions of responsibility within its ranks," is seen as "necessarily slow, given the present level of development of Algerian society."[6] In other words, the party does not have a concrete agenda for dealing with "social prejudices and retrograde conceptions" of women.[7]

The charter contains concrete recommendations about some concrete women: the wives of men who died during the war. It reveals that:

> pensions do not meet war widows' needs. Access to job training and social promotion must be given war widows to help them to fully participate in economic production. They must be given priority in the allocation of aid to rural reconstruction and urban housing. They are also entitled to free medical care.[8]

Nevertheless, a section of the charter covering war veterans specifically uses the concept in its masculine gender (*ancien moudjahed*) and fails to mention the needs of women veterans.[9] This could not be due to a linguistic habit of using the generic male term (*moudjahed*), because specific veterans' needs identified by the charter are *all* expressed in the masculine, yet women's needs (as, for example, help in obtaining a certification of participation in the war) are not mentioned, as might be expected given the charter's awareness of the feminine condition. The charter was also aware of the impact of red tape on a primarily illiterate population. For example, it denounced "bureaucratic formalism" which increased the gap between state and citizens, but failed to mention how it affected illiterate women, including those who served in the ranks of the F.L.N.[10]

The charter did not see women as a social group necessary to the task of building socialism, although a party organization, the National Union of Algerian Women, was hailed as "representing a revolutionary potential that should not be underestimated."[11] Admittedly, the charter did not conceive of male workers as a crucial part of the new socialist society either. Rather, it addressed abstract categories, such as self-management, and industrialization, and remained an ideologically undeveloped document that attempted to fit the Algerian socio-economic situation into a rudimentary notion of socialism lacking the breadth and imagination of utopian socialism. In addition, it passed judgment on Algerian culture from a modernist standpoint, not unlike that expressed by the French during the colonial era. It referred to a "low cultural level" and avoided an analysis of the positive aspects of Algerian culture *as a different culture*. Women were also seen as a problem, not unlike culture, inherited from history and about whom "socialism" was implicitly assumed to be powerless conceptually and empirically.

The new independent state had already been in operation for two years before the charter was issued. While the weight of the historical legacy may have been heavy, creating a new state also provided leaders with a chance to innovate. According to the charter, "we do not have a state tradition." It must be built. There was room for integrating women's needs into this state-in-the-making in new ways, instead of simply as members of a party organization. This was not done under the Ben Bella government, nor under his successors.

Yet one of the spectacular measures taken by Ben Bella was to request in 1963 that women donate their gold and silver jewelry to help the National Bank to build its reserves, at a time when national currencies were measured according to the gold standard. Within the Algerian cultural context, gold jewelry for urban women and silver for rural women constitutes an investment, a sign of status, and bears a sentimental value, as it usually represents a woman's dowry, and/ or gifts from parents and relatives. This means that the state asked of women a sacrifice, and women complied in great numbers. Dubbed *Fonds National de Solidarité* (National Solidarity Fund), this campaign was heavily publicized. At televised public meetings throughout the country, women walked up to party leaders and gave them their eighteen-carat gold chains (some of which were made of nineteenth-century coins), bracelets, anklets (some weighing half a pound), rings and earrings. How much gold and silver was collected is not known accurately. Nor is it known precisely what happened to it. In the past few years antique pieces of Algerian silver jewelry have occasionally appeared in a few jewelry shops doing business primarily with tourists. Rumor has it that these are parts of the collection of the *Fonds National de Solidarité* campaign. The ousting of Ben Bella in June 1965 helped to chalk up the campaign to mismanagement, one of the accusations leveled against him.

However, this was a significant event in the history of the relationship between women and the state. Women, as a group, were seen as necessary to the building of the state, but as contributors, not participants. The sacrificial view of women expressed by the wartime F.L.N. was thus given a clear content. Sacrifice, not duty complemented by right, was the cornerstone of the new state's view of women. Sacrifice does not always beget recognition. Indeed, in a critique of personality cult and of those who claimed a greater historical role in the revolution than others, the F.L.N.'s General Secretariat of the party identified as "historic" leaders only those who lost their lives during the war. No women figured among those he listed. That women also qualified as "historic" agents of the revolution was not acknowledged, the implication being that men made history, women sacrified their lives for history.

State, Women and Legitimation

Among Algerian leaders, the Charter of Algiers is but a trivial remnant of a short-lived political era. Yet, in its essentials, the charter provides evidence of continuity in perceptions of women at the political level, in the sense that no government after 1965 was able to transcend the problematic of sex/gender/state structure it so clearly revealed. This is due to a number of factors, among which the nature of Algerian socialism plays a crucial role.

Socialism in Algeria was unitary. Its first phase, implemented under Ben Bella, was mistakenly defined by its opponents as "scientific," and therefore atheist, primarily because of the presence of some French Communists in his entourage. Ben Bella's populist style hid the fact that the socialist doctrine he promoted stumbled on the issue of women. His successor, Houari Boumédiène, advocate of an "Islamic" form of socialism, rationalized the doctrine, no matter how ill-devised it was, without any fundamental change, leaving the conceptual and empirical roles of women in the new state in abeyance.

A new charter, the National Charter, issued in 1976, illustrates this point. A section entitled "the promotion of the Algerian woman," placed just after another dealing with "fighting social problems" emphasizes that:

> the Algerian woman's condition has improved significantly since the war of national liberation. However, to duly raise her status requires relentless efforts and courageous initiatives. Raising her status cannot be made to depend on the patriotic and social roles she played alongside her male companions in arms. Rather, it is an imperative act of justice and equity, a demand made upon us by the dialectic of progress, democracy, and nation building. It is also a clear consequence of her status as a citizen of free, revolutionary, and socialist Algeria.[12]

The National Charter thus recognized the unconditional rights of women, regardless of whether they took part in the war or not. However, just like its predecessor, it did not propose structural remedies for the ills it was quick to list. For example, the National Charter denounces:

> mental attitudes and negative legal structures that sometimes prejudice her [woman's] acknowledged rights as wife and mother, and her material and moral security." It also denounces "exorbitant and ruinous dowries, unscrupulous fathers who abandon their children to destitute mothers, or unjustifiably wrench their children from their mothers' affection; unmotivated divorces leaving women without alimony or health care; violence against women perpetrated with impunity; and exploitation of women by antisocial individuals" [meaning pimps].

But all these ills, according to the Charter, can only be solved by women themselves. "It is woman herself who must ultimately remain the best defender of her own rights and dignity through her deportment and qualities as well as a relentless struggle against prejudice, injustice, and humiliation." In other words, the plight of women is their own personal problem. "As for the state, it has already recognized the [Algerian] woman's political rights and is committed to her education and inevitable social advancement."[13] As in the previous charter, the National Charter was unable to fully integrate women in its conception of the new state. The ills suffered by women were recognized but unconnected with the other systemic sociocultural and economic problems identified in the society at large. Women were seen as a special social problem in need of a remedy that goes beyond the capacity of the state to help to solve in concrete ways. Their rights as abstract citizens were declared, because doing otherwise would go against the idea of progress which informed the struggle for decolonization, and the socialist orientation of the country.

Perhaps a charter is but a document that sketches the broad outlines of a governmental political program. Constitutions might be a better place to look for legally binding dispositions. Article 32 of the 1976 Constitution guarantees freedom to work to both women and men. Article 39 prohibits discrimination on the basis of sex, and Article 42 specifically guarantees women the protection of their political, economic, social and cultural rights. However, such protection was not provided in practice. For example, in 1981, a temporary restriction on women's ability to travel abroad alone was put into effect without prior warning.[14] In addition, although no government ordinance had been made public, passports were no longer issued to unemployed women during the same year.[15]

A university group of women, named Women's Collective of Algiers, sent a delegation of four women to the Minister of the Interior, who agreed that preventing women from traveling was unconstitutional and not authorized by the government.[16] The Minister refused to give written assurances that women would not be prohibited from travelling, but emphasized that he would exercise his right to prevent "people with a police record" from leaving the country.[17] It was a demeaning experience for the middle-class women, some traveling on business missions who were turned away at the airport for no apparent reason except that they were women.

In 1989, a new Constitution was issued by the government of Chedli Bendjedid, who initiated a gradual process of capitalist transformation of the economy. Inspired by political liberalism, this new document denotes a retreat from the previous charters and constitutions. Women are not mentioned, except under the term "Algériennes" in Article 31, which points out that the "fundamental liberties and Rights of Man and the Citizen are guaranteed. They constitute the common patrimony of all Algerian men and women." The concept of citizen is used in both the masculine and feminine genders in Article 30. However, Article 52 affirms the right to work to "les citoyens" without mentioning "les citoyennes," thereby creating the impression that only men have the right to work. Article 28 declares that all citizens are equal before the law "without discrimination on the basis of birth, race, sex, personal opinion, and other personal or social condition or circumstance." This awkward formulation essentially equates sexual discrimination, with infringement on freedom of speech.

The new Constitution does contain any article that commits the state to protect women's rights. Women are no longer considered a special category of people in need of special remedies. They are now subsumed under generic man, thereby implicitly denying the existence of problems specific to the condition of being female. In other words, the new Constitution makes women invisible. This is all the more remarkable in that it took place at the end of the United Nations Decade for the Advancement of Women, which drew the attention of the world's governments to the unrecognized and unanswered needs of women in developing countries. The international community had, by the time the new Constitution was issued, become familiar with the notion of gender inequality as well as the idea of women's advancement. Thus, in making essentially gender-blind pronouncements, the Constitution was out of step with the international consensus as expressed by the United Nation Decade for the Advancement of Women.

The 1989 Constitution is an instructive document not only because it represents an ideological shift from socialism to liberalism, but also as the culminating point of the sacrificial view of women held by the wartime F.L.N. From the standpoint of the advancement of women, the discursive inclusion of women in the Charter of Algiers, the National Charter and the 1976 Constitution was at least a recognition of their problematic condition. However, because women were not seen as one of the strategic groups necessary to the building of the future socialist society—these were identified in the masculine gender as peasants, workers and youth—but as a special and therefore marginal group, their participation in the new society was not raised as an issue. The lack of appreciation at the political theoretical level of the significance of the category "women" on a par with the categories of "peasants" or "workers" meant the erasure of women from the government's political agenda. Women could only exist as wives, mothers or daughters of men.

This theoretical/empirical caveat has provided the Algerian state with a chance to use women, *as a category*, in strategic ways to retain or defend its legitimacy. Tied to "historic" figures such as Ben Bella (one of seven men who started the revolution), or lesser known men such as Boumediene, revolutionary legitimacy began to erode as the old leadership died or dropped out of politics, the population grew increasingly younger, and the relevance of the F.L.N. to everyday life became dimmer. The Algerian state—an institution exhibiting bureaucratic features of the colonial, socialist and precapitalist states—has experienced a great need for legitimation as it weathered social and political crises. In the seventies, it was faced with a Berberist opposition which ostensibly wished to secure "cultural rights" for ethnic groups claiming Berber descent, but which held up the threat of dividing up the country into Berber and Arab territories. Subsequently, since the eighties, the Algerian state has had to contend with a disenchanted youth that took to the streets in violent demonstrations in October 1988, and a well-organized opposition from the religious right, as exemplified by the Front of Islamic Salvation.

A legitimation crisis not unlike that studied by Jürgen Habermas in relation to the late capitalist state has developed, provoking similar responses.[18] Under such conditions, the state, whether precapitalist or late capitalist, appeals to a "residue of tradition" to maintain social order. This residue of tradition is represented in the Algerian case by women and religion, the two having historically been linked together in the collective mind. The sacrificial view of women upheld by the F.L.N. could now be implemented for the sake of cultural authenticity. This is best illustrated by the passage of the 1984 Family Code, after eleven years of discussions and postponements.

The Family Code

Throughout the sixties and seventies a family code had been discussed by government officials in an attempt to rationalize what was perceived by judges and some lawyers as a confusing and anarchic family law, comprised of the *shari'a* and the various ordinances issued by the French colonial government amending it. In 1975, all colonial legislation pertaining to family matters was abolished. As a result, judges often found it difficult to resolve cases based solely on the *shari'a*. An environment of legal uncertainty was thus created, resulting in wide discrepancies in solving issues pertaining to divorce, alimony and child custody.[19] The opposition to the 1957 and 1959 colonial ordinances amending the *shari'a* was best summarized by Mr. Benhamouda, Minister of Justice in Boumédiène's government, who claimed that the "goal of the family code is above all to purify the structure of the family of all its un-Islamic elements."[20]

Drafts of a family code were drawn up in 1972 and 1979 but did not pass. Unofficial explanations for this failure invoked a struggle between socially liberal and conservative members of the government. At the time, the religious-right opposition existed but lacked the organization and social support necessary to put pressure on the government. President Boumédiène could not be said to have opposed the passage of a code during his tenure, since his own view of women was all but liberal. At the celebration of International Women's Day on March 8, 1966, he made a speech before a primarily women's audience, arguing that city women should count their blessings in comparison with the sorry lot of rural women. As a few women walked to the exit doors to leave in protest they were sent back to their seats by armed guards.[21]

It was not until 1984 that a new family code was passed. The history of its passage merits recalling as it reveals the dynamics and contradictions of tradition, revolution, gender and civil rights. A first draft was formulated in 1981 in secrecy. However, its approval was postponed, and a national commission was set up at the F.L.N. Party headquarters on April 29, 1982 to study the "organization of the family."[22] The commission was comprised of members of the party's Central Committee, the Ministry of Justice and representatives of the disciplines of theology, psychology and history. The code was not meant to be an instrument for ordering existing family relations but for rearranging them. Handing the task of examining and redrafting the code to the party was seen by some commentators as an unusual move, since traditionally it is the government that discusses legal texts.[23]

The decision to postpone the code was taken as a result of pressure placed on the government by women. The same independent group of about two hundred working women from universities which had objected to the arbitrary decision to prohibit travel abroad for women had met on March 8, 1979 in a small room made available to them by the General Union of Algerian Workers (in French U.G.T.A.), and passed a motion requesting more information on the composition of a commission initially set up by the Ministry of Justice to draft the code. They also requested that they participate in the formulation of the code. The motion was handed to the General Secretary of the General Union of Algerian Workers, and the General Union of Algerian Women (or U.N.F.A.).[24] In March 1981, a member of the government leaked a copy of a draft of the code to the Women's Collective, who began discussing ways of organizing against it. Six months later, the F.L.N. daily newspaper, *El Moudjahid*, reported the adoption by the government of a draft of a text on "personal status" to be presented to the National People's Assembly.[25]

The draft of the family code, euphemistically entitled "personal status," contained a number of articles that violated the letter and spirit of the 1976 Constitution which, in the mind of the new leadership, was already a doomed document, soon to be changed. The draft code institutionalized the unequal status of women in matters of personal autonomy, divorce, polygamy and work outside the home. Thus, Article 32 enjoins a wife "to obey her husband whom she must consider the head of the household." It also gives the husband "the right to demand that his wife breastfeed his children if she can, and take care of their education." A husband also "has the right to demand that his wife respect his father and mother and his relatives in general in a reasonable manner." Polygamy is not specifically prescribed, but it is condoned. Article 31 mentions that "If a husband has more than one wife, he must treat them with equity. He must provide each of them with a separate home."[26] In addition, Article 24 elliptically limits the number of wives a man can have to "that authorized by the *shari'a*," or four.[27] The regulation of divorce and repudiation is stated in unambiguous terms. Article 42 states that "the husband has the right to divorce. If he pronounces a divorce it is binding before the judge who must accept it in the first and last resort, that is to say without annulling it or allowing its appeal." However, if a husband "abuses" his right to divorce he is liable for "damages with interest not exceeding the amount of alimony due for a period of three years."[28] A wife does not have the right to divorce. She is "permitted to request a divorce" for a lack of payment of mandated maintenance, infirmities that prevent the consumption of marriage, physical mistreatment, grave violations of the law, refusal by the husband to share his bed with his wife, the husband's absence without a valid excuse, payment of alimony for a period exceeding four months or the husband's condemnation to jail for more than one year. In case of incompatibility a wife may obtain a divorce by exchanging her freedom for money paid to her husband, a practice the *shari'a* calls *khul'*.[29] Last, but not least, a wife can work outside her home only "if it is so stipulated in the marriage contract, and if the husband gives his authorization tacitly or specifically."[30]

In matters of child custody, marriage to a non-Muslim and procedural issues pertaining to the timing of remarriage, the draft of the family code follows the *shari'a* faithfully. For example, a mother may retain custody of her son until the age of ten, and of her daughter until she reaches puberty, although the legislator recognizes that "the interest of the child should be considered in the judgment ending custody."[31] A Muslim woman is prohibited from marrying a non-Muslim man, while a man is indirectly allowed to do so, since Article 49 states that a child must be brought up "in the religion of his father."[32]

This draft evidently bore the hallmark of social conservatism. Nevertheless, it contained some positive elements, none of which is incompatible with the *shari'a*. Thus Article 5 requests that "marriage is pronounced when one of the future spouses makes a request for it and the other consents to it." A woman's consent to marriage does not mean that she can contract a marriage on her own. She still needs a guardian to do so. However, Article 7 prohibits a guardian from coercing his ward to marry. A wife's absolute control over her possessions and assets is guaranteed by Article 31. Finally, Article 74 stipulates that at the death of her husband a wife becomes her children's guardian unless decided otherwise by her husband in his will.

In its essence, this draft of a new family law signaled to women that their rights as citizens were seriously jeopardized. The socialist society of equal citizens that the state had claimed to be building over the years seemed to have evaporated, and had given way to a society where men were legally empowered over women. Televised debates of the code at the People's National Assembly added insult to injury. Indeed, "A deputy pushed cynicism to its limits by advocating that women should be hit daily with a stick twenty centimeters long."[33] Reading the text of the draft and watching it debated on television shocked women (and some men) throughout the country. A woman expressed her surprise at the "retrogressive interventions made at the assembly that went beyond anything imaginable."[34]

A young woman reports a conversation with her mother to explain to her the gist of the code:

> ". . . a husband's authorization will be required to travel. . . ."
> My mother said: "Well, the husband must be asked, it is normal. . . ."
> I replied: "O.K., now you are a widow, and if you want to visit your daughter in Paris, what will you do? You will need your son's authorization."
> She said: "Me! How could it be! My son's authorization? But *I* brought him to this world, *I* married him off, and now *I* take care of his children, and you say I need *his* authorization! This is a topsy-turvy world![35]

Paradoxically, this feeling was shared by a number of men, members of religious groups at the time referred to by the general label of "Muslim brothers." They felt that the state's intervention in family law, no matter how mild, was a violation of the *shari'a*.

In an atmosphere of concern, if not panic, the Women's Collective sent a delegation to the National Union of Algerian Women to meet with its General Secretary, who reassured them that the code would not pass.[36] As it became clear that the code would most certainly pass, and that the National Union of Algerian Women was reluctant to press for its demise, the Women's Collective, joined by women in the professions and in the Administration, drafted a petition on September 28, 1981 to the People's National Assembly denouncing "the silence in which it was prepared and the absence of the people's consultation." It also stressed that "a draft formulated without the knowledge of the majority of the people can only satisfy a minority." It vowed that: "We cannot and shall not accept that our future be decided without our participation."[37] A copy of the petition was sent to women in the major urban centers in Algeria, and in France.

On October 28, 1981 a demonstration took place before the People's National Assembly, comprised of about one hundred women and five men. A second demonstration was held on November 16, 1981 led by former women revolutionaries such as Djamila Bouhired, Mériem Benmihoub, who is also a lawyer, and Zohra Drif, also wife of the president of the People's National Assembly. A delegation of twenty members was able to meet with two vice presidents of the Assembly, who defended the secrecy with which the code was prepared, asserted the right of their body to legislate regardless of pressure, and recommended that the matter be taken up with the National Union of Algerian Women who allegedly participated in the formulation of the draft. On their way home the petitioners decided to pay a visit to the Union, where they were told that its Secretary would not meet with more than three of them, instead of twenty, and insisted on seeing them privately rather than at a meeting with the members of the Union's council.[38]

Another demonstration before the People's National Assembly was routed by the police on December 14, 1981. A last and larger demonstration took place on December 23, 1981 on the steps of the landmark building of the main post office, where signs displayed demands that went beyond the cancellation of the code. Demonstrators demanded the implementation of the National Charter and the 1976 Constitution, as well as the right to be informed, and to work. They also denounced "silence," and the state's "betrayal of the ideals of November 1 [1954]."[39]

At a meeting held on January 21, 1982, the women war veterans "express once more their discontent and decide to appeal to the President of the Republic in his capacity as guardian of the constitution." They reminded the President of Articles 39, 40 and 41 of the Constitution , which guarantee women's equality with men and the protection of their rights, and Article 127, enjoining the People's Assembly to defend the socialist principles as outlined in the National Charter.[40]

There was something poignant about the flurry of activities that women undertook during 1981. Their appeals to the revolution, socialism and logic only underscored their powerlessness. There was no independent organization to defend their rights. The fact that former women revolutionaries joined the fray in a last-ditch effort to test the extent of their moral power revealed the utter vulnerability of women as a social group. Indeed, they hung by the thread of the state's moral obligation to some of them in their capacity as former fighters for an independent Algeria. As is the case with individuals who have only good intentions and the belief in lofty principles on their side, instead of the material means (such as organization, numbers, money), they lost. After being postponed for revision, the family code was passed without a struggle on June 9, 1984, perhaps not accidentally during the holy month of *Ramadan*. Was this a way of catching women by surprise at a time when they were far too busy to regroup, and when all activities slow down? Or was it simply a symbolic gesture towards the community of religious leaders and theologians, to signal to them the government's pious mood by choosing the proper timing for a legal text that duplicates the *shari'a* in its essentials? Whatever the answer to these questions, the new code constitutes a historical landmark in women's *prise de conscience* of their condition, and represents the first unambiguous governmental attempt at implementing its sacrificial view of women.

The final version does not differ in a fundamental way from the 1981 draft. However, it tones down its language and amends a few of its dispositions. It modifies its previous definition of marriage as an act for the purpose of procreation. Article 4 states that "one of its goals is to create a family based on affection, kindness, and caring, morally protect the spouses, and preserve family ties." Article 7 changes the age of marriage for a woman from sixteen to eighteen and for a man from eighteen to twenty-one. Although this is a welcome move it does no more than institutionalize a demographic trend. But Article 8 specifically invokes the *shari'a* to condone polygamy, which it regulates by emphasizing that a husband must "justify his action" and secure the consent of his wife, who may be permitted to divorce should she object. Article 37 enjoins a polygamous man to treat his wives with equity. He is no longer obligated to provide them with separate homes. Article 11 reiterates the fact that a woman needs a guardian (who may be her father, a male relative or a judge) to contract marriage. She also needs a dowry paid to her before the marriage becomes legal. Article 48 retains the husband's right to divorce, but also allows divorce by mutual consent. The husband's right to divorce is no longer expressed in absolute terms, and an attempt at reconciliation must precede a divorce judgment. Article 51 institutionalizes divorce by repudiation by spelling out the penalty for a man "who has divorced his wife three consecutive times" as prescribed by the *shari'a*. Presumably, since the code states that divorce must be pronounced by a judge, repudiation, a verbal act, is no longer an issue.

However, the number of times a man divorces invoked in this Article, as well as the specific penalty which prohibits reconciliation unless the wife has married a third party are characteristics of repudiation described in the *shari'a*. Article 65 makes it possible for a mother to have custody of her son until the age of sixteen as long as she has not remarried. A mother may retain custody of her daughter until she "reaches the legal age of marriage," or eighteen. Article 75 maintains a father's obligation to pay child support. Article 87 makes the mother the full guardian of her children upon her husband's death, thereby removing the restriction imposed in the 1981 draft. The new code does not subject a woman's ability to work to her husband's approval. In matters of adoption of children and inheritance the code appears to follow the *shari'a* closely, although only an extensive knowledge of the complexity of the *shari'a* on this matter could ascertain that this is indeed the case.[41]

Women's protests in 1981 drew attention to the issue of equal rights, and were instrumental in causing the government to amend the text of the code, but this fell short of changing its framework, which remained that of the *shari'a*. It would be tempting, as some commentators have done, to conclude that the code is not an entirely negative legal text, that it protects, even if partially, women's rights to divorce, child guardianship and custody. However, within the context of Algerian political history since 1962 stressing equality of citizens regardless of sex, and the official recognition of the need to raise women's status, the code is an infringement upon women's rights to full citizenship. Indeed, unable to reconcile the principle of equality before the law embedded in its Constitution with the Quranic assumption of the natural empowerment of men over women at the heart of the *shari'a*, legislators acted as members of precolonial Algeria. In this respect, the code is an anachronistic piece of legislation that erased with the stroke of a pen the historical changes that had taken place over a hundred and fifty years. It attempts to restore social relations of a bygone era that contemporary social structures, including the family, could not accommodate. The spectacle of women lawyers and judges having to litigate family cases in court on the basis of the code illustrates the absurdity of the social project it was meant to serve.

The code attempts to reinforce the family in the life of Algerian women and men. As an editorial of *El Moudjahid* pointed out, the family is a social "cell" in need of "protection and preservation" from social ills.[42] Women emerge as the instruments of protection of the family headed by a man, to whom his wife owes "obedience" and "consideration." She must "respect her husband's parents and his relatives." In return, she has the "right to visit her parents and receive them according to custom."[43] It is possible to read these prescriptions as responses to existing problems in a society experiencing rapid socioeconomic change. Individual complaints about a dilution of family ties and an erosion of social values are legion. However, the solution proposed, which emphasizes "social solidarity" and legislates feelings, betrays the government inability to address structural issues directly.[44] The family is seen as the cause of problems originating outside of it, and which have in fact affected it. The hierarchical model of family proposed, where the father's role is instrumental and the mother's expressive, is itself fraught with potential conflicts that can rend instead of reinforce its structure. Indeed, given the nature of the Algerian economy, fewer men could be breadwinners, and fewer women are content with "obeying" their husbands.

Whatever the deficiencies of the family code, it did serve the function of raising working women's consciousness. It made them realize that they had taken the implementation of their rights for granted. Perhaps more importantly, they became keenly aware of the fact that they could not be represented adequately by the F.L.N.-sponsored National Union of Algerian Women. Attempts were made by working women in the aftermath of the code to create their own associations, as will be discussed in the next chapter.

Gendered Development

The family code is but one expression in the legal system of the dynamics and contradictions of an economic mode of production that has, since 1965, rested on abstract, ostensibly gender-blind principles. While the general orientation of the Algerian economy was until 1978 socialist, in the sense that land, heavy industry, commerce and banking were either state-owned or controlled, its content was developmentalist. The choice of development strategy was related less to the socialist ideal of economic equality than to the goal of increased labor-saving and capital-intensive production.[45] Establishing an industrial infrastructure was given precedence over all other economic, political or social issues. This meant that the disjuncture between socialism and development (seldom recognized in the relevant literature) added a new dimension to the structural silence that had historically characterized women. Indeed, the sacrificial view of women embedded in the Algerian brand of socialist ideology was transformed into a structural exclusion of women as a group in need of affirmative action by the state's development practice.

The transition from sacrifice to marginalization was made possible by a focus on the technical side of development, perceived as a disembodied, degendered, purely instrumental process of acquisition of control over the means and methods of production. It could be reasonably argued that unemployed and unskilled men were also sacrified by a model of development that privileged high technology over labor and industry over agriculture. However, where jobs under this model are generally scarce, practice reveals that they tend to be allocated to men.

Algeria is hardly the only country in the Third World whose development policy did not factor in women. Development experts have, in the last fifteen years, documented the ways in which Third World governments *as well as* international development organizations have unwittingly embarked upon projects that resulted in the economic marginalization of women by reinforcing their invisibility in the production process, which rests on their ill-paid (or often unpaid) participation.[46] The specificity of the Algerian development model was that it promised women and men a leap into the world of industrialization— hailed as a cornucopia of jobs, food and well-being—after a relatively short transitional period, and in an autonomous fashion. But the new industry was highly automated, agriculture suffered from endemic underemployment and state bureaucracy was inflated. However, the influx of petrodollars from 1965 to 1980 enabled the state to not only finance its development projects but also provide free health care and education, and subsidies for basic foodstuffs. A general climate of relative welfare obscured the fact that families and individuals still struggled to make ends meet.

Within this context, women found jobs in the sectors of the economy least affected by the development policy or created to administer its modalities, namely the state apparatus (that is, the government and the state-owned enterprises), international organizations and/or foreign businesses based in Algeria and the professions. This constitutes a reversal of a trend in Third World societies, where women's employment is concentrated in agriculture. Official statistics indicate that women comprise six percent of the labor force, most of whom (eighty six percent) are in white-collar jobs.[47] In comparison with other socialist societies this is a low figure. However, it does not include women who are engaged in the informal sector of the economy, or unpaid members of family businesses.[48] The proportion of women engaged in the informal sector increased fourfold between 1977 and 1985. There is little information about the nature of the activities these women carry out, although many are known to take in sewing, embroidery and pastry making. However, their increasing numbers are a reflection of the worsening of the Algerian economy and its structural adjustment.

Rural women have usually worked on their family farms. Traditionally they were responsible for weeding fields, tending lentil crops and vegetable gardens, raising chickens and taking care of animals. The agrarian reform initiated by the Boumédièe government, based on land redistribution and the construction of "socialist villages" equipped with water facilities and electricity, brought about changes in women's lives. On the one hand, access to amenities lightened women's domestic burden. On the other hand, the introduction of machinery benefited men, and the rationalization of production resulted in diminishing women's roles in agriculture. Some of them have complained that they feel "useless now."[49] However, this trend is counterbalanced by the increased participation of women in all phases of agriculture in areas where men have emigrated either abroad or to nearby urban centers. In an attempt to stem the tide of migration and to encourage efficient farming the government offered plots of land to homesteaders through an arrangement that would grant them ownership. It is unclear how many women were among the takers. The recent policy shift towards a market economy has been accompanied by a greater privatization of the land, employing women as well as men as seasonal workers.

A number of characteristics of women in the labor force distinguish them from women in other Third World societies, especially the Middle East. First, the wage-earning population is generally (eighty percent) literate, half of whom have at least a high school education. Among the unemployed, educated women figure in higher percentages than men. For example, thirty nine percent of unemployed women had had a secondary education (against 12.6 percent of men) and 7.4 percent a postsecondary education (as compared with two percent of men).[50] This means that the particular structure of the Algerian economy makes women compete with men with lesser education and skills thus turning women's educational advantage into a liability. Second, women are equally represented with men in professions such as the law, where they also rise to the rank of judges. Third, there are no legal barriers to entering any profession. Fourth, the practice of credentialism that has marked the administration enables women to enter a job at a salary level commensurate with the degree received. However, individual employers have on a number of occasions hired men at higher salary levels than women with equivalent degrees, thus violating the law and presented women with a comparable worth issue.[51] Fifth, the state-controlled economy enabled individual women, until the late seventies, to partake in import–substitution by setting up fashion designs, knits and ready-to-wear businesses. Sheltered by the state, some of these businesses have proved lucrative.

A case in point is provided by a woman of working-class background, married to an employee of Algeria's Electricity and Gas Works, and who once wore the veil. With money borrowed from a friend she bought a knitting machine and began to copy French designs, catering to the need for attractive national products expressed by wives of members of the government, whom she charged inflated prices. In time, she expanded her operation, importing more machinery from Switzerland, hiring and training young women from rural villages west of Algiers to operate them, and opening a second boutique at Riyad El Feth, Algiers' duty-free commercial center. At a time when buying property was severely restricted, she was able to obtain a permit to purchase land, on which she built a house with a long-term, low-interest (two percent) loan from the state, designed by a French architect and distinguished by its marbled floors imported from Italy. Two of her sisters are also owners of less spectacular but just as lucrative garment businesses. Nevertheless, for every woman's success story there are numerous stories of men who set up equally successful import-substitution businesses. What women's success stories reveal is that a gender-blind model of development has implicitly universalistic aims which may make it possible for the women who can to take advantage of it. Indeed, having no competition from abroad, essentially protected by the state, these women were able to carve out a niche for themselves. Garments do not constitute the only business women engage in. In Algiers, for example, women entrepreneurs have also tried their hands at tourism, cosmetics and movie theater management.

The fact remains that for women who have no capital to start a business and who need to work outside their homes, opportunities for starting viable businesss have been limited. Since 1979, when oil revenues began to dwindle as a result of diminished demand, the economy slowed down, imports of foodstuffs have fluctuated, aggravating an already existing situation of relative scarcity, and the black market has thrived. A national deficit of twenty-six billion dollars was announced by the government in the last four years making hopes for the much-touted sustainable development a remote possibility. For women, this means that jobs will be scarcer although their demand for them will increase. In addition, the government's self-imposed structural adjustment policy has meant an end to medical drug subsidies, galloping inflation helped by currency devaluation and higher prices for foodstuffs and other commodities. The transition to a market economy has not meant an easier availability of such commodities. Rather, it has signified increased participation of international capital in an economy that prided itself on its independence, and higher prices for consumer goods. As happened in other Third World societies subjected to structural adjustment policies designed for them by the International Monetary Fund, it is women who, as a vulnerable group, are feeling the crunch of the state's attempt at meeting its debt obligations.[52] Shortages of commodities during the socialist years compelled women and children to wait in long lines to acquire needed goods. The transition to a market economy, coinciding as it has with a budget deficit, also means shortages of commodities (such as semolina, coffee, almonds and flour) the import of which is controlled by a state strapped for hard currency it does not wish to allow to be spent freely. For women lines are still long and family budget must be managed with less.

Children, Housing and Water

Gender-blind in its theory, the Algerian model of development is gender-real in its consequences. Among these, runaway demographic growth and long-lasting housing and water crises. At the World Population Congress held in Mexico City in 1974, the Algerian delegate expressed the government position by stressing that the issue for Algeria was not population growth but development.[53] This view resonates with a school of demography that rightly stresses the correlation between higher standards of living and lower fertility. It is also true that Algeria experienced an expected baby boom after its long and bloody war of decolonization. However, the doubling of the population in less than twenty-five years must be seen as a direct consequence of a political economy that put a premium on planning on petrodollars and left civil society to its own devices. In a sense, the state could afford to ignore the demographic dimension of its development policy only if half of the population were to be removed from the pool of job seekers and implicitly entrusted with the task of making and raising children. Carried over from the colonial era, bonuses continue to be paid to working heads of households for their children, thus making their earnings family wages.

Since the onset of the economic crisis, the state has begun to address the demographic issue. Centers for the Protection of Mothers and Infants (P.M.I.) providing primary health-care services for mothers and their infants have been used for dispensing information about child-spacing and contraceptives. In 1982, a program of population control was formulated in cautious terms, emphasizing child-spacing, and the study of the determinants of fertility as they relate to development.[54] A study of the first six years (1975 to 1983) of this incipient population policy indicates that the women who sought the services offered were city dwellers with an average of five children each. The study also reveals that even though the Islamic Superior Council issued an opinion declaring contraception permissible if initiated by individuals to meet their personal needs, contraception can be viable only if accompanied by a transformation of women's social status.[55] This points to the relative role played by religion when development policy does not fully involve women in its parameters.

Given the scarcity of jobs and the low remuneration of white-collar positions—women's domain—it does not seem unreasonable for a woman with an average of seven children to stay home and raise her children.[56] It is important to realize that, despite its vagaries, Algerian socialism did result in providing health care to those who needed it, medical drugs at low prices and free child immunization. All these essential services are in danger of being restricted. Drugs, for example, are now more difficult to obtain and at highly inflationary costs.

There are as many forces pushing women to get out of their homes to earn a living as there are to tie them down to their homes. A housing shortage in urban centers is one such force that women find confining. Individuals are compelled to live in extended families, an arrangement that had been on the wane. There have been reports in Algiers of family members taking turns to sleep in beds due to a lack of space, or sleeping on roofs and balconies in the summer wherever possible. Lawyers state privately that a high proportion of the divorce cases they handle are caused by tensions resulting from crowded living quarters. The severity of the housing question is well illustrated in a short story written by a former female cabinet member, Leila Aslaoui, where a brother is led to kill his sister over a disputed house.[57] New housing projects built by the state have not met demand. In the past ten years, private builders got in on the act, charging rents above the capacity of those who need them the most. Still, the preferred solution, for those who can, is to build their own houses. The influx of migrant workers' remittances from Europe exchanged on the black market has given an additional boost to the building trade.

One of the least appreciated consequences of the housing crisis is the daily pressure it has placed on women, who must constantly clean and tidy up after children and male adults, cannot afford to stay in bed if they are ill and sometimes must suffer incest quietly. Occasional cases of incest are whispered about by female doctors, who attribute them directly to the crowded conditions under which many city women live. Some of the victims refrain from reporting their abuser to the police not only because of the scandal this might cause but also because they lack the physical space to escape to.[58] Thus structural silence is compounded by situational silence.

The housing shortage is worsened by an equally serious water crisis that has plagued Algerian cities for the past thirty years. The population of Algiers, for example, has experienced water cuts regularly since the late sixties. Oblivious to women's needs and their schedule of domestic activities, the City cuts water for most of the day, turning it back on around midnight and sometimes later. This causes women to lose sleep waiting for the water to be restored; they store it in a variety of vessels and sometimes in bathtubs. Families who could afford them also set up cisterns hooked to their water pipes to catch the precious liquid as soon as it is turned on. A dam that the state built in the last few years on the outskirts of Algiers relieved the pressure somewhat. However, cuts persist and the lack of running water for women with large families has caused them great grief. Indeed, it is difficult to pour water that had been stored in pots to wash up. It is equally difficult to keep a neat house when water must be taken out of different pots and pails, leaving a trail of droplets no matter how careful one is. During the summer, showing becomes difficult, forcing young men to go to the beach regularly to take advantage of public showers. There is always the *hammam*, but to use it daily is a prohibitive cost for many families. Apart from being a vital utility, water also holds a mythic/symbolic significance in the cultural lore. Traditionally, stagnant water was avoided because of its malefic potential. Running water symbolizes purification and renewal. Finally, a shortage of water is identified with times of scarcity and poverty. Yet today one may not be poor but suffer from water shortage. For women, water shortage has meant an additional strain. An Algiers psychiatrist reports frequent cases of depression among women who find it difficult to cope without running water.[59]

Humanizing Development

The United Nations Development Program has, since 1990, spearheaded a conception of development, termed "human," that takes into consideration not only economic growth but also social welfare as measured by life expectancy, literacy, health care and a "decent standard of living."[60] Thus a country that scores high on growth may score low on health care or literacy. This view may be a corrective to the development-as-growth conception, but it does not go far enough; it does not recognize the gendered nature of development no matter its qualifier. To be "human," development must be measured in terms of gender. This is so because, as a category of analysis and an empirical reality, gender has proved to sum up dysfunctions, implicit or explicit contradictions and inequities inherent in development programs and projects.[61]

The Algerian case is an illustration of this point. The state started out investing in its human resources by expanding education to all and launching an extensive training program during the first fifteen years. This policy, combined with socialized health care, would have made the Algerian development policy balanced, in the sense that it did not rely solely on economic growth. Women made enormous strides in education, where their numbers have quadrupled since 1962. However, they still register a lag with men. The Human Development Report for 1990, which lists Algeria among the countries scoring a medium position on a scale ranging from low to high, indicates that the net primary school enrollment ratio is eighty-one for females and ninty-one for males.[62] This compares favorably with countries such as Morocco, India or Pakistan.

Women are eligible for training abroad, but the bulk of scholarships has generally been awarded to men. At a conference I organized in 1970 for students sent by the government to study geology, physics, engineering and biology, there was no woman in a group of sixty. A scholarship awarded to a female student at the University of Algiers in 1967 by the African American Insitute was cancelled because the Ministry of Education at the time failed to approve it. This may have been a case of bureaucratic incompetence. But women have complained that their sex has disqualified them from getting training scholarships. It is easier for a woman to receive a scholoarship to complete a doctorate in France. But this is so because up until 1988 doctorates in the social sciences, for example, could not be completed in Algeria. Now that the state is strapped for money, men too are finding it more difficult to obtain training abroad. A few women who received specialized training and found jobs commensurate with their qualifications realized they were assigned tasks for which they were overqualified.[63]

Finally, the very concept of work for women is in need of developing to prevent prejudices against female workers. For example, in 1980 an investigation revealed that 1,300 young women who worked in a plant manufacturing electronic products in the provincial city of Sidi Bel Abbès had been at the center of controversy. They were perceived as immoral by the larger community and subjected to a number of pressures by male relatives. Prospective husbands insisted that marriage contracts include a clause forbiding their wives to continue to work at the plant.[64] Yet this was not simply the result of some cultural prejudice against working women. It was part of an old Algerian attitude towards *industrial* work. During the colonial era, work in manufacture was associated with a loss of status, and identified with the French colonial working class. This aristocratic view, a legacy of Algeria's agrarian past, persisted even when Algerian men joined their colonial counterparts as industrial workers. Women who work in a plant incur a double prejudice, as workers and as women doing a devalued man's job. Human development requires a revaluation of industrial tasks in societies with changing economic systems. Short of this, industrial managers will continue to turn this prejudice to their favor by hiring women at lower pay than men.

9

Consciousness, Culture and Change

A trend in the social sciences has accredited the notion that culture holds the key to understanding what a simpleminded economism failed to grasp, namely that there is no causal relationship between material change and social change.[1] When pushed to its logical conclusion, this view transforms culture into a preformed totality having a determining power over the minds of those who are assumed to live not in it but under it. Yet culture, in colonial and postcolonial societies, as elsewhere, is a reflexive process shaped by individuals interacting in various social spheres and at different temporal levels, and shaping them in turn. When seen as a process, culture is inextricable not only from material life, but also from consciousness, a phenomenon easily forgotten in the feminist literature on women in the Middle East.

To argue that Algerian culture was affected by colonial—to be distinguished from French—culture does not simply mean that it was impoverished and became "fossilized," as the official F.L.N. interpretation has it. What appeared "fossilized" was already a patterned way of solving problems of the day. It means that for a period of over one hundred years a culture made up of precolonial material mingled with new accretions to make a coherent, albeit contradictory, totality in flux. This makes cultural decolonization a complex attempt at teasing out those elements (linguistic, ideational *and* psychic) that gave Algeria its native-colonial cachet.

Decolonization is not simply the process of removing colonists from power and replacing them with native people. Nor can it be reduced to building new state institutions to administer formerly colonized people. It also means managing native culture suppressed by the colonial society and facilitating its change and transformation. This

166

is no small task, as it gets entangled in the political strife that usually accompanies the establishment of a new government. During the war, F.L.N. leaders knew the importance of cultural development and change when they envisioned the future of an independent Algeria. The Tripoli Program, for example, advocated the "restoration of national culture and the gradual arabization of education on a scientific basis."[2] Similarly, the government of Boumédiène launched a "cultural revolution" to complement the "agrarian revolution."

However, the term culture in both instances was used as a synonym for the expansion of literacy in Arabic, the "preservation" of cultural artifacts. Echoing the Tripoli Program, Ahmed Taleb Ibrahimi, a former minister of culture defined the cultural revolution as "a return to our roots, to authenticity in order to reconnect with our past which, under foreign domination, was masked, obscured, and distorted."[3] Although he cautions that a rediscovery of the past must not be understood to signify a rejection of change, he does not provide any guidance as to how the past can illuminate the present, therefore leaving the issue of decolonization unresolved. The notion of culture as a value and ideational system was left unexplored. Nor were the ways in which colonial culture affected the psyche of Algerian people, including their leaders, addressed in a programmatic fashion. Instead, culture officially meant "restoration" of an "Arab-Muslim" society that had already been there *in its Algerian form*. In other words, the specificity of the Algerian condition as it had been affected by a radical colonial policy of acculturation was neither seriously appreciated nor remedied. Somehow, the substitution of Arabic for French in schools was thought to do the trick. The colonial government, too, had begun its policy of acculturation with the introduction of French as the language of instruction. But it also supplemented it with an all-French curriculum steeped in a technological environment that established the supremacy of French culture, in its colonial form, over native culture. In this sense, the French language was only one part of the implantation of a *hegemonic* culture. The Algerian state's linguistic project was naive in comparison and fraught with problems, the most serious of which being a Berberist (which often means anti-Arab if not anti-Muslim) opposition claiming its own dialect as a national language.[4]

How does all of this affect women? Under condition of incomplete or inadequate decolonization, individual consciousness appears to embrace the particular and shy away from the universal. The government may emphasize "nation-building," but individuals focus on their ethnic affiliation. Women demand equal rights, men insist on privilege. Cultural strains and contradictions rend a social fabric already weakened by years of fighting. Relationships between women and men offer an excellent site in which to study the dynamics of culture, consciousness and incomplete decolonization. The ways in which women and men perceive themselves and one another reflect changes that have taken place not only in their political and social environments, but also their cultural habits. Algeria provides an example of a society where new life-styles have emerged, affecting time and space, and where different forms of consciousness oscillate between old and new cultural contents. These changes cannot be understood without a brief analysis of the sociocultural context that has prevailed since 1962.

Context of Cultural Change

A basic medium of change in the lives of women and men since the independence of Algeria is television. Its use even in the poorest urban homes has made it an essential fixture of everyday life. It is not uncommon to turn the set on while families are having dinner or entertaining friends. Unemployed women's time has become a function of TV time. Domestic activities are thus arranged according to TV programs. The centrality of television to families compelled state censors to edit out love scenes from European and American films deemed embarrassing to the older generation. Television programs are an eclectic assortment of foreign films, primarily from the U.S., including serials such as *Kate and Allie, Beauty and the Beast, The Bill Cosby Show,* and at one point *Dallas,* as well as Egyptian serials or variety shows from neighboring countries. National TV productions are few and far between, as budgetary constraints make imports more economical. Apart from foreign films and situation comedies, TV also broadcasts, usually late at night, rock concerts catering to youth. In the last few years, dish antennas have made their appearance on private homes and apartment buildings, where tenants share in the cost of obtaining them. Thanks to this new symbol of modernity, Algerian women and men have access to unedited French, Spanish and Italian programs, sometimes displaying naked women.[5]

This media situation underscores Algeria's cultural vulnerability. Women and men are daily exposed to messages produced primarily in industrial countries rooted in a different cultural tradition. At the same time, religious programs are broadcast whose context is in contradiction with these messages. These contradictions are experienced as a tension created by the disparity between one's lived reality and the world of films and situation comedies. Women feel this tension more deeply than men, since TV is their most important form of entertainment as well as the source of their information on the outside world.

Men are also subjected to the conflicting messages from foreign films offered by movie theaters, where sex and violence against women go hand in hand, and an ascendant religiosity that emphasizes chastity for women. Growing up female or male in an environment that depicts women as sexual objects, chaste, pious and free (for there are broadcasts of foreign women in sports) is a most confusing experience. The confusion may have reached a climax when a young native woman, Hassiba Boulmelqa, won a gold medal at the Olympic games in the summer of 1992, thus bringing publicity to the nation and eclipsing male members of the Algerian team.

Caught between conflicting images of femininity, women have attempted to order their lives on their conception of modernity. This began with a rearrangement of their lives within the confines of the apartment, a change from the house built around an open courtyard and providing space for oversized pots and pans used in cooking for large families, doing the laundry in wooden vats etc. Urban migrations forced families to live in apartments abandoned by departing colonists at the end of the war, and to adjust to smaller quarters. Gas stoves, steam cookers, refrigerators and, more and more frequently, washing machines have made life easier for women, and contributed along with the school schedule of their children to bringing housewives, including the illiterate among them, into the *time* frame that characterizes "modern" life. These physical changes have been counteracted by the water crisis, as discussed in the previous chapter.

Changes in space, time and greater access to household appliances have coincided with an expanded awareness of the world, conveyed not only by the media but also by opportunities for travel abroad, as well as contacts with nearly one million emigrants to Europe, many of whom visit their relatives back home every summer. Last but not least, the very fact of Algeria's independence, seen as a radical change from the past, created a frame of mind open to adopting life-styles hitherto associated with the French, but now seen as "modern." What was repressed during the colonial era as inauthentic could now be expressed as a sign of a new time. For example, more often than not, young urban women meet their husbands before marrying them. Wedding ceremonies often dispense with proof of the bride' virginity, and more frequently combine one "traditional" celebration held for women and men separately, and another one where both women and men mingle and dance to Western music.

Expressions of Cultural Change since 1962

Cultural change since 1962 is the culmination of incremental change that took place throughout the fifties but did not become visible until the war ended, thus removing the restrictions that had prevented its full expression. The war had compelled individuals to reorder their priorities and even change their life-styles. For example, the F.L.N. had recommended that weddings be celebrated in the intimacy of the family, without the usual music and festive celebrations, as a sign of respect for those who were dying everyday for the independence of their country. Restrictions of this kind created a crisis of postponed hedonism, which awaited the end of the war to finally make up for lost time.

A popular musical form called *rai* is the best example of this search for pleasure and the expression of desire. *Rai* performers are usually young women and men often singing (in duos) lyrics celebrating love and romance, although sometimes addressing social problems in the same manner as rap singers. *Rai* music became prevalent in the early eighties. Yet it was already popular in Western Algeria in a different form. In the fifties and sixties, a female working-class singer, Fatma Remiti, accompanied by flutes and drums, sang boldly about her loves, graphically depicting her sexual romps. Taking their inspiration from her, the younger generation of *rai* singers began to sing of their sexual frustrations within a society they find unresponsive to their needs. One of the leading *rai* singers, Chab Ahmed, refers to the social group to which he belongs and about whom he sings as the *mrifiziyn* (an Arabized version of the French word, *refusés*) or misfits. Included in the *mrifiziyn* are "youth and women."[6] The concept *rai* means, in colloquial Arabic, commonsense, opinion or advice, and was used in an old song by Remiti. At first confined to Western Algeria, *rai* singers' popularity spread to the rest of the country to the dismay of religious leaders and upright citizens, who see in it one more sign of the disintegration of values as well as a symptom of cultural impoverishment.

The search for pleasure is often expressed in small yet psychologically significant ways. Where the sexual division of labor extends to the consumption of physical pleasure, cigarette smoking may afford the pleasure of symbolically overthrowing the established order. An old attribute of masculinity, it has also become, among many female students and occasional career women, a sign of liberation. To smoke is to signify one's status as an independent woman and to claim equality with men. The pleasure is greater and unmitigated if a woman is to smoke in public, instead of the privacy of one's or a friend's home. If smoking may be harmful to one's physical health, kissing in a public park is not, and it too has been observed on a number of occasions in Algiers parks, during lunch break.

Humor is another area where change has occurred. Slim, the well-known caricaturist, has for years satirized Algerian life. On occasion he addressed the woman question, poking fun at men. For example, one of his comic strips refers to a man named Diassa, whose wife was selected to share a space voyage with a Russian cosmonaut for five days. Naturally the husband refused to let his wife go alone, despite government pressure. That is until an official suggested paying him a large sum of money in foreign currency. The husband immediately gave his authorization. Thus "Algeria's honor was safe, except for Daissa's."[7]

Similarly, Zemmouri, a comedian, has parodied his countrymen's customs. He also made a film *Prends 10,000 balles et casse-toi* ("Take 10,000 bucks and scram") which, among other things, addresses a typical problem among parents who encourage their daughters to acquire careers, tolerate the fact that they have male friends at the university, but expect them to travel with a chaperone and marry according to the old ways.[8]

A Freudian psychologist who studied this problem explains it in terms of a conflict due to rapid acculturation in the values of "modernism" and a desire to maintain traditions, a source of psychic safety and comfort. In this sense, rapid acculturation is also felt as "deculturation"—a loss of traditional values—which triggers resistance evidenced in some well-to-do parents' insistence that their daughters not receive phone calls from male friends, or that their sons live with them after their marriage.[9]

What these changes indicate is a willingness to raise the issue of women that culminated in their entry into Algerian feature film as a major theme. Algerian filmmakers have explored this theme in the last fifteen years, generally portraying women as subjected to the domination of their husbands or fathers. The film, *A Wife for my Son*, based on a book bearing the same title, is a case in point.[10] Missing is an in-depth analysis of structured gender inequality that would show both the strengths and vulnerabilities of various groups of women in society. Male directors and producers have had more difficulty in handling the subject of women than they did the war. They could provide a different interpretation of the war, and describe the suffering it imposed on individuals. But when addressing the woman question, they lose their originality and become indistinguishable from their French counterparts. The first Algerian film to have featured women prominently as active agents in the history of their country, *The Battle of Algiers*, managed to provide no information about their biographies—as it did for Ali-la-Pointe, a major male protagonist—or the process through which they became urban guerrillas. Their participation was presented as arising *ex nihilo*, and confined to taking orders. Typically, they spoke very little, thus highlighting women's silence at the very time that their actions spoke loudly.

Women and the Return of the Cultural Repressed

Cultural change in a society undergoing rapid social change is a source of intra- and interindividual conflict. It affects different groups differently and causes various reactions, all of which are in one way or another related to women's changing roles. Indeed, women *are* at the core of the cultural continuities, mutations, contradictions and inconsistencies. The entry of women into the worlds of school and work has made them singularly conspicuous, considering their past invisibility. Since 1962, the presence of women in the public sphere, no matter how limited it is in absolute terms, is the most significant aspect of postwar Algeria. This has coincided with an increased urbanization process that has uprooted rural families in search of a better livelihood, and marginalized rural populations by making them dependent on cities for their material and cultural survival. In addition, the passage from a primarily agrarian to an industrializing society is accompanied by a change from a community-based to a cash-based society, where money has increasingly become the measure not only of things but also of people. Finally, these profound economic changes have affected women's (and men's) conceptions of themselves. Women, urban as well as rural, expect to live their lives differently from their mothers, by resisting cohabiting with their in-laws, choosing or influencing the choice of their husbands, getting an education and/or working outside their homes.

Women and men live in a tug-of-war between the demands of a new material life requiring freedom of movement, expression and thought, as well as *individual* advancement, that often counter the persisting cultural demand for the preservation of family-based solidarity and hierarchical relations, rightly or wrongly identified with religious values. In a typical pattern, women emerge as the standard for the evaluation of the distance that separates the "old" from the "new." This is so because they were the only social group in the colonial era that was physically suppressed, making their visibility in the postcolonial era a dramatic if not traumatic event for men. Furthermore, the family and its maintenance are seen as intimately linked to the roles of mother and housewife. Any woman who steps out of these roles or questions their primacy is perceived as threatening the integrity of the family, and by extension, that of the culture at large.

Within this context, it is not surprising to note a number of contradictory attitudes among fathers, who are open to the education of their daughters but are unable to conceive of the freedom of movement they require, even when they become of age. Contradictory attitudes are also demonstrated by young men, who demand of women the wearing of a *hijab* or giving up a career and sometimes male friends, as conditions to marrying. Better still, some young men let their mothers arrange their marriages for them. This was the case of a man with a Ph.D. in nuclear physics, who married a woman chosen for him by his mother and whom he had met once. He found out after his wedding that she was illiterate, a fact kept hidden from him by the bride and her family. He did not divorce her, however, but undertook to teach her how to read and write, thus unwittingly fulfilling Ibn Badis's dream.[11]

A more important sign of cultural contradiction and change is provided by the emergence of unwed mothers as a social problem. In 1970 the number of unwed mothers was 6,706, and this number has been increasing ever since, although accurate statistics are difficult to come by.[12] The intractability of this problem is due to the fact that many unwed mothers prefer not to give birth in a hospital or clinic to protect their identity. It is not so much the number of unwed mothers as their emergence that is significant, because of the rarity of its occurrence in the past. Prior to 1962, a widowed or divorced woman could have a baby twelve months after her husband had left or died and attribute its affiliation to him.[13] The legal doctrine of the "sleeping child" helped to protect sexually active mothers without husbands. With changing times, widowed and divorced women have difficulty getting remarried, and may be heads of households, a condition making them conspicuous when a new baby is born long after the disappearance of a husband. However, the doctrine of the "sleeping child" does not apply to unmarried women who become pregnant. In the past, such cases were handled differently depending on the family involved. But their occurrence was generally rare, making this a dreaded but unlikely problem for the average family to face.

By the late sixties, unwed mothers began to be talked about in major cities. Their condition reflects the social changes that have affected Algerian society, ranging from lesser individual restraint in the expression of desire to women's greater vulnerability to men's sexual demands in return for promises of marriage or favors in a highly bureaucratized environment. Although unwed motherhood is primarily an urban phenomenon, rural areas have their share of it. A study of fifty unwed mothers (including widows and divorcées) carried out in Algiers indicates that they varied in age between sixteen and thirty, and included unemployed (forty-six percent) as well as employed women (forty-four percent). They represented a cross section of the population, although over half of them were working-class women. While some of them (eighteen percent) became pregnant because of a contraceptive failure, the majority did not use a contraceptive. Employed unwed mothers, most of whom work in the garment industry, often claim they were raped.[14]

Unwed mothers may and often do give birth in a hospital where their anonymity is protected. The law entitles them to be admitted to one clinic in the seventh month of their pregnancy free of charge. During their stay they cannot have visits or receive mail, ostensibly to protect them from possible family retaliation but perhaps also to contain a socially embarrassing problem, and prevent its institutionalization. However, their treatment by hospital or clinic personnel reflects society's ambivalence towards sex outside of marriage when it is publicized by pregnancy. Women report their nurses express their disapproval of their behavior and resent having to serve them. Other patients occasionally object to sharing a room with unwed mothers. One patient insisted that an unwed mother hide under her sheet whenever her husband came on a visit, thereby betraying the anxiety felt before sexual transgression, making the culprit/victim a temptress.[15] Families' reactions to out-of-wedlock pregnancy is generally subdued. Mothers are the first to know about daughters' condition. They may or may not tell fathers, although there is little doubt that fathers get to know of their daughters' predicament.

Since the most important problem is to salvage one's reputation, family members cooperate in finding a solution, which may be to arrange a quick marriage, send the daughter to distant relatives living outside of Algiers, or keep the pregnancy within the family until the birth of the baby. In most cases the baby is aborted when possible, or abandoned (seventy-six percent) after its birth. However, for the women who became pregnant while away from their families, the panic and fear of social opprobrium lead them sometimes to simply kill their infants. Between 1965 and 1971 there were 664 cases of infanticide and there is no evidence that this number has not increased since then. These were cases prosecuted by the courts, excluding those that do not come to the attention of the police.[16] Infanticide is also a function of young women's guilt for having transgressed a social taboo that traditionally played a central role in gender relations. It is mirrored in the claims made by many unwed mothers who became pregnant for the first time that they were still virgins, and did not understand what happened to them. Some even requested that their hymen be restored by a doctor. Many denied they were pregnant until their body told otherwise, thus missing a chance to abort that could have spared them their trauma. Finally, some women even pushed their denial of their pregnancy to acquiescing to their family demand to see a doctor to determine the cause of their bodily change. They chose a generalist to whom they lied about their condition (in order to avoid the right diagnosis and detection) until it becomes overwhelming.[17] This denotes ambivalence towards the pregnancy as well as the family, which the young women want to shock and comfort at the same time. More importantly, this kind of behavior may signify rebelliousness, expressing itself in the most extreme form possible.

Like teenage pregnancy in industrial societies, out-of-wedlock pregnancy in Algeria lends itself to numerous explanations. However, one explanation provided by Mahfoud Boucebci, who had the merit of studying the subject, is worth recalling for its unabashedly male-centeredness. Noting that about one-third of the women in the small sample studied came from homes where the father was either absent or unemployed, he argues that mothers in such families become the imaginary repositories of the paternal phallus. The "phallic mother" displaces the "castrating mother" in the mind of the daughter, who wishes through pregnancy to have a homosexual relationship with her mother. "The absence or effacement of the father disturbs the process of development and identification of the unwed mother. There is no aggressivity towards the mother, at least for a while."[18] Furthermore, "The man's role is then considered a hindrance or useless. This is why the unwed mother's partner remains anonymous. It is often an occasional companion, or a man whose situation prevents him from getting married." The author proceeds to quote a woman who tells of a man she met through a friend and who departed for France without leaving his new address.

Ignoring this information, he states that his respondent could have "easily" found the man's address. "She preferred not to mention her pregnancy and silently sought refuge with her mother," thereby somehow proving that she was a homosexual, having chosen a "phallic mother" over a possible husband.[19] Boucebci's concern for the plight of the father leads him to demonize women. Thus the father is seen as the "guarantor of the social superego" whose authority is severely undermined by his low economic status, whereas the mother, the keeper of family traditions, sees her nurturing role reinforced. The mother channels all of the child's wishes for identification. The daughter wants to identify with her mother, be like her. She needs to be a mother and head of a family. This demand, greater in the working woman who to various degrees supports her family, is reinforced by a feeling of frustration caused by her identification with a mother socially diminished by being traditional. The daughter seeks and rejects tradition at the same time. . . . Unable to question her father's role, the daughter projects onto the world of men her frustrations and claims against a husband, in divorce or extramarital affairs. Uncertain as to whether she could dominate a husband, she unconsciously searches for a partner that can be neither a husband nor a father, but solely an impregnator, a means to have a child. The daughter will have thus accomplished what her mother could not. She will have succeeded where her mother failed in the sense that she will not only have vanquished and dominated man [*sic*] but will have annihilated him. However, she will feel incomplete. For, she may have fulfilled her psychic need, but has failed socially. She has a child, but no hearth. She will therefore come back to her mother, blend into her, with or *without a child*. (emphasis added)[20]

This last statement is followed by an interview with a young woman who mentions that her mother was the head of her family and her father, an immigrant worker in France, sent money regularly, but visited the family for only two weeks a year.

In a general sense this interpretation is a good example of the symbolic violence that can be exercised on women in the Third World when models of psychological development that have long been denounced in Western societies for their inadequacies and sexist contents are blindly applied to women in different cultures. In a more specific sense, this interpretation essentially victimizes unwed mothers by diagnosing them [the author is a psychiatrist] as suffering from a psychic condition, unconscious homosexuality, caused not only by mothers usurping the economic role of fathers as breadwinners, but also by working young women. The inconsistency of his psychological interpretation, which lumps together physically absent fathers with economically disabled fathers, is matched by the apparent lack of clinical data to support his claims. None of the statements made by the women quoted in the text can lend themselves to a Freudian interpretation, given the Algerian context. Indeed, war widows, wives left alone by men who emigrated to Europe and many divorcées have swelled the ranks of female heads of households, calling for a redefinition of the author's uncritical reference to men as "the guarantor[s] of the social superego."

The author leaves the reader in the dark about the young man growing up in a fatherless, "phallic mother's" home. Is he too a homosexual, transferring his frustration with his symbolically vaginal father onto other men he uses as women? Or does he turn his frustrations with his "phallic mother" against other women, whom he ends up beating? Whatever the answer to these questions, the fact remains that Boucebci blames the victims for their plight. Most importantly, he silences them by choosing to disregard their claims and drowning their voices out with his expertise, borrowed from dubious sources. By also divorcing pregnancy from its socioeconomic context, and using it as an abstract condition of womanhood which "achieves its completeness" only through it, he makes it into a natural phenomenon with perverse implications. Furthermore, by interpreting pregnancy as a homosexual condition born of an unfulfilled desire to dominate men, he projects onto women men's desire to dominate and control women. Penis envy is seen as being realized when a woman gives birth to a male child, another penis! What is surprising about Boucebci's conception of women is his lack of understanding of the social construction of femininity and masculinity in his society. His desire to salvage masculinity as an ordained and normative condition is paramount and well illustrated by his assertion that the pregnant unwed mother cannot find happiness with her "phallic mother." The daughter "will miss heterosexual exchange when with her mother which she will later find with a male partner. He will represent for her a more attractive model in all respects; As a lover he will symbolize the long sought father."[21] Ultimately, it is the man, whom the unwed mother sought to dominate and compensate for, who has the last word. A nonworking wife is the answer to the anomic situation of the working daughter of the "phallic mother."

It is precisely work, a rather scarce resource for women, that Boucebci blames for pregnancy. Indeed, he believes that women's entry in the labor force is "massive" when in fact it is quite limited. He further points out that educational opportunities for girls have enabled them to "enter the world of the street hitherto considered the world of foreign men and women."[22] By forgetting to mention the role played by Algerian men in making women pregnant, and emphasizing work and education as possible explanations for the psychological condition that leads to out-of-wedlock pregnancy, he provides more ammunition to those among his contemporaries who oppose women's access to jobs.

The anxiety aroused by unwed motherhood in the larger society extends to their abandoned children. Boucebci provides a grim description of the conditions under which such children live when left in the care of Algiers and Wahran hospitals. They are generally raised in a purely mechanical manner, centered on the satisfaction of their basic physiological needs. Seldom cuddled or given physical stimulation, many do not develop normally, being unable to smile or react to stimuli. When their environment changes, either through better institutional care or foster parenting, their development improves and approximates that of normal babies.[23] It is perhaps in view of the problems encountered by abandoned children that the 1984 family code (Articles 116 and 120) allows adoption of children of unknown parents but insists that those with known parents retain their last name.

Women are also at the center of revivals of occult rituals which had been on the wane during the war years. In urban centers, especially Algiers, the ritual of the *wa'da* attracted the attention of researchers such as Noureddine Toualbi, who studied its functions in some detail. *Wa'da*, or "treat" in colloquial Arabic, was initially an offering to God or to a saint when an individual's wish came true. In Algiers, it is a ceremony held usually by women—but more and more men participate in it—over a three-day period to invoke a plurality of *jinns* believed to descend on the third day and speak through a woman richly dressed and wearing a mantle of the *jinn*'s color. In the popular culture there are white, red, blue and sometimes purple *jinns*. The *jinn* then grants the individual her wish. The ceremony, which gathers a number of women, is usually hosted by one family, and includes elaborate meals and cakes, the sacrifice of at least one lamb depending on the status of the host, and seances of fumigation and incantation.[24]

Toualbi claims that the practice of the *wa'da* is widespread among well-to-do families in Algiers, although it is also practiced by other socioeconomic groups. He attributes its frequency and the increased participation of men, as audience and performers, as a means of relieving a "cultural anxiety" precipitated by rapidly changing values conflicting with old ones. He sees it as a way of restoring the wholeness of one's identity in the face of disruptive change. However, Toualbi did not interview any women, therefore transforming a female ritual in the process of being appropriated by men into a therapeutic, albeit anachronistic, psychological device that helps men to deal with their divided lives through appeal to the occult. It is tempting to see in the reemergence of the *wa'da* in cities like Algiers a feminization of the culture not unlike the broadcasting of the *boqala* game. Indeed, female rituals are now attracting men, who find emotional comfort and solace in them. Psychological explanations, such as the one provided by Toualbi, himself a psychologist, are plausible but also speculative, and sometimes dead wrong.

A great deal of the anxiety noted by the author is intimately linked to women. Instances of impotence and obsession with a wife's alleged power to hurt a husband by casting a spell on him have been documented by other researchers. A study carried out in a village in the eastern region of Sétif reveals that a new generation of professional exorcists, charging a set fee, has arisen, dealing with a mixed clientele. Men generally attempt to escape women's assumed powers as wives or relatives. Women hope to escape the sexual embrace of a *jinn* who is said to have "mounted" them. Interestingly, women report being unable to ward off the sexual attacks of *jinns*. Men, on the contrary seem to be more successful. Indeed, a man who reports having been "kidnapped" by a female *jinn* who decided to marry him allegedly told the judge she took him to: "according to Muslim law, it is the man who is the master of the house (*Rab el Beit*)." The judge agreed, and the female *jinn* had to return the man to his normal life.[25] Thus men's status is recognized and reinforced in the supernatural world.

Other manifestations of social delirium in an environment fraught with socioeconomic change also implicate women. A self-styled prophet claimed that a saint forced him to straighten up his community. One of his tasks was to stamp out city ills, such as "having a father sitting in a café with his daughters," young men wearing their hair as long as girls', or girls in miniskirts.[26] That modernity threatens individuals' beliefs about sex and sexuality is evident in these examples. Algerian social scientists interpret appeals to exorcists and other healers as signs of imperfect urbanization among individuals who live in predominantly rural areas, or among economically successful migrants to large urban centers. The fact remains that these practices have always existed in rural and urban areas, although the typical exorcist lived in a small town. Perhaps what is remarkable about their persistence is the fact that they are claimed by many, as Toualbi's data indicates, as part of one's religion when in reality Islam prohibits occult and magical practices.[27]

The category "woman" thus becomes indistinguishable from the magical, the purely religious and the profane, seen as the sphere where men lose their psychic balance and women their prudishness. In other words, women are culture personified. In a reversal of the anthropological wisdom, expressed by Claude Lévi-Strauss, that women represent nature while men represent culture, the loss of cultural identity mentioned by Algerian social scientists is in effect the loss of the old conception of womanhood. This is a crucial trait of Algerian life, for it implies that the development of present-day culture is predicated upon the reaffirmation and maintenance of ideal models of womanhood that may not be attainable in an industrializing society.

Mothers, Daughters and Time

The antinomy between the lived reality of development and the immutable model of acceptable womanhood conjures up a temporal conflict. Young women born during and after the war live in a different time frame from their mothers and fathers. The justification of the old model of womanhood is meaningless to them. Their mothers, regardless of their educational levels, already find themselves astride two time frames. In attempting to merge them they often experience a sense of loss. Talks with women in their late fifties and sixties reveal feelings of inadequacy and redundance mixed with envy before the new life-styles based on the conjugal family, the inclusion of regular leisure activities in one's schedule and a greater freedom of movement. The sense of redundancy is stronger among illiterate women, who feel that time has passed them by. Expressions such as "what are we good for now" (*ahna 'alash durk*)? are commonplace among them. Sometimes a widowed mother lives the new time through her daughter's success in marriage or career.

However, the frequent differences in education between mother and daughter are so great that the gap results in a relationship fraught with alienation. Mother is respected, often looked upon as a casualty of a bygone era, but also experienced as a personal liability. An executive secretary wondered how a woman like her seventy-year-old mother could have managed to raise her and her three brothers. Yet her mother was no different from the majority of women her age: illiterate, dressed in traditional clothes, well-mannered and devoted to her children. The educational and generational gaps are greater among professional women, thus making time a crucial dimension in understanding women's and men's perceptions of themselves and one another. A twenty-eight-year-old social science instructor felt her mother, who could read and write, was hostile to her independent life-style and supported her fundamentalist brother against her. One day she left her parents' home surreptitiously for a European university, where she had obtained a scholarship, taking along her older but less-educated sister. While this is an extreme case of mother-daughter antagonism, it illustrates the depth of the resentment and difficulty of communication between women belonging to different time frames. Thus development time has drawn young women further from their mothers, without necessarily bringing them closer to men's time.

Marriage, Divorce and Nostalgia

Signs of changes in marriage and divorce since 1962 have been noticed and analyzed by Algerian social scientists. A major feature of marriage is the persistence of the dowry and its increase in value. As mentioned in the previous chapter, the F.L.N. tried during the war to limit the value of the dowry to ten thousand francs or one hundred dollars. Yet there were parts of Algeria such as Cherchell, west of Algiers, where the dowry was fixed at a symbolic twenty-centime coin, as required by an old custom established by the patron saint of the town, Sidi Ma'amar. A similar custom was created by another saint, Sidi M'hammed Ben Yahia in the vicinity of Relizane in western Algeria.[28] These cases notwithstanding, dowries have gone up, driving the cost of marriage often to prohibitive levels. Apart from the dowry, the trousseau and the marriage ceremony have become ostentatious ventures among well-to-do families, and emulated by other socioeconomic groups. A bride may receive not only gold jewelry but also such items as a new fancy car registration in her name, which is then exhibited before guests in lieu of the car.[29] The bride's parents reciprocate by trying to best the groom's presents in an Algerian version of the potlatch.

The spectacular aspect that marriage has acquired is all the more striking in that it often involves couples who have met and dated but who leave the specifics of their wedding to their parents. Interpretations of this phenomenon vary with the gender of the writer. Toualbi argues that ostentatious weddings provide a ritualistic way of "using a traditional cultural item in order to satisfy a modernist ambition."[30] The traditional custom of sitting the bride, dressed in rich clothes, before female guests only to admire her beauty, is maintained but extended to the groom who, in an unusual departure from custom, joins the guests and places the wedding ring on his bride's finger.[31]

A feminist, Souad Khodja, analyzes this practice as parents' desire to assert their waning authority and role in maintaining the traditional form of marriage based on the involvement of mothers in choosing a bride and arranging all ceremonies. As young men choose their wives, the role of mothers in brokering a marriage is diminished.

They recoup it by taking charge of wedding ceremonies, thereby symbolically reintegrating marriage into the traditional domain. She further argues that the ascendant class, the petty-bourgeoisie, lacking a style of its own, mixes traditional bourgeois and Western cultural elements, thereby emphasizing quantity over quality to mask the poverty of its own class culture. Khodja claims that this custom results in a "new form of domination of women under the guise of liberation."[32] Both interpretations are plausible, thus pointing to the complexity of the Algerian cultural situation.

However, both neglect the fact that ostentatious weddings existed during the colonial era. It is the ritual that is changing, from a once entirely gender-segregated to a gradually mixed set of practices. As the individual demand for a "modern" life-style is felt, customs are usually perceived by many young people as "traditional" and therefore old and passé. This is partially the result of the anomic cultural environment in which they live, which overvalues Western *traditions* and negates their own. Thus, rather than developing ways to modify and transform local practices, they see them as impervious to change and needing replacement by not-so-new Western practices. The Western white wedding gown is no newer than the "traditional" Algerian wedding dress. But it represents a triumphant culture to which many a man and woman aspire. Ostentatious weddings represent a formalistic attempt at salvaging a cultural practice based on women's passage from virginity to womanhood through wifehood. Once virginity is no longer *the* issue (and this is generally the case among urban well-to-do and increasingly among middle-class families) the ritual loses its meaning that must be somehow compensated for. Marriage used to be a long-planned affair involving multiple intermediaries and relatives, and took place in several stages beginning with the search for the ideal partner, followed by engagement and culminating in the double wedding ceremony, one held at the bride's and the other at the groom's. It is now a much less exacting endeavor, taking a relatively short period of time: another reason, perhaps, to celebrate it in a way that makes it remembered.

The historical significance of the dowry, however, is not sufficiently appreciated by its commentators. Feminists see it as an antiquated custom that objectifies women. Men see it as a hindrance to getting married if they do not have the means to afford it. Traditionally the dowry covered a number of gifts, some of which are no longer applicable: money (to help the bride's parents partially defray the cost of her trousseau), gold or silver jewelry, foodstuffs, furniture, cattle, servants, and land. In Algeria the first three gifts are predominant, although a study suggests that in the Tlemcen area in western

Algeria, the large number of women who own arable land bought with their dowry may be a sign that in the old days women received land as their dowry.[33] More "modern" dowries specifically include a "honeymoon trip abroad."[34] The dowry is the sum total of all these donations bearing different names, some of which are payable upon signing the marriage contract, others by installment. Since the major part of the dowry is theoretically not returnable in case of unjustified divorce initiated by the husband, the greater the dowry, the greater a woman's ability to tide herself over until she gets married again. Thus, the dowry played the role of instant alimony the wife paid herself. Gold jewelry, as part of a dowry, plays the role of old-age insurance for women with no independent income. In addition, even within marriage, women often sold or pawned some of their jewelry to defray the cost of medical care or other emergencies whenever their husbands could not or were reluctant to help them. Husbands may pressure their wives to use up their dowry in marriage, thus recouping the cost of their marriage.[35]

The dowry was not and is not a "bride price" paid to parents to compensate them for the assumed loss of a worker, which in urban settings marked by large families was meaningless. In rural areas, where women are also agricultural workers, dowries have traditionally been small and comprised of a few pieces of silver jewelry and clothing, and/or a modest sum of money. The fact that some usually impoverished fathers have used the monetary part of the dowry for other purposes instead of remitting it to their daughters for the purchase of a trousseau does not detract from the original function of the dowry. In urban settings the bride's parents match the groom's donations and often surpass them, often incurring debts as discussed above.

Returning or keeping a dowry after marriage is often a litigious process. The most serious cause of a man's failure to honor the dowry agreed to, and for a woman to reimburse her husband, is the lack of virginity in a wife. The lack of consummation of a marriage gives a woman the right to keep half of her dowry.[36] Evidence shows that a man may change his mind about a dowry or a woman, and charge her with having been deflowered before the marriage in order to get his money back, and this despite a "virginity certificate" provided by the bride but contested by the groom.[37] The wife is then compelled to go to court which must determine whether she was a virgin or not. The link between dowry and virginity in first marriages is such that many *cadis* in Tlemcen, reputed for its social conservatism, but also in similar cities, require a virginity certificate before drawing up a marriage contract as a way of avoiding future litigations.[38] The family code devotes four articles to the dowry, none of which mentions virginity. However, it is unlikely that *cadis* who continue to operate alongside civil judges will change this practice.[39] Nevertheless, under the family code women may theoretically appeal nonpayment of their dowry for an alleged lack of virginity. But litigations involving payment or restitution of dowry do not end with the consummation of marriage. There are cases of divorced women who sue for the payment of a dowry agreed to but never fully paid, enabling a husband to marry again without awaiting the conclusion of a divorce.[40]

If the dowry is a source of endless legal conflicts, why is it maintained? In her serious study of the role played by the dowry in marriage, divorce and work in Tlemcen, Chafika Dib-Marouf argues that the dowry is part of an antiquated system of cultural and aesthetic significations pointing to the changing roles of women in society. She sees the new emphasis on expensive and elaborate trousseaus as a way for parents and their daughters to show that the dowry given by a man is not "a 'purchasing price' but an exchange of equivalent material goods. . . . The woman's trousseau largely compensates for the 'right over her person' that the dowry presupposed."[41] Perhaps; nevertheless, Dib-Marouf documents the clothing, rug and jewelry industries that thrive in Tlemcen among women as well as men *for the satisfaction* of dowry requirements and brides' paraphernalia. In addition, she also demonstrates that young women employed in the food and garment businesses claim to work primarily to gather a trousseau. In functionalist terms the dowry sustains and fuels a local economy based on an old tradition of embroidery, silk and wool weaving. This gives the dowry more and not less enduring meaning.

It is true that some young couples forego the dowry altogether by reducing it to a symbolic wedding ring. However, the problem still remains to be explained as to why the legislator made the dowry a condition of marriage. Not requiring it would have meant establishing a principle of equality between the spouses. There is a sense in which the dowry represents, for the legislator, a way of institutionalizing inequality at the same time as it implicitly purports to compensate for it. Indeed, when combined with the requirement that a husband must support his wife, the purpose of the dowry becomes more evident. Whatever its amount, it cannot help a divorced woman to survive for long, especially if remarriage is not immediate, which is now often the case. Hence the acrimonious struggles over the disposition of the dowry noted by Dib-Marouf. Conversely, given the scarcity of jobs for women, it might even make a marriage attractive to a woman who might otherwise delay it. A question arises when dowry is still demanded by women who do not need it, either because they have professional skills that would help them to support themselves should they divorce, or because they are well-to-do. An answer to this question may lie in conceptions of self (and family worth) in an environment where gift-giving is seen as a *measure* and not a *token* of one's status, affection or appreciation.

Like the dowry, divorce has undergone some changes in the past thirty years. It has always been easy for a man to divorce a woman. However, the practice, especially in urban centers, has been generally curbed by a number of sociological factors, including the economic cost of marrying again and the pressure felt by parents to stay together, even if unhappy, for the sake of their children. The willingness to divorce was a function of the spouses' social class. Thus rural and urban lower-middle- and working-class women have traditionally been more vulnerable to divorce by repudiation than other women. The social cost for a husband who used his right to divorce without restraint was minimal for these classes. The wives' male relatives wielded too little influence to be effective in preventing a divorce, except by appealing to the good offices of a religious authority who acted as a moderating force.

Divorce increased dramatically (thirteen percent) between 1966 and 1976, from 85,767 to 114,896. This last figure does not include the number of pending divorces, which reached 119,096.[42] For the year 1983, two tribunals in Algiers had a total of 2,800 divorce complaints.[43] While reasons for divorcing may vary, some are outstanding for their frivolity and arbitrariness. A man claimed he was divorcing his wife because "she does not wake up in the morning to make coffee."[44] A woman claimed her husband divorced her while she was visiting her parents for a few days. Upon her return she found out he had brought home a new wife.[45] There are numerous cases of women who were divorced or abandoned just after the independence of the country by husbands who became members of the new administration and wanted to have younger wives to fit in their upwardly mobile lives.[46] However, women too (especially the middle-class and literate among them) sue for divorce, for reasons ranging from their unwillingness to share an apartment with their in-laws to incompatibility.

In most cases, judges concede that women are vulnerable to husbands' "patent abuse of their power." Often a husband does not appear in court. He hires a lawyer who represents him, and may marry again while his wife is tied down by the court's decision, which may take several years.[47] The family code has only aggravated this situation by upholding a husband's right to divorce without restriction. High illiteracy rates among women aged twenty and over constitute another aggravating factor, in the sense that it makes women more dependent on men for their livelihood, although illiteracy is also relatively high among men in these age groups.[48] Women with education have found a way of taking advantage of the *shari'a* by divorcing a man in civil court and marrying another according to the *fatiha*, or religious pronouncement, which makes a marriage legitimate (and socially acceptable) but does not require its registration. This happens among women who wish to avoid the risk of losing the custody of their children if they marry again, or retain a deceased husband's pension benefits, which they would lose otherwise.[49] Marriage *fatiha*-style has been used by men as a way of legitimizing sexual activity with women other than the wives whose names appear on the original marriage contract. A man who marries according to the *fatiha* may not pay his wife (who in strictly religious terms is legitimate) a dowry or alimony, since recourse in court necessitates a marriage license.

Custody battles have increased, with divorces highlighting women's vulnerability to men's positively privileged legal status. Drawing attention to this issue, Leila Aslaoui, who, as a former judge in Algiers had firsthand knowledge of how women fare in family courts, wrote a short story describing the plight of a woman who lost custody of her four children. As a result, she lost her sanity and became homeless, living on the streets of Algiers shouting the names of her children.[50] Keeping one's children beyond the age mandated by the law is a function of one's ability to secure good legal representation and use influence, which are class-related advantages. Where class is not a controlling factor, male privilege becomes a salient feature in determining the outcome of a custody battle.

Polygamy, which the family code does not specifically mention in its definition of marriage but accepts and regulates, has fluctuated since 1962. As mentioned earlier, this was a primarily rural and limited practice during the precolonial era. It has, however, never been stamped out and provides individual men with a more acceptable option than divorce, thus enjoying the best of the old marriage and the new one. Its emergence as a topic for concerned women lies in the fact that it is practiced by men *despite* the resistance of their first wives. It is unclear whether polygamy has been on the rise, or it is simply more visible because it stands out as a symbol of gender inequality in an environment where the great majority of people live in monogamous marriage. Dib-Marouf argues that it is a mark of "couples' failure to live together."[51] She also explains its apparent visibility in urban centers as related to the practice among men of marrying a brother's widow—a practice used often after the war.

She also attributes it to rapid wealth accumulated by men after the independence of Algeria.[52] The institutionalization of polygamy, even if it is practiced by a minority of men (less than two percent), remains, with the restriction of women's right to divorce, a monument to the failure of the Algerian state to build a just and egalitarian society. This is an issue that could have been resolved in terms of the very *Quran* on which it is based. Indeed, there are valid interpretations of the *Quran*, according to which, when a subject is treated in the *Quran* by more than one *sura*, the last one should be binding. In the case of polygamy the last *sura* recommends monogamy.[53]

Wife-battering, an ever-present preoccupation among women, has become an issue occasionally discussed in newspapers. *El Moudjahid* reports that women complain that their husbands beat them with their fists, heads (as one hits a soccer ball), feet, or use weapons such as knives or razor blades. A man may beat his wife to compel her to wear a veil, refrain from wearing makeup, or give him her consent to marry a second wife.[54] A medical doctor claims that menopause, which some men do not understand, as well as disease-induced impotence, may cause violence.[55] References are made to stress induced by alcoholism, drugs, cramped quarters or unemployment as factors that might explain wife-battering. These are plausible reasons, but they tend to excuse wife-battering. In the absence of a national survey of wife abuse, it is difficult to tell which men are more prone to it and why. Battering is not confined to wives. It sometimes includes mothers, coworkers and shoppers. A woman was beaten because she failed to pay a bill she owed a storekeeper.[56] I interviewed a forty-six-year-old woman in 1982 who had been slapped by a male coworker in the administration of the district (or *wilaya*) of Mostaganem, with whom she did not get along. Wife-battering is a cause for divorce, but few women leave their husbands unless they have an independent source of income.

Women-battering, like all battering, is punishable with imprisonment and a fine only if the victim spent more than fifteen days out of work.[57] This disqualifies the majority of women who do not hold a job. There is no study that documents violence against young girls and unmarried women, whether daughters or sisters. Cases of brothers assaulting their sisters because they have come home later than allowed are not uncommon. A female head of a garment business reports that some of her female employees who travelled by bus from in Algiers a village nearby were authorized to leave the plant early for fear of arousing the ire of their brothers, who benefited from their salaries. This case highlights the lag between changing roles of women who earn a living and men's consciousness of their power as the keepers of women's virtue, even when they can no longer support them. However, there are also brothers who defend their sisters from what they perceive as excessive parental authority. I interviewed a female-headed family of eleven in Mostaganem, where a mother opposed her eleven-year-old daughter's desire to continue to appear at musical concerts where she sang *cha'abi* (old-style popular music). The eldest brother reminded his mother that she was "blocking" his sister's future, and wasting her musical talent that had received public recognition.

Women in Men's Imagination

Change as well as continuity in contradiction mark native male writers' conceptions of women. During the early colonial period, when men began to write in French, they used women characters as symbols of their cultural concerns: to assimilate to French culture or to retain one's identity. The best example of this trend is represented by Mohammed Ould Cheikh, author of *Myriem dans les palmes* ("Myriem in the Palm Grove"). Myriem is the daughter of an Algerian woman, Khadija, and a French military man, Captain Léon Debussy, who despises Algerian culture. Characters in the novel express the French critique of Algerian culture as well as a lukewarm defense of it. Jean Debussy, son of the captain, rails against Maghrebin men who "neglect" their wives. This is why, he maintains, "they leave you to marry foreigners or Frenchmen." A native character, Hamdi, replies: "For us men are masters whom women must obey." In spite of the freedom that French culture allows women, Khadija "remained Muslim: she dresses in Moorish clothes and practices her religion with fervor." She insists that her daughter, Myriem, marry an Algerian man, "to spare her the libertine inconveniences of modernism."[58] Myriem realizes her mother's wish, and her brother, Jean-Hafid, marries a Moroccan woman. They thus signify the triumph of Algerian culture and identity, preserved and passed on by the mother.

Women as tropes for culture, identity and nation will continue to be used in postcolonial society. Well-known contemporary authors, such as Mohammed Dib, or Kateb Yacine, wrote about women as symbols of the nation suffering from the inequities of the colonial order, or the redemption of a colonized society searching for its soul.[59] At times, women are also portrayed as threatening symbols of deception and division, as is the case with Malek Haddad, whose *Le quai aux fleurs ne répond plus* recounts the story of a member of the nationalist movement whose wife had an affair with a legionnaire while her husband was in exile in France.[60] A thorough analysis of images of women in the numerous novels written in the last hundred years is beyond the scope of this book. However, some writers, such as Rachid Boudjedra, express a love-hate relationship with women in their novels that needs discussing for its value as an exemplar of male attitudes towards women in contemporary Algerian society.

Boudjedra links up with the tradition begun by the Young Algerians at the turn of the century, who took up the woman question not so much because they understood it, but because it constituted for them an embarrassing cultural problem that had been already defined as such for them by their colonial peers. In *La répudiation*, the narrator feels sorry for his repudiated mother, whose apparently passive reaction towards his father irks him.[61] Since there is really no plot in the classic sense of the word, and no information about context, the reader is left to her own devices to figure out how the events criticized actually unfolded. The lack of analysis of how the act of repudiation occurred, how the mother *felt* about it and how her family (about which the narrator says next to nothing) handled it, enables the author perhaps to highlight its fundamental arbitrariness. However, this is done at the expense of the mother, who is silenced.

Boudjedra's view of women other than mothers is purely instrumental. Men are sex-crazed, and perceive women as sex objects whom they pursue wherever they find them, including at home. Women are seen as breasts, buttocks and vaginas needing "penetration." The narrator makes love to his multiple cousins, and his stepmother—all of whom are willing—stopping short of his mother. Women's assumed acquiescence to men's sexual appetites is seen as part of their vegetative lives, their boredom and sheer stupidity. Thus women have no sense of self; they exist only for men's pleasure. Boudjedra reifies women while purporting to address their condition. An apparently critical text reinscribes men's prejudices against women by failing to unravel their constructions of women. Whether the men in his novel epitomize the typical Algerian male is an empirical question. Some do, some do not. What is certain is that in real life they have feelings. In the novel they do not.

In *Journal d'une femme insomniaque* ("Diary of an Insomniac Woman"), Boudjedra speaks in a woman's voice about her female condition, symbolized by menstruation. The themes of blood and the color red—already present in *La répudiation*—reach their fullest development in *Diary*. Menstruation signifies, for the narrator, a "wound" in need of healing, a "monthly misery," a red flood and "death."[62] The narrator, a medical doctor and head of a clinic somewhere, indulges in a stream of consciousness that reveals her to the reader as narcissistic, afraid and contemptuous of men, whose genitals disgust her. Her aunt is a neurasthenic lesbian, her younger brother an occasional homosexual—a theme explored almost word for word in another novel, *Le démantèlement*—her mother an archaic, lifeless creature unaware of her misery.[63] The narrator's hatred and "phobia of men"—an unrecognized sign of her fundamental homosexuality, which the author strongly hints at—makes her wish for them to get a "good prostate cancer."[64] Taking tender care of mice is the pastime of the narrator, presented as a sick woman living in a sick society.

The author marshals all the ills of Algerian society in one text, delivered in a monologue attributed to a woman, which enables him perhaps to express his own misgivings about his society. However, by speaking in an assumed woman's voice about essentially female issues such as menstruation, work with men, to marry or remain celibate, he reencodes men's conceptions of these issues. Yet for women menstruation is also a sign of youth and a source of empowerment. His description of menstruation reeks with disgust and contempt. His characterization of the narrator as narcissistic is simply the expression of a common man's assessment of women's condition that transcends the boundaries of Algeria.

Implicitly women do not love or cannot love. Sex is brutal. The idiosyncratic character of the *Diary* is illustrated in the author's projection of the father-son problematic relationship explored in *La répudiation* onto the father-daughter relationship. In reality, the father-daughter relationship is far more complex and diverse than the one discussed. The mother-daughter relationship described is unreal in its fuzziness, and thus lacks plausibility. This portrayal of women and Algerian society is not new. It was done before and after the independence of Algeria by colonial writers. It tells more about the author than about his subject matter. Boudjedra's critique lacks originality and does not enlighten women or men about their problems. The pathological model used as an explanation of these problems adds another burden on women desiring to change their society, since they will have to deconstruct one more myth about themselves. Boudjedra does not truly have a conception of women. Like Algerian filmmakers who treat the subject of "women," he provides a social critique *through* women who are thus objectified.

This insidious expropriation of women's moral outrage that characterizes Algerian men's writings is tangled up with a nostalgia for gender relations of the past. Malek Alloula's *The Colonial Harem* best illustrates this trend. The book reproduces postcards that colonists made of Algerian women striking sexy poses *à la* French, purportedly to reveal Frenchmen's orientalist imagination. More importantly, the author claims that by making the picture available to the world (which includes contemporary "orientalists") he "return[s] this immense postcard to its sender" thereby achieving his own "exorcism." In fact he has achieved none of this. The narration he provides to guide the reader's interpretation of the pictures betrays his own feelings about bared women's bodies, for whom he at times expresses his desire. It is *he*, and not Frenchmen (who incidently also published nude pictures of French women) who conceived of the models as part of a colonial "harem."

In his attempt at explaining colonial fantasy, Alloula speaks in the name of both the photographer and the French soldier who bought the pictures to send home, thereby substituting his male desires for their male desires. He tells his readers of the "logic of desire" and, reluctantly, of "the kernel of truth," represented by the fact that some real women *did* pose for the pictures assumed to be mere props of the colonial imagination run amok.[65] His language is highly sexualized, fraught with terms such as "penetration" and "violation," as he relives for his readers the emotions of the colonists.[66] How does this double take help Algerian women? Alloula dug up the colonial pictorial archives and "violated" Algerian women once more by making titillating pictures available to a wider audience than the original. His narration cannot transcend the contemporary thirst for the eroticization of any woman's body. When his book came out, a number of students at the upper-middle-class college where I once taught bought it for its "pornographic" import, not its assumed value as a monument to colonial fantasy. It is a work of inverted colonial nostalgia that silences women by appropriating their outrage. Since the publication of the Colonial Harem, colonial postcards have turned up among Algiers street vendors in large numbers. Algerian professional photographers have also begun to produce postcards depicting veiled and half-veiled women from various parts of the country as souvenirs for tourists to send home.

A common perception among women and men is that in Algeria feminism is a man's affair. A distinction must be made between supporting women's quest for a more egalitarian society that protects their rights, and writing critically from a male-centered perspective about women. A trend among urban men insists on sexual freedom, not so much in order for women to have control over their bodies, but for men to have freer access to women's bodies. One of the first acts of the sociopolitical liberalization in the early eighties was the emergence of beauty contests at Zéralda beach, west of Algiers. Freud's authority is often invoked to denounce the consequences of the denial of sexual freedom.

Men's wish to pry women away from the code of sexual conduct which they paradoxically also want to see maintained often betrays a reluctance to accept women as equals even when they are no longer convinced of their primacy over women. This ambivalence is best illustrated by a poem written by a reader of *El Moudjahid* entitled "You . . . Woman!"

> You . . . You always led me to believe that *I* managed, com-manded, governed, reigned, conquered, built, wrote, thought and lived. In short, you led me to believe that I was the strong man, the real master of the ship of life, when in reality I could only aspire to be a quartermaster on calm seas. As soon as storms befell us, I found you to be the captain of our ship in distress.
>
> I want you to know that I cannot do without you. You, passenger with your sail blowing in the wind, you, Captain. I want to acknowledge your strength, your genius.
>
> But, between us.
>
> Between you and me only.
>
> Allow me to pretend that I am in command of the outside world. Let me pretend to make History, to be the rainman since you know that in reality *you* are in command.
>
> Let me believe, let me dream. Be what you have always been.
>
> A woman . . . Woman . . . Woman.
>
> To the tip of your fingers.
>
> To your very lips.[67]

There is no need to subject this poem to psychoanalysis. Suffice it to say that the author projects onto women his own fears, which he transforms into women's strength. His appeal to women to be complicitous in his project to keep them at bay is an echo of the sacrificial view of women studied in the previous chapter.

Women's Ambivalence

Ambivalence also affects women's attitudes towards change. In 1985 a young sociology student sent me a note expressing her feelings about women's freedom of movement:

> During the last few months I have noticed that the young Algerian woman has entered a space that is usually male. I am not saying that women have invaded cafés. However, it

is true that women are everywhere. I cannot remember when
I saw so many women in restaurants, tearooms, pizzerias,
theaters, alone or with companions, at 7 or 7:30 P.M., an hour
considered late for the majority of women. I also see high
school students at a late hour on Thursday afternoon [when
schools are closed]. .... It is inconceivable to me that they
can make such a radical break with their heritage only because their parents allow them to do what they want.

It is not always the case that parents "allow" their daughters to
be outdoors in the evening. However, this student echoes concerns
expressed by mothers who were once students under the colonial era,
but claimed none of the freedoms that their daughters demand. These
mothers worry about their daughters' cavalier attitude towards family values and propriety. They often refer to young women as having
been "let loose" (in Arabic: *entalqoo*). Being let loose is risky, since
it connotes a condition of normlessness. The exaggerated concern
expressed by the author of the letter only dramatizes the conflicting
feelings that a woman may experience when her sense of specialness,
deriving from being "free" to walk the streets, is banalized by the
presence of other women who enjoy the same freedom. It is as if when
freedom of movement becomes multiple it is no longer experienced
as freedom. Is the implication that an unveiled woman feels free only
when surrounded by veiled women?

Looking for a Husband

In the past three to four years a new phenomenon has emerged
among women and men: personal ads. Generally young unmarried
women and men (some of whom are middle-aged bachelors, widowers
or divorced) place ads in newspapers published in Algiers and provincial capitals such as Qasantina, looking for a mate. The popularity
of this practice is due to the fact that it offers a way of bypassing
relatives in choosing a spouse. In addition, it compensates for the
lack of a social mechanism that would permit women and men to
meet outside the framework of the family. Finally, it offers individuals
a safe way of meeting one another, since ads are screened by the
papers that carry them.[68]

A perusal of an Algiers weekly, *MAG 7*, indicates that a cross section
of women seek a relationship with a man for the purpose of founding
a family. A number of men seek women who have an apartment, a
response to the housing shortage. Some women appeal to prospective
respondents not to write back if they are not serious, because they

are "sensitive" and might be hurt. These ads also reveal frequent entries from unmarried professional women in their forties. Finally, sometimes women, just like men, request a partner who lives as an immigrant in France.[69] Editors of personals receive thank-you notes and gifts from readers who met through the ads. Perhaps what is remarkable about this new practice is its timing, at the height of the religiose movement's rise in politics. In this context it takes on a countercultural characteristic. A number of entries from women emphasize that they are "practicing" Muslim women, thus inscribing a religious code outside the normative religiosity claimed by the movement.

10
Women's Rise to the Word

Three major antithetical events have marked women's lives in the last fifteen years: The rise of women as a subject of study in academic institutions, the creation of women's associations and the emergence of political parties based on religious platforms. In the seething cultural and political caldron that sums up contemporary Algeria, women were able to enter a new social space in ways that betray political sophistication. Using the history of nationalism, and taking advantage of the youth revolt of October 1988, women laid down the foundation of a movement that gradually integrates them in academic studies and political life.

Academic Feminism

Women as a field of study emerged before the women's movement, in the late seventies in universities, among female students writing theses and dissertations, often chaired by male faculty members. The Institute of Foreign Languages (especially French), the sociology department of the Institute of Social Studies in Algiers and the *Centre de Documentation des Sciences Humaines* in Wahran were the first privileged sites of scholarship on women. In an effort to contextualize women's roles in the postwar era, women first sought to understand the relationship between gender and nationalism. Using literary and paraliterary texts, Mériem Cadi-Mostefai, for example, studied images of women during the war.[1] Using the linguistic-structuralist methodology, Chérifa Benabdessadok critically analyzed the F.L.N.'s discourse on women, also during the war.[2] Neither reported encountering opposition from male faculty members. Djamila Amrane surveyed the files of the Ministry of War veterans to identify the roles played by women during the war.[3] These topics were considered legitimate within the political context of the time, still dominated by the socialist ideology. Early sociological theses dealt with issues such as the emergence of the *hijab* among university students, or the impact of urbanization on families who migrated to Algiers after 1962.[4] Seminars and roundtables organized around feminist issues were first held at the Institute of Political Science in Algiers, and followed up at the University of Wahran in 1980. Since then, more dissertations, articles and books have been written about women from diverse perspectives. A remarkable feature of Algerian women's scholarship is its attempt to distinguish itself from French feminism. This stance is dictated not only by a sociopolitical climate that makes male intellectuals and religious opposition leaders ready to accuse women of mimicking Western women, but also a history of ideological manipulation of women for consolidation of the past colonial order. Feminist *criticism* was spearheaded by the University of Wahran where women questioned gender-bias in census data, investigated the meaning and extent of work for women, explored female participation in political life and so on. It is in Wahran also that the first feminist journal, *Isis*, appeared. On March 8, 1984, the Workshop for Research on Algerian Women (or *Atelier de Recherche sur les Femmes Algériennes*) was formed by a group of female intellectuals eager to mark the celebration of Women's Day with the concrete act of writing and publishing. The workshop issued two anthologies comprised of articles and essays by faculty members from the Universities of Algiers and Wahran, as well as students expressing their views on a variety of topics, although historical and cultural themes predominate.[5] These anthologies are edited collectively and, therefore, do not bear any one woman's name on the front cover, thereby highlighting women's desire to break away from conventional rules of publishing.

The Rise of the Women's Movement

The women's movement emerged out of the controversy that marked the draft of the family code in 1982. The televised debates at the National People's Assembly and the cavalier ways in which government officials and the police handled demonstrators objecting to the code impressed upon women the urgency of organizing themselves to defend their rights. The F.L.N. party-controlled Union of Algerian Women failed to represent women's interests with the vigor required under the circumstances, and thus lost whatever legitimacy it still had. The passage of the code in 1984, with a few amendments to pacify the women's opposition, consecrated legal inequality between women and men. More importantly, it marked the year of the rupture between women and their government and women's radical questioning of the state's legitimacy. Indeed, a number of studies carried out by women had focused on the resilience of gender inequality, and expressed hope that legislators would take it into account in drafting a new code to remedy it. Furthermore, newspapers and literary works had explored the feminine condition and highlighted the power differential between women and men.

Based on their reading of official texts, such as the National charter and the Constitution of 1976, women felt that their rights had been recognized and could not be infringed. The code changed all of that. It became apparent that the postsocialist government could not care less about what women felt or thought. Having no representation, women were sacrificed to those who did: conservatives whose religiosity made them allies of an opposition still underground at the time and liberal assemblymen afraid of antagonizing a rising tide of religious militants.

On March 4, 1985, a group of working women, still reeling from the passage of the code, formed a provisional committee supporting equality between women and men. In an effort to draw attention to the significance of women in the struggle for their country's freedom, the committee called for a rally in the Casbah of Algiers at the place where Hassiba Ben Bouali died during the battle of Algiers in 1957. On May 16, 1985, a group of about forty women—intellectuals, professionals and housewives—formed the Association for Equality between Women and Men under the Law. It took its inspiration not from the National charter or the Constitution, but from the African Charter for the Rights of Men and Peoples, and the Universal Declaration of Human Rights. It thus signaled the founders' intention to move the woman question outside the confines of the Algerian state and into the context of internationally recognized human rights. Working through members living both in Algeria and France, it was able to secure support from groups of Algerians in France interested in the woman question, among whom was Mohammed Harbi, a former advisor to President Ben Bella and a historian living in exile in Paris. Relying on dues of one hundred and fifty dinars, or about seven dollars, the association publishes a xeroxed newsletter which it circulates among its members.

The association's demands include the abolition of the family code, the unconditional right to work, the abolition of polygamy, an efficient protection of abandoned children, equality with men in majority age, divorce and sharing of common property. Its ambition is to represent women nationally. Hence its statutes specify that it is open to all women "regardless of political, philosophical, or religious persuasion."[6] Its goal of inclusiveness is also attested to by Article 11, specifying that its membership extends to "foreign women married to Algerian men and living in Algeria." It received the indirect approval of former well-known revolutionaries such as Djamila Bouhired and Fettouma Ouzegane, who signed a petition they circulated objecting to the passage of the family code. However, the association could not have any legitimacy unless it became legal. It was not approved by the Ministry of the Interior until 1991. It was helped in this by the youth rebellion of October 1988, which compelled the government to experiment with a democratization of its political institutions. The state gave citizens the right to form associations freely, thereby making it possible for women to organize themselves outside the framework of the party.

Two other associations formed simultaneously with the preceding one. They are the Association for the Emancipation of Women, whose president, Ms. Selima Ghezali, a professor of French at an Algiers Lycée, is also editor of a women's magazine *Nyssa*, and the Association for the Defence and Promotion of Women's Rights. Less radical in its demands than the other two, the Association for the Emancipation of Women is founded on the belief that there is more to gender inequality than legal rights, and focuses on women's self-understanding, men's attitudes towards women, and so on. Divergences of opinion on strategy led the first president of the Association for Equality, Khalida Messaoudi, to form a splinter group under the name Independent Association for the triumph of Women's Rights.

In the last few years a number of women's organizations have sprung up throughout the country, one of which is an association for "support to women's associations," thereby emphasizing the need to strengthen an unprecedented movement born among women and for women. Indeed, all these associations constitute a veritable revolution within the Algerian context that did not have a native women's movement in the past. Considering the difficulty of finding locales, having access to xerox machines (already a commodity in limited supply), getting funds, printing materials in an environment where political passions have reached a paroxysm, women's associations denote commitment and courage.

The establishment of feminist associations coincided with the rise of a multiple party system that numbered in July 1991 fifty parties, which indirectly boosted women's militancy in the sense that it provided them with bargaining power in seeking support from some of the parties in return for giving their own endorsement. In addition, a liberalization of the press helped women's organizations to publicize their views on issues. Public politics are thus thrust upon them, making some of them political associations defending womens' interests rather than the classic Western-style feminist organizations focusing on narrowly defined feminist issues. The Association for Equality before the Law between Women and Men illustrates this point. In October 1988 it took part in demonstrations protesting the government's repression of the youth rebellion, and supported youth's demands for the democratization of the political system. Later it called for an end to the Gulf War and to the state of siege decreed by the Algerian government in 1992 after cancelling legislative elections which the Front of Islamic Salvation (or F.I.S.) had won. All major associations also met from May 17 to 18, 1990 and moved to protest, among other things, Article 54 of a new electoral law passed in April 1991 enabling spouses to vote in each other's name. This was rightly interpreted as giving husbands the right to vote in their wives' names. Women also protested Article 50 of the law, which limited the right for Algerians residing abroad to vote by subjecting them to complicated procedures to secure vote by proxy.[7]

Literary Expressions

The emergence of academic feminism and the women's movement helped to kindle interest in the rediscovery of past feminine expressions and the analysis of mounting literary voices. Four women writers in particular need to be discussed because of the different facets of women's lives and thoughts that they reveal. During the colonial era, two native women had dabbled with fiction: Djamila Débèche and Assia Djebar. Of the two, Débèche was perhaps more attuned to women's needs and interests than Djebar, although both found it difficult to disentangle themselves from the colonial culture. Débèche was a French-educated woman who attempted to bring about changes in the lives of her compatriots within the colonial system. The review she founded, *L'action*, bore the slogan: "The evolution of Algeria depends on the combined efforts of her sons and daughters." Her goal was to "look into the conditions under which our least privileged Muslim sisters live; concern ourselves with the children's future; take interest in everything that is related to Muslim homes and families."[8] In her entreaties to the colonial society to teach Arabic to native children and give women the right to vote, she referred to the French as "the pioneers of 1830."[9] References such as this one, combined with her unquestioned conviction of the superiority of the French ways, made her the female counterpart of the French-educated male intellectuals of the thirties and forties known as assimilationists. However, they rarely addressed the woman question except in rhetorical terms, whereas she put her education at women's service. Perhaps reflecting upon her own status as a native woman who made good in the colonial society, she wrote that there were only two options for the Algerian woman: to have a career, thus becoming "totally assimilated," or to choose her culture, and therefore give up her career. She pondered why "neither Europeans nor Muslims understood the young emancipated woman."[10] She advocated the education of women and the teaching profession as ways of redressing the gender and colonial imbalance. Through teaching women will "confirm the adage according to which the brotherhood of men can be made possible only if women take care of it."[11] In other words, women teachers will bring together Algerian and French men. As discussed in previous chapters, this was the favorite theme among colonists, who reduced colonial domination to a cultural issue symbolized by women.

Débèche's novels, *Leila, jeune fille algérienne*, published in 1947, and *Aziza*, published in 1955, recount the adjustment problems experienced by a French-educated native woman which, in their essence, are not so different from the problems of contemporary women caught between cultural conservatism and self-affirmation. Unlike novels written by men such as Mohammed Ould Cheikh, hers do not delve into mixed marriages. Typically, her heroines marry native men.[12] In both novels she develops the theme of the orphaned woman, which will be explored in the independence era by writers such as Rachid Boudjedra, in *Diary of an Insomniac Woman*, and Yamina Méchakra, in *La grotte éclatée*.

Assia Djebar, better known today than Débèche, wrote her first novel *La soif* (*Thirst*) at about the same time as Débèche published *Aziza*. She was immediately hailed by the colonial press as the Algerian Françoise Sagan, not so much for her style, which was still in its infancy, but because of the theme she chose, a young woman probing her desires, and the timing of her novel, three years into the war, when the battle of Algiers was raging. Unlike Débèche, who addressed the cultural conflicts experienced by young women, Djebar's character evolves out of space and time, oblivious to the constraints of the war. Perhaps this novel reflected the author's own sheltered and privileged life as the daughter of a well-to-do family who physically could blend easily into French society but could not erase her Algerian origins. Or it could be argued that she simply wished to show that the war did not have the same impact on all women, an idea she developed further in *Les enfants du nouveau monde*. But Algerians criticized her lack of political awareness at a time when other young women were sacrificing their lives for their country. Outside the Algerian context, this first novel would undoubtedly make Djebar the equivalent of Zora Neale Hurston. Whatever the characterization of Djebar's early work, it represents the author's rejection, expressed in subsequent novels in one form or another, of native women's life-styles. The litany of complaints about "tradition" and Islam stifles her characters' voices, and turns them into pitiful, empty-headed puppets. The assumed "naivete" she attributes to women in *Les alouettes naives* is the counterpart of Boudjedra's characterization of women as "idiotic."[13]

The rejection of Algerian culture lock, stock and barrel infuses her more historical writings with a nostalgic view of colonialism. The book, *Femmes d'Alger dans leur appartement*, best illustrates a primary feminist perspective that is remarkable for its decontextualized, uncritical and abstract character. The author attempts a realist reading of women's lives through a painting by Delacroix. She somehow considers the painting as an expression of the lived reality of a group of women who had been coralled in one room to satisy the curiosity of a French painter. Eager to provide historical evidence of women's "oppression," she failed to see in the painting the product of the collusion of two men, a defeated native and a colonial artist. She equally failed to decipher the ways in which the women reacted to their *de facto* unveiling before a conquering stranger. They appear stiff, with vacant looks in their eyes, as if they did not see the painter. In fact, they hid from him while still facing him without their veils on. If there was any sadness portrayed, it is unclear whether the painter put it there, or it was there to express displeasure at posing. Indeed, the painting could easily be seen as ushering in a new mode of apprehension of native women by colonists. They were made to "pose" for French men, be models of embodied difference, and thus lose their individuality. *Femmes d'Alger dans leur appartement* constitutes another way of silencing women, this time by a woman.[14]

La chrysalide, a novel by Aicha Lemsine, represents the opposite pole of the range of feminist expression. Her characters assume their culture while trying to change it. She superficially explores the themes of polygamy and pregnancy out of wedlock, which she resolves with a sleight of hand, portraying the father of the heroin, Faiza, as more tolerant and accepting than the mother.[15] Faiza is an educated woman who grew up reading, among other things, *Jane Eyre, Wuthering Heights*, and Greek mythology. Through her brother she discovers Karl Marx, only to be reminded that he did not believe in God and was himself considered one by communists, thus making him unacceptable to a Muslim.[16] The book strikes a note of colonial nostalgia by attributing changes in customs to a benevolent French woman who symbolizes a benign colonialism. Written in a linear and accessible style, the book became an instant success, especially among young women and men. Its very success has also subjected it to intense critical scrutiny. Christiane Achour wrote an extensive analysis of the book, which she sees as a romance novel harking back to the colonial fiction centered on the exoticism of natives' lives.[17] She further points out that the book's lack of historical context, its summary rejection of selective customs as "superstitions" and its language peppered with Arabic expressions denote its ideological character, a product of the "national bourgeoisie." Achour's critical analysis is astute. However, it still does not explain the success of the book. For young women who sometimes read romance magazines such as *Nous deux* and *Femmes d'aujourd'hui*, or mysteries by Duc des Cars, Lemsine's book provides a similar escape outlet, with the difference that characters and situations portrayed are familiar to them. It is not overtly political, and it provides reassurance to both women and men by portraying them as loving and forgiving, although at times getting in one another's way.

Another critic of Lemsine's book, Souad Khodja, sees it as articulating a distinct model of "moderate emancipation" for women, which she feels is ascendant in contemporary Algeria.[18] According to this model, adopted primarily by bourgeois families, women combine features of Algerian and Western customs deemed least extreme in matters such as dress, culinary habits, and education. For example, a woman is expected to know how to cook Algerian and French dishes, avoid decolletés and short skirts and refrain from smoking or drinking. She may choose a husband who is acceptable to her family, pursue her education and even work, but must be mindful of the fact that being a "diploma-ace," in Lemsine's words, may not get her a husband. Khodja carried out interviews with twenty-eight university graduates who held managerial positions to find out whether Lemsine's conception of women was shared by Algerians. She found out that her respondents were eager to forego payment of a dowry, favored contraception, and would permit their wives to work, therefore breaking away from "tradition." However, she dismisses her findings as unreliable on the grounds that her talks with women confirm her in the belief that few men, for example, would marry women of whom their mothers did not approve. Further discussions with her respondents indicate that their ideal of a woman corresponds to the one portrayed in *La chrysalide*. Like Achour, Khodja attributes this model of womanhood to a rising bourgeoisie still searching for itself, and of which Lemsine, the wife of an ambassador, is the mouthpiece.

Unlike Djebar and Lemsine, who evince strong signs of colonial nostalgia, whether epistemic or substantive, a little-known author who is also a psychiatrist, Yamina Méchakra, breaks new ground in writing. Her only book, *La grotte éclatée* ("The Exploded Cave"), written as a poem of sorts, recounts the story of an orphaned woman raised by French nuns who joined the F.L.N. as a nurse/fighter.[19] Her style is pungent, concise and often stirring. She evokes the many moods and feelings experienced by women and men fighting while searching for themselves. The war and the "people" are used as metaphors to signify women's hopes and disillusions. The story is filled with vignettes of the lives of women and men. The female narrator speaks harshly of men within the context of the struggle against colonialism. In many ways, her narrator is more powerful in her contextualized critique than in Boudjedra's *La répudiation*. This power derives from her gender, reinforced by her enhanced status as a fighter who is in a position to judge men by the standards of the revolution which she protects. There is not enough information about the author's biography to relate her ideas to her social class, except that she was born in a town in the Aurès mountains and that, as Kateb Yacine notes in the preface to her book, she had a "cruel and tormented life" having seen her father tortured by the French and a man left to die from exposure, tied to the mouth of a cannon. Like Boudjedra's narrator, Méchakra's also spends some time in a psychiatric hospital, after having seen her cave explode and her son maimed. Mental illness told in a woman's voice stems not from psychosexual problems as in Boudjedra's novel, but from "the explosion of the cave" symbol of the family, the nation. The narrator explains the meaning of madness: "I claimed madness. I wanted to free myself from others, myself, memory."[20] In a telling image she sums up what she got for her pain: "I left the hospital. I was promoted lieutenant. Two stars on my armless shoulder."[21]

However, just like Lemsine, the author does not have only an Algerian audience in mind, judging from footnotes explaining the meaning of transcribed Arabic words, some as common as *meskine*, or "poor," that needed no clarification for Algerians.[22] This preoccupation with audience (greatest in Lemsine's novel) may very well be related to the degree of colonial nostalgia present in women writers' books. Nostalgia reinscribes the colonial interpretation of women in texts that claim to be feminist, thus preventing authors from exploring gender inequality with fresh eyes and formulating a new problématique of sex, gender and politics. Méchakra avoids the nostalgia trap by setting up her narrator as a rebel against colonial paternalism and men's callousness towards women. Her notion that everything that is said about the people, the revolution and, therefore, women, must be distrusted as "fabrication" ("invention" in the text) is a welcome starting point for women writers interested in articulating a new worldview.[23]

Mention must be made of a writer, Leila Aslaoui, whose only ambition is to portray the world of women and men as it is lived daily, based on her experiences as a judge. Although her style is often awkward and strained, she provides, more than other writers, a rare insider look at the interface between state (the justice system), gender and family in a society riddled with social problems. Unwed mothers commiting infanticide, housing shortages pitting sister against brother, child custody battles among other things are recounted pretty much as they unfold in court room situations. Her understanding of the uneven ways in which the legal system shapes gender relations, and the vagaries and elusiveness of the notion of justice make her work a valuable resource. By avoiding colonial nostalgia she succeeds in addressing the Algerian reality on its own terms and demystifying it.[24]

Feminist Theory

Working in relative isolation from academic feminist trends in other parts of the world, Algerian academic feminists have formulated their own theory to account for gender inequality and its reproduction in contemporary Algeria. It is a theory that bears the marks of its rapidly changing political environment as well as a keen awareness of the dangers of mimicking Western feminists. Thus it tries to throw off the epistemological shackles of its colonial heritage with various degrees of success. This gives rise to some noteworthy situations whereby a feminist relies on a postcolonial French text on Islam while at the same time claiming that she is eager to break away from anti-Muslim prejudices.[25] This may be partially due to the fact that many academic feminists write in French, and may not have enough mastery of Arabic to explore original texts. Besides, Algerian social science is still dominated by a French tradition that has yet to be transcended or displaced.

Algerian feminist theory focuses on the relationship between culture, politics and development. Culture is seen as comprised of "traditions," mental attitudes and religion. A distinction is made between "traditions" which account for the organization of the family, restrictions on women's freedom of movement, or excessive dowries, and "religion." Feminists vary in their treatment of religion and the role it plays in gender inequality. For example, in a lucid fashion Chérifa Benabdessadok deconstructs the dichotomy "tradition-modernity" which assigns Islam to "tradition" and everything else to "modernity."

She eloquently argues that this is a continuation of a debate in Islamic history that pitted partisans of the "old" and those of the "new." She sees the contemporary equation of "modern" with "Western" as a convenient excuse for politicians and theologians not only to avoid the issue of in-depth social change, but also to impose their own superficial conception of "modernity" and "tradition." She argues that insistence on this view impedes historical evolution, thereby blocking more viable alternatives. She points to the principle of *ijtihad*, which in Islamic thought means "sustained effort" for renewal, which men have neglected in their perorations about women.[26] In a similar vein, Chafika Dib-Marouf points out that the dichotomy "tradition-modernity" as a methodological device is too reductive and needs to be replaced with an interdisciplinary approach "inspired" and not "borrowed" from existing social theories. She used with some success Marcel Mauss's concept of the "total social phenomenon" to study the dowry as expressing the complexity as well as the historicity of the feminine condition, which comprises not only religion but also law, economics, sociology and psychology.[27] Less critical of theoretical models but equally nuanced in her understanding of the religious factor is Souad Khodja, who agrees with Germaine Tillion that Islam introduced liberal ideas about women into Maghrebin societies, which were subsequently subverted by a reactivation of the old traditions typical of Mediterranean cultures.[28] She asserts that "there is a big difference between the teachings of Islam and their application in Algeria today."[29] However, she faces a contradiction when she bemoans the erosion of "traditions" which she thinks provided women with some degree of "protection" from abuse. She cites, as an example, men making it a point of "honor," in the past, to pay dowries they agreed to. This may very well be an idealization of the past, as the very laws regulating dowry payments and reimbursements can be taken as recognitions of the custom's conflict-ridden potential.

In demystifying the dichotomous notion that a woman is either "Algerian," whatever that means, or "Westernized," feminists expose the ideological nature of prevailing conceptions of women. The concept "Western" is a grab-bag category that includes all the excesses attributed to industrialized societies, such as sexual license, alcohol abuse, and a general lack of family values. Academic feminists agree that there is no typical Algerian woman. There are multiple ways of being a woman in a society in the throes of rapid change. According to Benabdessadok, there is no "traditional" woman or "modern" woman. Every woman is engaged in a process of adaptation to a complex situation where new and old attitudes towards life and self are interrelated.[30] In a more formalistic fashion, Khodja sets up a typology of modes of representation of "emancipation" upheld by women, which she thinks are "far from being a systematic imitation of Western women."[31] Apart from the "moderate" model exemplified by Lemsine's *La chrysalide*, she identifies three more, universalistic, traditionalistic and Islamic-purist.[32] The "universalistic" model is upheld by women eager to break away from the normative pattern of relations between women and men mediated by marriage as the fulfillment of women's lives. These women adopt a life-style in keeping with their education and desire for autonomy. This is evidently a minority model. The "traditionalistic" model is said to be represented by Mostéfa Boutef-nouchet's problematic dissertation on the Algerian family, in which he outlines in absolute terms the typical family, where the woman plays an entirely expressive role, subservient to her husband and children.[33] His caricatural portrayal of women in the family militates against taking it as the embodiment of an actual reality, as Khodja did. It tells the reader more about Boutefnouchet's antifeminism than about the family. The "Islamic-purist" model characterizes women who, by conviction or conformity, reject "Western" conceptions of modernity and attempt to shape their lives according to their religious beliefs. A woman marries a husband chosen from a community of devout young men many of whom are affiliated with the religiose movement. She opposes contraception and "Western" dress, and wears a *hijab*. This typology is itself somewhat caricatural and rigid. It has the merit, however, of showing that Algerian society is far too complex to lend itself to facile generalizations. It also indicates that, as in other societies, womanhood is multiple.

The intersection between culture, religion and development is seen as expressed primarily in the resilience of veiling and the emergence of a relatively new form of veiling borrowed from the Middle East (which in fact is a new dress code), the institutionalization of polygamy, restrictions on the right to divorce, limited access to jobs, the persistence of social prejudice against working women, the appearance of separate cafeterias for women and men in some workplaces, neglect of unwed mothers and their children and sexual harassment on the street. Development is equated with industrialization, urbanization, the expansion of education and the introduction of new lifestyles.

The state emerges in academic feminist writing as a key institution in subverting women's rights and reinforcing prejudices against them. The family, although agreed to be in transition, is perceived as sustaining the state's lack of responsiveness to women's needs. Thus, Khodja asserts that many young men would not marry a woman without the approval of their parents, especially mothers. Finally the media and the school system (which uses textbooks portraying characters playing sex-typed roles) provide the ideological framework for the reproduction of gender inequality by the stereotypical images they generate in the minds of children and the general public.[34]

Feminist theory places little faith in the transformative power of development on young men's consciousness, which it relates to the particular ways in which they are socialized. It does not yet have an elaborate perspective on psychosexual development. It was left to men to fill this gap which, as discussed in the previous chapter, has resulted in the creation of new stereotypes. It is expected that academic feminists will eventually take up this challenge.

There are no distinctly identifiable schools of thought among academic feminists at this stage of their intellectual development. However, there is an incipient although subdued Berber-centered orientation that can also be detected in feminist writings, including novels. This can be inferred from the ubiquitous presence of the character of El Kahina in discussions of Algeria's past as well as in literature. This is a reflection of the political divisions that have rent Algerian society in the last few years, some of which focused on the assertion of a distinct Berber identity. A trend among what might be termed a Berberist movement that has the tacit support of members of the women's movement is decidedly anti-Arab and anti-Muslim. Aware of the divisive potential of this issue, individual women of Berber descent consciously try to distance themselves from the Berberist movement.

French Appropriation of Feminism

As Algerian women are trying to make their history, attempts are made to people their past with women somehow claimed to be precursors of a diffuse feminism. I shall leave to others the task of defending the ideas and works of French colonial women who in one way or another contributed to the mythitication of Algerian women. Contemporary French writers with roots in the colonial period have already undertaken to salvage from some feared oblivion the names of colonial women or European women who lived in Algeria before her independence. Isabelle Eberhardt, the young Russian woman who converted to Islam, married an Algerian man and died in a flood trying to save him, has always aroused the imagination of writers. During her short life she travelled through the Algerian south more preoccupied with her personal identity problems than with colonial abuses of natives. She exemplified the nineteenth-century Western woman who sought to both lose and find herself in a strange culture.[35] Presumably, her notoriety came from colonists' ire for her transgressing the colonial sexual code that prohibited a European woman from consorting with or marrying native men. However, the enduring interest in her life is in no small measure due to the land and society she chose to settle in. It is always a source of astonishment to many that a European woman could live among "Arab" people dressed as a man. This apparent exploit is meaningful only against the backdrop of the perceived undifferentiated mass of natives, females as well as males. Ultimately, it is Algerian society that makes the reputation and notoriety of European women.

Aurélie Picard, a French woman who married the head of a religious order near Laghouat in the Algerian south, served the colonial administration as much as she found satisfaction in being a self-styled representative of French taste and manners. Unlike Isabelle Eberhardt, Picard had no interest in Islam nor respect for Islamic culture, and died a Catholic. Jean Déjeux, who included her among illustrious Algerian women, explains: "Aurélie [Picard] Tidjani appears in Algerian contemporary history as a strong and compassionate woman who remained French and Christian and naturally loved her country of birth, France."[36] This flattening out of Algeria's history erases the meaning of colonialism that mediated the relationships between European women and native women and men. The complicity of the Tidjani Sufi order, A Muslim institution, in the colonial project of domination goes a long way in explaining the anomalous presence of a Catholic woman at its head. Déjeux offers a one-sided view of a life that was lived for France's glory. Yet, once more, it is the native society that gives meaning to a European woman's notoriety.

Similarly, Fanny Colonna, A French social scientist, published an expensive edition of photographs taken by a Thérèse Rivière, during an ethnographic mission in the Aurès Mountains in 1935.[37] The selection of these pictures is inscribed in a larger anthropological design that privileged Berber-speaking regions, of which the Aurès is a part. More importantly, it implicitly purports to add another "illustrious" woman to the feminine European pantheon in Algeria. While no nationalism is intended, it is important to realize that the recentering of these women in postcolonial Algeria's panorama has the *effect* of neutralizing the significance of contemporary Algerian women who have just emerged out of the colonial silence. The "we were there before you" attitude preempts and appropriates native women's historic space.

11

Between God and Man

> The preacher and woman are, in my opinion, the foundations
> of a solid and serene future because of their function as social
> educators.
>
> Kamel Hamdi[1]

The dramatic entry of women into the collective consciousness since the war is paralleled only by the equally dramatic rise of religiosity in politics. The concept of "fundamentalism" commonly used to refer to this phenomenon is a misnomer in the sense that groups who use religion for the purpose of seizing power do not advocate the fundamentals of religion. If they did they would have to uphold the *Quran* against erroneous interpretations of women's roles in society held by their members. In addition, the concept is deceptive since it implies that religion as practiced is in violation of some assumed fundamental principles of which these groups are the guardians. Yet a close look at the agenda of the Front of Islamic Salvation (or F.I.S.) and its practices during its control of city councils from 1990 to 1991 reveals that apart from a stricter enforcement of culinary restrictions, such as drinking alcohol, and conservative dress code, its focus was on a redefinition of state power and legitimacy rather than what are the basic tenets of pietistic life. Concepts such as "intégrisme" and "Islamism" used by French scholars and French media are equally inadequate. "Intégrisme" assumes that the aim of religious opposition is to bring about integrity in social and political life. To accept this assumption is to downplay the actual power ambitions of the oppositional groups and blur the distinction between ideology and practice. The concept of "Islamism" seeks to distinguish between Islam as a religion and its use as a political weapon.[2] However, by using essentially the same term to refer to the two orders of phenomena it remains confusing. I will use the concept of "religiosity" in politics and the expression, "religiose" movement, to identify the groups involved in order to emphasize the manipulation of religion as a tool of justification and acquisition of political power. Understanding the religiose movement in Algeria requires an analysis of the interface between social class, politics, sex and economic crisis.

Intellectual Roots of the Religious Movement

Algerian intellectuals and government leaders often express surprise at the swiftness with which the religiose movement rose in political life, and perceive it as alien to the Algerian tradition. Yet, in its cultural project and the roles it assigns women, this movement is an heir to the 'Ulama movement discussed in chapter 5. It was also prefigured by the Association Al Qiyam (or Values) which during the first three years of Algeria's independence agitated for the enforcement of a strict Islamic public morality in opposition to a perceived Communist threat. The association declared that:

> any political party, regime, leader that was not grounded in Islam was illegal and dangerous. Communist, secular, and Marxist-socialist or nationalist parties (the latter because they endanger the unity of the Muslim world) cannot exist in the land of Islam.[3]

The Association found support among members of the ruling F.L.N.

There is also a tradition among Algerian intellectuals of the colonial era born of their desire to counter a French anti-Muslim discourse to bend over backwards to demonstrate Islam's power to answer contemporary questions. Malek Bennabi was perhaps the most articulate proponent of this view.[4] His ideas have resurfaced in the aftermath of the youth rebellion of 1988 and informed some of the debates on the role of religion in everyday life. Similarly, Dr. Ahmed Aroua, who belongs to the same generation as Malek Bennabi, has also been an advocate of the relevance of Islam to contemporary life. His best known book, l'Islam et la science, suggests that "Muslim society should fill the gap that separates it from its own cultural roots and the knowledge acquired by contemporary civilization." It can do so only by "blending faith with science that it must acquire urgently and thoroughly."[5] The author emphasizes the danger that contact with the West poses to Muslims. He notes that in the postcolonial era individuals are guilty of "a refusal to be ones' self, and the introjection of an external ideal. Colonial alienation which was rooted in material need has given way to a more serious ideological alienation grounded in the self."[6]

Social Foundations of the Religious Movement

The religiose movement is comprised of a number of groups sharing a strong distrust of the existing government capacity to solve social, cultural and economic problems, and a belief that the establishment of an "Islamic state" is the *only* possible solution to these problems. The groups differ on the means to achieve this goal as well as the modalities of its implementation. The Front of Islamic Salvation is the most visible in the movement because of its militancy and the fiery oratory of one of its two leaders, now in jail, Ali Benhadj. It won the ruling majority in the people's National Assembly in 1991. However, fearing the demise of the F.L.N. party, the government cancelled runoff elections, made sweeping changes in electoral law, and finally moved to ban the F.I.S. Two other major groups include *Da'wa* (or "Cause"), led by Mahfoud Nahnah, and *Ennahda* (or "Renaissance"), led by Abdellah Djaballah.

There is a consensus among Algerians and foreign observers that the rise of the religiose movement was caused by the economic crisis that Algeria has experienced since the mid-seventies, as a result of the falling prices of its oil exports, which revealed the government's general mismanagement of the economy. This view is bolstered by the fact that the rank and file among the F.I.S., for example, is typically comprised of young, disaffected and unemployed men living in cramped households with no hope of improving their lives. Furthermore, the most radical mosques where leaders of the F.I.S. used to preach about the inadequacies of the state happen to be located in poor and populous neighborhoods such as Bab El Oued and parts of Belcourt in Algiers. This is true. However, the F.I.S. is far from being a working-class or poor people's movement. Its membership cuts across all social classes, as it has become one of the institutions, along with the *Da'wa* and *Ennahda*, that crystallize and channel a trend among Algerian men and some women to assert their cultural identity. Responding to the notion that Algeria's problems are economic in nature, Abdellah Djaballah asked: "Is it true that the crisis experienced by Muslims today is an economic crisis? No, it is not. It is a crisis of consciousness, of civility. Our crisis comes from the fact that we strayed from God and the behavior pattern of his Prophet."[7] However, economic issues are also seen as playing a role in the regeneration of Algerian society. As Abassi Madani, the co-leader of the F.I.S., put it:

> Islamic justice can only be applied in an Islamic state capable of providing all citizens with a decent standard of living.

> Before cutting off the hand of a thief, we should educate him
> first, give him adequate housing, a job, and assure him of all
> the conditions necessary for him to lead an honest life.[8]

The act of cultural self-assertion that has marked Algerian life in
the last ten years is a multifaceted response to a series of structural
changes and state-directed policies. First, the industrial development
policy launched by the government in 1965 helped the emergence of
two social classes: one comprised of technocrats and managers trained
in foreign universities at the state's expense and in control of the
state's apparatus; the other, a class of entrepreneurs and businessmen
engaged in import substitution and/or commerce, who benefited from
the controlled socialist economy to monopolize a market of cheaply
made commodities (clothes, linen, shoes, construction materials, cosmetics, and so on) sold at relatively high prices.[9] At times members
of the technocratic class also invested in private enterprises, thus
signalling the existence of interlocking interests between the two
classes. Both classes indulged in conspicuous consumption, creating
invidious comparisons and resentment among the struggling middle
and working classes. While technocrats and managers (referred to in
Algeria as *"cadres"*) unabashedly displayed their taste for things
French and American, complete with golf courses, entrepreneurs who
worked harder at making money and, in the past, worried about
losing it should the state change its mind about letting them do
business freely, generally kept closer to their petit bourgeois background by retaining ties to mosques and the social conservatism they
imply. The oil crisis that began in the mid-seventies (referred to in
Algeria as "the crisis") endangered the power base and life-styles of
technocrats and managers, who now faced social unrest as unemployment and basic commodity prices rose. Independent of the state for
their source of income, entrepreneurs and businessmen were little
affected by the "crisis." If anything, their role as manufacturers of
goods and at times exchangers of Algerian money for hard currency
was enhanced. The religiose movement found sympathetic support
among entrepreneurs and businessmen who channeled some of their
surplus into the building of neighborhood mosques. The Algerian
government has often accused Iran and at times Saudi Arabia of
providing financial support to the movement. But it has not looked
into the internal sources of financial support that might prove more
crucial than any external aid. The creation of a multiparty system
brought to the fore too many new parties with overlapping goals
centered on a rhetorical assertion of democratic liberties to be acceptable to entrepreneurs and businessmen, whose needs for political/

economic security have always been known. A party such as the F.I.S., in its inception, was far more acceptable because its ideology emphasized the conservation, not change, of basic values which include doing business and making money.

The public display of religious activity, as expressed in men donning long white robes on Fridays and attending mosque regularly for prayer, growing beards and taking time off from work to pray, has affected all age groups but primarily young *men*. It is a defiant act towards a government seen as not only incompetent and corrupt but also culturally alien to the people. It is paradoxical that a movement that attracts impoverished young people also finds acceptance among older and richer groups. Yet this is only one more expression of the notion of the "*oumma*" or community of Muslims which is part of the Islamic ethos. It is also a measure of the extent to which leaders of the F.I.S. have been able to capitalize on what the majority of Algerians have in common, namely a yearning for homegrown values, a sense of solidarity, a desire to belong.

These yearnings were all the more important in that Algerians traveling in France or their immigrant relatives were subjected to many racist vexations; the French media anti-F.I.S. campaign and news of attacks on Muslim countries, such as the bombings of Tripoli in Libya and Iraq by the Reagan and Bush administrations, conveyed a heightened sense of a culture in disarray and under siege.[10] The only place to flaunt one's cultural identity as an act of bravado is at home against one's government, perceived as the representative of a "Western" world staunchly opposed to all things Islamic.

Living by some sort of Islamic ethics is widespread in the movement and has given many a sense of specialness as well as direction. For example, a taxi driver who displayed prayer beads and played a cassette of the *Quran* tried to explain to me why the fare he charged me was reasonable. He mentioned that he was "allowed," implicitly by the religiose group to which he belonged, to charge no more than a given fare for a ride of specified distance. Figured in his high fare was the cost of car parts that might need replacement and could only be imported. He also pointed out that if he did not have any small change he was allowed to let the passenger pay an amount lower than the meter indicated instead of keeping the change (as is done in other capitals such as Cairo or Damascus). Another taxi driver agreed that an Islamic ethics would apply to both women and men. If women should wear a *hijab*, men should also wear long robes, and cover their heads. When asked why *he* was not wearing a robe, he explained that he wore one only on Friday, the rest of the time he kept it hidden, neatly folded in his glove compartment for fear of alleged persecution by the police. Young male students from a high school in Blida, one of the centers of the religiose movement, told me that living by the *Quran* and the Traditions provided an alternative to Western life-styles, fraught as they are with unbridled materialism, drugs, prostitution, and pornography. When asked whether contemporary social problems were too different from those posed to early Muslim societies to be solved in similar fashion, they explained that the *Quran* and the Traditions provided guidelines that were applicable to all human situations.

The idea of clear guidelines or rules is often brought up as a positive feature of a Muslim society. A successful lawyer who valued French education for his children pointed out to me that "we have rules, they [Westerners] don't." By this he meant that moral rules grounded in religion and internalized by individuals suffuse Muslim societies, whereas Western peoples rely on the application of legal norms that lack moral authority.

The Religiose Movement's Political Agenda

A review of selected statements made by the religiose movement indicates that its goal is to redefine the nature of political legitimacy by advocating a state modeled after the organization of the early Muslim community established by the prophet Muhammad rather than any past Algerian state. It would be wrong to dismiss this view as simply millenarian or ahistorical. It is in fact grounded in Islamic political philosophy, although it bypasses the mishaps of the concretization of this philosophy when applied by conquering Muslims ruling other Muslims, as was the case of the Ottomans in Algeria.

The principle of legitimacy advocated by the leadership of the F.I.S. does not lie in the people but in God. It is God who is sovereign, not the people. This means that Western-style democracy based on the expression of the will of the people is unacceptable, because it privileges the power of man over the power of God. In fact, as Ali Benhadj, a F.I.S. leader put it: "Democracy is heresy."[11] He further argues that majority rule may not be compatible with the rule of the idea of the good. "If democracy means freedom for some, it also means the rule of fifty-one percent of the people. If fifty-one percent think drinking alcohol must be tolerated, then it will be. This is what democracy is about."[12] Opposition to democracy is in fact rejection of the secular basis of the state. Secularism is seen as a system whereby the law, according to an Algerian Islamic scholar,

> simply ratifies the evolution of mores instead of protecting and controlling them. Thus, prostitution, elective abortion,

homosexuality, usury and gambling, alcohol and drugs, are not only tolerated by the law but also legalized under the pretext that public opinion runs in their favor.[13]

Thus majority rule cannot coexist with the application of the *shari'a*, the expression of the will of God for the betterment of man.

The critique of the formalism of Western-style democracy is reinforced by the notion that this is a non-Muslim invention tied to colonialism. As Benhadj put it:

> Parties are unanimous in claiming that we should take a special care of this embryo that was conceived for them in France. But for us, it is Allah who governs, not the people. Should we give charity to a rich man who begs? No. We possess the Book of God. Why should we ask for charity from the West or the East? Why stretch our hand before dictators, Communists, liberals, and democrats? When Israelis debate their affairs do they seek solutions in the *Quran* or the Bible? Has anyone seen a European look for solutions in the Muslim's Book?[14]

According to this view, Muslims need no Western-style democracy; they have their own democracy, or *shura*, based on the consultation of various interest groups and scholars. Behind the rejection of Western-style democracy lies a strong yearning shared by many Algerians for a political community and system that evolved out of their own past history. The establishment of a postwar state modelled after both the French colonial government and Eastern formerly socialist states unadapted to the realities of the postcolonial era was lived as an imposed alien entity requiring the use of French, an equally alien language, despite a cosmetic "arabization." To a large measure, the popularity of the religiose movement until recently lay in its accurate and powerful critique of the cultural vacuum in which Algerians have lived since 1962, as well as the recognition that Algeria was still a cultural colony. The "West" looms large in the pronouncements made by leaders of the movement as a comparative referent point against which to gauge the failures of the state to foster and sustain a coherent culture and economic system. The "West" is also used to draw parallels between the native state and its colonial predecessor by pointing to the similarities in their reaction to Islamic religiosity. Often the F.I.S. presents itself as a victim of the age-old battle waged by colonists against Muslims. This strategy resonates very deeply among Algerians sensitive to prejudices against their religion. Also very astute is the critique of the halfway modernist/Westernist stance of the state, which identifies Islam as "the state religion" yet governs according to secular principles. This prompted Mahfoud Nahnah to point out: "Either the Quran is assumed in its entirety or it should be dropped. What is astonishing is that in most Arab and Muslim states leaders and authorities write: 'Islam is the state religion'."[15] In a nutshell the religiose movement exposed the inner contradictions and cultural ambivalence of the leadership of the state, thereby providing a cathartic relief of sorts for its supporters.

Women in a Native Sate

Powerful as this critique might be, it leaves out the significance of women to a rebuilding of the Algerian state along Islamic lines. The F.I.S. rejection of the foundations of the modern state *could* signify a desire to invent a new state more suited to the needs of the Algerian people. But it does not, because it has little room for women as members of the consultative bodies that implement the idea of the *shura*. Women also do not matter as participants in the debates/sermons over what exactly the role of women is under the *shari'a* publicized over the last three to four years.

All the leaders of the movement have expressed opinions about the roles assigned women in the future Islamic state, thus making it very tempting to argue that women are central to the religiose movement. In fact, women constitute only the most visible (because of their specific history) and clear-cut issue these groups are able to handle according to their ideology. Pointing to the controversial nature of the woman question, a commentator sympathetic to the movement notes that a misunderstanding exists between women, leaders of the movement and religious figures which he claims is fostered by "hidden groups."[16] Yet there is little that is hidden about religiose leaders' conception of women. It rests on the twin issue of the *hijab* and work. Defending himself against accusations that he was a sexist, Ali Benhadj points out that "Woman is a gem who raises generations of men, lions struggling against the enemies of Islam. All those who use women as an issue are not real men, but effeminate men."[17] There is no doubt that masculinity and femininity are opposite principles in this statement. Women are important for their reproductive capacity. Thus "Woman is a nest for man and the bearer of heroes. . . . I say that woman is better off at home. When I say that woman must stay home, some have distorted what I mean. They say that I am the enemy of women. What people say does not interest me."[18] However, the coleader of the F.I.S., Abassi Madani, seems to disagree with his peer when he mentions that "The Algerian woman is very competent. She proved it by giving us her powerful support during the elections. Do you think we will penalize her for it? We are here to provide solutions not to discuss false issues. It is true that some people get carried away by their emotions and say that women must stay home."[19] However, he too has misgivings about women working outside their homes. "There have been experiments with work among women in various societies such as the one mentioned by Gorbachev whereby women worked in agriculture, industry and scientific research, but at the expense of the family. The Soviets are rethinking their policy on this matter."[20] To prevent the alleged collapse of the family that might result from women taking up jobs, Madani offered to pay "the poor woman who must work to support ten children if she so desires to enable her to devote herself to her educational task." The allowance paid would be financed from the savings that the future state will realize by cutting down on police personnel.[21] At first glance it seems as though Madani advocates some welfare measure to help poor female heads of households. However, he does not mention the creation of day care services that might help women who wish to work, thus signalling his opposition to work regardless of women's social class.

Echoing a general sentiment held by legal Islamic scholars, the leader of the *Ennahda* group, Abdellah Djaballah, believes that:

> Islam freed woman from servitude and conceives of her as an essential element in the building of an Islamic society. However, Islam has given woman rules derived from the *shari'a* that offer her the objective conditions for success in her mission. She is a responsible being just like man but within the confines of her (feminine) nature and her abilities. This is why we believe that we must rely on woman and enable her to participate in our societal project.

After recounting the number of women who took part in public affairs during the heroic period of Islam, he concludes that "there is no objection to a woman occupying positions of responsibility if she is qualified. Scholars [in religion] allow her to exercise any function except that of president of the state."[22]

This is the most "liberal" position expressed by a leader of the movement despite its contradictions. A leader of the *Da'wa*, Mahfoud Nahnah, expressed his view of women in the most unusually graphic fashion: "A woman clad in a *hijab* is for me preferable to a thousand Friday sermons. She is a moving tank [*sic*]. Europeans show great respect to a woman in a *hijab*."[23] On the issue of the *hijab*, Madani advocates a moderate attitude. He rightly pointed out that: "The issue of the *hijab* is linked to Muslim faith which is based on consent and education. What can be achieved through education dispenses of its opposite [meaning coercion]. So we aim for conviction not coercion or punishment."[24] This is a laudable aim if it is implemented faithfully. However, making conviction a goal is akin to proselytizing.

During discussions I held with a number of university students in 1991, I was told that in poor neighborhoods in Algiers, young girls are persuaded to wear a *hijab* by members of the F.I.S., who offer it to them free of charge. It is true that opponents of the F.I.S. the have used the issue of women as their major weapon to undermine the religiose movement's claim to power. This use of women by men in their ideological battles is in keeping with the historical tradition established since the colonial era. Excesses in charges and counter-charges only dramatize the fact that women continue to be the trope through which power struggles unfold. A tragic example illustrates this point. In 1991, in the southern town of Ouargla, a single mother and her two children died in a fire allegedly set by members of the F.I.S., who accused her of prostitution. Defenders of the F.I.S. denied the charge and pointed to a disgruntled and estranged companion as the culprit.[25] No matter who the culprit was, violence against women was finally reported by the press not for what it was but for being committed by the F.I.S.

Women are not silent agents of this process that pits men against men. Some of them are members of the religiose movement. They too attend mosques on Fridays, usually on a mezzanine. Older women who traditionally did not attend mosque now do so on Fridays, where they listen to *imams* and get news from other women. There is a sense in which the mosque has displaced the *hammam* which used to be the place where women gathered together. Despite the existence of women among its members, the movement remains a men's movement for the purpose of creating a new state for men's benefit. While some younger women are members of the movement by conviction, many are relatives of male members, making their involvement somewhat suspect. The hallmark of religiosity for a woman is the *hijab*. Discussions with female students at the University of Algiers reveal that some believe that it is a religious duty for a woman to wear a *hijab*. One, who wore a *hijab*, pointedly told me that "it is colonialism that led Algerian women (implicitly such as myself) astray by neglecting the veil. We know better. We know what our obligations and duties are." Echoing the F.I.S. position on this mater, another student made the point that she recognized the fact that to live as a good

Muslim she should wear a *hijab*. However, she is personally not ready to do so. She would rather not wear it without being "convinced" that this is the right thing for her to do at this time. At a focus-group meeting in Algiers comprised of well-to-do young housewives and a middle-aged professor at an Algiers professional school, a consensus emerged that the *hijab* was an obligation to be discharged if a woman was ready for it. My devil's advocate argument that the *hijab* might concretize the principle of gender inequality in an age of equal rights was squashed by an appeal to faith. The *hijab* is for believers. A young mother began to recite in Arabic a long and beautiful poem that flaunts gender difference to support her argument.

One cannot dismiss these expressions of difference as just so many justifications of a social order deemed "oppressive" to women. However, this still begs the question as to what to make of those who do not think they are unbelievers by refusing to wear the *hijab*, and can invoke early Islamic history for examples of women who flaunted the veil. It is the linking of the veil with faith and faith with the foundation of a Muslim polity, which was spearheaded by the F.I.S. that essentially distorts the nature of the incipient debate on the woman question and threatens to silence it. Likewise, it is the appeal to the divine source of political power that threatens to further curtail women's roles in society, since the *shari'a* is presented simplistically as the word of God instead of man's attempt to create a legal system he deemed close to God's word. Aware of the boldness of their assertions, one of the leaders of the F.I.S. rightly claimed that "We are not Islam. We are Muslims and even though we intend to give Islam a concrete meaning we are not Islam."[26] This is a sensitive point that goes to the heart of the Muslim problématique in the contemporary Middle East. What is Islam, if each group engaged in a political quest for power sets out to implement its tenets, yet denies it represents it or accounts for it? Is Islam one or many? If it is many why is it that one modality is chosen over another? What gives one modality the power to assert itself over another?

State, Political Mosque and Women

It is often claimed that there are two almost antithetical traditions in Islamic thought, one that emphasizes *taqlid* or social conservation in legal if not social matters, another that underscores *ijtihad* or effort for renewal if not change.[27] Yet one is hard put to provide concrete examples of societies in the Middle East that have availed themselves of *ijtihad*. This concept remains largely a matter of assertion and exhortation to rhetorically defend against religiose groups. For instance, the Algerian government had a quarter of a century within which to elaborate a family law based on *ijtihad*, yet opted for one essentially based on *taqlid*. But in mounting a defense against the F.I.S., it appealed to the very tradition of *ijtihad* it failed to promote. Somewhat as a rearguard action, in the mid-eighties it hired a doctor of theology from Al Azhar University in Cairo, Sheikh Mohammed Al Gozali, whose lectures were broadcast on television. His message was one of moderation on social issues under which he subsumed women's roles in society. He felt that a woman could carry out:

> her social functions as teacher, medical doctor, business-woman capable of managing her property, etc. This is normal and unquestionable. To seclude a woman and prevent her from acquiring an education is criminal. What is not permitted is the degeneration of mores which leads some faithless men to unscrupulously assault the honor of others. . . . Many men look upon women with contempt. These men do not have faith and know nothing about it; they are part of a wayward and mindless trend.[28]

However, after he returned to Cairo, where the government show-cased him as a moderate theologian, he testified in court at the trial of Islamic militants in July 1993 that "a secularist represents a danger to society and the nation that must be eliminated. . . . It is the duty of the government to kill him."[29] Presumably a "secularist" woman would incur death as well. Recently, an Algerian woman married to a Belgian man was killed with her husband in the city of Blida by members of the religiose movement.

Similarly the Algerian media have given ample coverage to lectures by Sheikh El Kardaoui. On the subject of women he emphasizes that they constitute half of society and can hardly be ignored. He reasons that "We fear only the debates that are detrimental to woman and prevent her from asserting herself. It is not possible for a society to take off using one wing only, or breathe with one lung. We are opposed to those who plan to seclude woman and distrust her. Islam sees her as a daughter, wife, mother, and member of society."[30] For El Kardaoui, the *hijab* is a matter of personal choice and conscience. Thus

> the Muslim woman must wear it if she is personally convinced that this will bring her peace with God and with herself. . . . The *hijab* we see today is the expression of a woman's personal choice just as there are choices that women

make in seeking freedom. She chose this way of dressing according her conscience, freely.[31]

There is some truth to El Kardaoui's remark. There have been numerous instances of young women who insist on wearing the *hijab* despite their parents' opposition. Peer pressure, desire to avoid harassment on buses and on the streets, and faith have been invoked by a study devoted to the subject matter.[32]

What is remarkable about this religious counterdiscourse aimed at a religiose socio-political project is that it is carried out by men. No woman has entered the political mosque. It is as if the word attributed to God and said by multiple men silenced women, perhaps fearing the charge of unbelievers. Newly formed women's associations are prisoners of their modernist discourse of *rights*. In a terrain where the notion of right gives way to the notion of faith, they feel disabled, and reveal their cultural weakness as well as the inadequacy of their strategy, based as it is primarily on wresting the protection of rights from the state. Indeed, the leadership of the women's associations rejects the religiose discourses without engaging its authors on their terrain. The "political mosque" has eluded them, just as the secular political parties have given them only rhetorical support.[33] As they stand now, the women's associations cannot enter the political mosque to energize it with a feminist input because to a great measure they neglected to educate themselves in the language and history of Islam which have become the monopoly of the religiose leaders. So far feminists have reacted with awe and shock. Some have even felt that appeals to feminist associations in France and elsewhere might deliver them from an impending danger. But if there is danger it must be faced from within. A feminist fluent in the history of Islam and the *shari'a* might provide a much-needed perspective in a debate that has remained exclusively male. Indeed, the political mosque has of late published books addressed to women informing them prescriptively, among other things, of their obligations to their husbands and children, but essentially socializing them in the political culture of the future Islamic state.[34]

Women's *circumstantial silence* was not imposed upon them. They created it by failing to engage in self-criticism and recognizing that they are part and parcel of the cultural vacuum denounced by the religiose movement which rendered the quest for a sense of self as futile as the assumption of a ready-made modernist identity. Women failed to score a revolution of their own by missing the opportunity of being the cultural conscience of Algeria through using their own historical circumstances as a metaphor of the impoverishment of

Algerian culture, and a model for its renaissance in a new form. Instead, they waited for men's political failures to reveal to them their implicit complicity before they awoke to a feminist discourse that had already been scripted elsewhere.

In the unfolding tragedy that has beset contemporary Algeria, women's ability to secure a space necessary for them to play a role as arbiters, peacemakers, and agents of social change has been seriously curtailed. Their own survival is at stake violence targeting them *as women* has become a test of power between rival factions, religiose and secularist. Once considered the most important and viable religiose opposition, the Front of Islamic Salvation party has been eclipsed by new factions such as the Islamic Armed Group, comprised of younger men, perhaps former volunteer fighters in Afghanistan, who have claimed responsibility for the killing of male intellectuals, foreign nationals, policemen, servicemen, and members of the government. This group has also been blamed for the assassination of women married to foreign men, or engaging in activities deemed un-Islamic, such as reading tarot cards. A few weeks ago, the Islamic Armed Group posted signs on Algiers street walls and dropped leaflets warning women to wear the *hijab* or risk death. This was no idle threat as two students were gunned down at a bus stop, on March 30, 1994, because they did not wear a *hijab*.[35]

Other groups, such as the Organization of Free Young Algerians, a secularist vigilante group operating with the complicity of factions within the ruling F.L.N. party, have carried out reprisals against relatives of suspected members of the religiose movement. They too issued posters warning women against wearing the *hijab* and have killed two women as a direct response to the Islamic Armed Group's action. In another but more deadly replay of their past, women have emerged as the symbols of cultural integrity—Islamic or secular—and conflicting interests between men. The sacrificial view of women upheld by the government has finally reached its ultimate expression: the physical immolation of women on the altar of men's battle for power and control in the names of God and democracy.

Conclusion

There comes a time when the mind prefers what confirms its knowledge to what contradicts it. Then the self-preservation instinct reigns and spiritual growth is stunted.

Gaston Bachelard[1]

This book is meant to open up a new space for Algerian women. Concluding it would be both presumptuous and premature. An attempt will be made instead to draw lessons from the Algerian experience. There is a sense in which the history of Algerian women stands as a metaphor for an abstract feminine condition that transcends culture and social class. Ideologized and mythified by *all* men and women that took a fancy to them, artists, filmmakers, poets, fiction writers and social scientists, their lives are a constant struggle to impose their basic right to be . . . themselves.

The history of Algerian women exposes the antinomies and contradictions at the core of liberal feminism, whether practiced by American women, Middle Eastern women or Algerian male writers. It reveals that the liberatory discourse rests on the assumption of a fundamental inequality between women that can only be grasped in terms of a specialized language of "oppression." This conceptual condition is at once asserted and called forth thus relegating Algerian women to a quarantined space. The problem is that such a space had already been built for Algerian women during the colonial era by men and by women who claimed an abstract sisterhood with them. Algerian women find themselves struggling against the ghosts of history as well as their modern reincarnations.

The historical injustice that defined Algerian women's lives is compounded by an epistemic and philosophical injustice. It is one thing to shoulder the burden of colonialism, recognizing that one was not responsible for it. It is another to have to confront a condemnation of one's existence continuously, and like Sisyphus ceaselessly labor to assert the possibility of freedom. Few women in the Third World have had to contend with the expropriation of their moral outrage

223

by so many women and men ostensibly speaking for them but in fact speaking against them. Silence in Algeria is both deadening and eloquent. It is deadening by the sheer weight of the concepts that have condemned Algerian women to an irremediable caricatural existence. It is eloquent in that it has led to actions that women have taken throughout their history, the time design they clung to, the changes they continue to make in their lives as their voices are persistently quelled.

Five major findings having theoretical implications emerge out of this study. First, Algerian women, like other women, are not a context unto themselves. Their roles and statuses are shaped by historical as well as structural forces such as modes of production (peripheral merchant capitalism and colonial capitalism), imperialism/colonialism (Ottoman and French), kinship structure and Sufism. The diversity of modes of being female which characterized precolonial Algeria gave way to a more unitary existence. This trend was reinforced by the fundamental economic changes that affected Algerian society in the nineteenth century. Transformations of the structure of the family and its functions impacted on women who paradoxically needed the family the most when it became unable to serve their needs. At the same time that women were pried loose from the bonds that tied them to their menfolk, they were also pushed back into the family fold by an inhospitable colonial social system.

Second, colonialism was not a benevolent system of government that served women's needs. Colonialism was a mode of production as well as a system of political and cultural domination. There is no evidence that it favored native women over men. Politically it did too little too late to bring about legal change for women. It ushered in the ideologization of women by rhetorically addressing their condition as reflecting the failure of a doomed native culture, seeking an abstract alliance with them, yet doing little to provide equal education, training and jobs. At the same time, it defined women who did not fit the stereotype of the "Muslim" woman as prostitutes, and gave social enclaves (such as the *M'zab* in the south) free reign over women, who could be forced to marry a man chosen by their fathers. In general, colonial policy benefited men more than women.

Third, religious values as they affect women can be asserted at conjunctural times. Such values may, under historically specific conditions, be inoperative. The spectacular entry of women into the war of decolonization took place unchallenged by religious authority. More importantly, the very act of stepping outside the family and into the world of war is evidence against the scripturalist view of Islam, according to which women's vocation is the home. The rise of the religiose movement must be explained in terms of the contemporary conjuncture of events as well as the lack of resolution of the issue of cultural development in Algeria—an issue Algerians inherited from their colonial past and have refused to face squarely since their independence. This movement is an heir to the tradition established by the colonial government of defining group identity in religious terms and essentializing the identity thus constructed. For over a hundred years, difference between French and native people was socially, politically and legally infused with a religious content, thereby effectively preventing the emergence of a conception of self among natives that could transcend the boundaries of Islam, seen as the source of authenticity in opposition to the perceived inauthenticity of foreign *qua* Western cultural domination.

Fourth, the Algerian case demonstrates that culture is identical with the concept of woman. The common perception that women are the keepers of the family in the Middle East is not borne out. It is not so much the family as culture that appears crucial in Algeria, where women are seen as the embodiments of cultural authenticity. The F.L.N. as well as the religiose movement have repeatedly identified women with culture. The colonial history of Algeria as well as the rapid socio-economic changes it has undergone since 1962 make the issue of culture paramount. The 1984 Family Code is an expression of the identification of women with a culture perceived in danger of transformation towards an abstract "Western" model. Similarly, the religiose movement made it very clear that women embody the specificity of Islamic culture. Finally, the secularist opposition to the religiose movement also uses women as symbols of a narrowly defined secular culture, thus completing women's alienation from a political system in disarray.

Fifth, women's rights may not be implemented or protected without the state's active participation. At the same time, the state can and will use women to further its own political interests. The Algerian state recognized the importance of promoting women's interests, undertook gender-blind educational policies that to a degree benefited women, but fell short of protecting their rights as citizens. In the end, it attempted to placate an emerging religiose opposition by formulating a family law that restricts women's rights in matters of marriage, divorce and inheritance. This highlights the necessity for women to create their own pressure goup, if not party, in order to impinge on the state's political consciousness. In an age of incipient democratization, organized promotion of group interests is a *sine qua non* of political visibility.

Finally, silence and time are categories of analysis that ought to be developed in the study of women cross-culturally. They create the conditions of possibility of the transindividual subject that makes intersubjectivity crucial to the study of "other" women. Algerian women have historically acted and conducted their lives in ways that have been discursively obscured. To come to terms with the fact that their lives have been as meaningful as "ours," that they do not live in cultural quarantine, it is essential that explorations of silence and time, two complex and intricate categories of existence, begin in earnest. Women's silence helped to preserve Algerian culture during the colonial era and maintain psycho-social boundaries between the French-qua-Christians and the Algerians-qua-Muslims. Women's rise to the word in post-colonial Algeria is threatened by violent silencing.

Notes

Notes to Chapter 1

1. Jean-Paul Sartre, *Search for a Method* (New York: Vintage, 1963), p. 37.

2. The use of the concept "Western" in this book does not connote any ontological meaning. It refers to individuals who inhabit the space identified as the "West" which happens to coincide with industrialization and/or past colonial empires. The concept of "Third World" is as inadequate as "West" especially now that the so-called "Soviet Bloc," which occupied the space of a Second World, no longer fits the Cold-War terminology.

3. Fatima Mernissi, *Beyond the Veil* (New York: Shenkman, 1975); Nawal El-Saadawi, *The Hidden Face of Eve* (Boston: Beacon Press, 1980).

4. Rosario Morales, "We Are All In The Same Boat," p. 91. in Cherrie Moraga and Gloria Anzaldua eds., *This Bridge Across My Back* (N.Y.: Kitchen Table, Women of Color Press, 1983), p. 91.

5. Mitsuye Yamada, "Asian Pacific American Women and Feminism," *Ibid.*, p. 71.

6. Sheila Rowbotham, *Women, Resistance, and Revolution* (New York: Vintage, 1974), pp. 244–247.

7. Pierre Bourdieu, *Outline of a Theory of Practice* (Cambridge: Cambridge University Press, 1977), p. 21.

8. Michel Foucault, *Language, Counter-Memory, Practice*, D. F. Bouchard, ed., (Ithaca: Cornell University Press, 1977), p. 154.

9. Audre Lorde, "On Open Letter to Mary Daly" in Elly Bulkin, M.B. Pratt and B. Smith, *Yours in Struggle* (New York: Long Haul Press, 1984), pp. 94–97.

10. Gayatri Chakravorty Spivak, " 'Draupadi' by Mahasveta Devi," in Eliza-

227

beth Abel, ed., *Writing and Sexual Difference* (Chicago: University of Chicago Press, 1982), pp. 261–282, especially translator's foreword.

11. Pierre Bourdieu, *Outline of a Theory of Practice*, p. 2.

12. See Ranajit Guha, ed., *Subaltern Studies VI: Writings on South Asian History and Society* (Delhi, Oxford and New York: Oxford University Press, 1989);

13. Patricia Hill Collins, *Black Feminist Thought: Knowledge, Consciousness and the Politics of Empowerment* (New York: Routledge, Chapman and Hall, 1991).

14. See Marnia Lazreg, "Feminism and Difference: The Perils of Writing as a Woman on Women in Algeria," in *Feminist Studies*, vol. 14, No. 1, Spring 1988.

15. Margaret Smith, *Rabi'a the Mystic and Her Fellow Saints in Islam* (Amsterdam: Philo Press, 1974), pp. 148–154.

16. Reuben Levy, *The Social Structure of Islam* (Cambridge: Cambridge University Press, 1959).

17. I am indebted to Stephen Kern's *The Culture of Time and Space 1880–1918* (Cambridge: Harvard University Press, 1983) for helping me to appreciate the significance of perceptions of time and cultural change.

18. Lucien Goldmann, "Genetic Structuralism" in *Sciences humaines et philosophie* (Paris: Editions Gonthier, 1966), p. 151.

19. *Ibid.*, p. 60.

20. In anthropology Clifford Geertz argues for the maintenance of such identities by emphasizing that researchers' relation to natives is purely cognitive. See his *Local Knowledge: Further Essays in Interpretive Anthropology* (New York: Basic Books, 1983), ch. 8.

21. Lucien Goldmann, *The Hidden God: A Study of the Tragic Vision in the Pensées of Pascal and the Tragedies of Racine* (New York: Routledge and Kegan Paul, 1964), ch. 1.

22. Barrington Moore Jr., *Injustice: The Social Bases of Obedience and Revolt* (New York: M. E. Sharpe), pp. 500–505.

Notes to Chapter 2

1. The literature on El Kahina is abundant. For a summary see Jean Déjeux, *Femmes d'Algérie: Légendes, traditions, histoire, littérature* (Paris: La Boîte à Documents, 1987), ch. one.

2. See, for example, Yamina Mechakra, who presents a female character/ narrator as a niece of aunt Daya, a name assumed to be El Kahina's. The narrator refers to Arris, a town in the *Aurès* mountains, as the symbol of resistance. See *La Grotte Eclatée* (Alger: Entreprise Nationale du Livre, 1986).

3. See Jean Déjeux, *op. cit.*, pp. 120–133.

4. Pierre Boyer, *La vie quotidienne à Alger à la veille de l'intervention française* (Paris: Hachette, 1963), p. 229. See also Déjeux, pp. 157–169.

5. Arsène Berteuil, *L'Algérie française* (Paris: Dentu Librairie Editeur, 1856), vol. 1, p. 352.

6. Tailliart, *L'Algérie dans la littérature française*, (Paris: Librairie Ancienne Edouard Champion, 1925) p. 20.

7. *Ibid.*, p. 26.

8. *Ibid.*

9. "Les Aventures de Thédenat Esclave et Ministre d'un Bey d'Afrique (XVIII s.)," *Revue Africaine*, 1948, p. 336.

10. *Ibid.*, p. 338.

11. *Ibid.*, p. 340.

12. Pierre Boyer, *La vie quotidienne*, p. 229. This practice is reported by a number of authors.

13. *Ibid.*, pp. 228–229.

14. *Ibid.*, p. 228.

15. Lucien Chaillou, *L'Algérie en 1781: Mémoire du consul C.-Ph. Vallière* (Toulon: chez l'Auteur Villa "Beau Site," Valbertrand, 1974).

16. *Ibid.*, p. 75.

17. Général du Barail, *Mes souvenirs* (Paris: Plon, 1894), vol. 1, p. 283.

18. Pierre Boyer, *La vie quotidienne*, p. 160.

19. M. Morelet, *Les maures de Constantine en 1840* (Dijon: Imprimerie Darantière, 1876), p. 9.

20. Mohammed Hadj-Sadok, "A Travers la Berbérie Orientale avec le Voyageur Al Warthilani," *Revue Africaine*, 1951, p. 318.

21. *Ibid.*, pp. 318–20.

22. *Ibid.*, p. 361.

23. *Ibid.*, p. 375.

24. Léon Roches, *Trente deux ans à travers l'Islam* (Paris: Firmin Diderot, 1884), vol. 1, p. 43.

25. *Ibid.*, p. 49.

26. Mohammed Hadj-Sadok, "A Travers la Berbérie," p. 368.

27. *Ibid.*

28. *Ibid.*, p. 369.

29. Pierre Boyer, *La vie quotidienne*, pp. 94–95.

30. *Ibid.*, p.168.

31. Allan Christelow, *Muslim Law Courts and the French Colonial State in Algeria* (Princeton: Princeton University Press, 1985), p. 51.

32. Emile Dermenghem, *Le pays d'Abel* (Paris: Gallimard, 1960), p. 102. Echoes of Arab courtier love may be found in French Occitanie of the twelfth century.

33. *Ibid.*, pp. 34–38.

34. Emile Dermenghem, *op. cit.*, p. 71.

35. *Ibid.*

36. Isabelle Eberhardt, *Notes de route* (Paris: Eugène Fasquelle, 1923), pp. 186–94.

37. Pierre Deloncle, *La caravane aux éperons verts: Mission Alger-Niger* (Paris: Plon, 1927), p. 17. See, also, pp. 62–64.

38. Rolland, *La maison sous les palmes*, p. 53, quoted in Taillart, *L'Algérie dans la littérature française*, p. 479.

39. Quoted in Emile Dermenghem, *Le pays d'Abel*, p. 89.

40. *Ibid.*, p. 92.

41. Etienne Dinet and Slimane Ben Brahim, *Khadra: La danseuse des Ouled Nail* (Paris: H. Piazza, Editeur, n.d.), p. 11.

42. *Ibid.*

43. *Ibid.*, p. 8.

44. Saadia et Lakhdar, *L'Aliénation coloniale et la résistance de la famille Algérienne* (Lausanne: La Cité, 1961), pp. 116–128.

45. Mathéa Gaudry, *La femme chaouia de l'Aurès: Etude de sociologie berbère* (Paris: Librairie Orientaliste Paul Geuthner, 1929), p. 121. The practice described in this book was not radically different from the way it was prior to the French invasion.

46. *Ibid.*, p. 274.

47. *Ibid.*, p. 125.

48. *Ibid.*, p. 124.

49. *Ibid.*

Notes to Chapter 3

1. Gabriel Esquer, "L'Algérie vue par les écrivains," *Simoun*, 1925, p. 3.

2. Eugène Fromentin, *Une année dans le Sahel* (Paris: Plon, 1884), p. 224.

3. Esquer, p. 3.

4. *Ibid.*

5. *Ibid.*

6. *Ibid.*

7. Pierre Boyer, *La vie quotidenne à Alger à la veille de l'intervention française* (Paris: Hachette, 1963), p. 10.

8. Quoted in Esquer, p. 2.

9. Esquer, p. 113.

10. Eugène Fromentin, *Une année dans le Sahel*, p. 224.

11. Jules Lemaitre, *Les petites orientales*, quoted in Charles Tailliart, *L'Algérie dans la littérature française* (Paris: Librairie Ancienne Edouard Champion, 1925), p. 470.

12. Clément Lambing, *The French in Algiers* (New York: Wiley and Putnam, 1845, trans. Lady Duff Gordon), p. 6.

13. Augustin Berque, "Les Intellectuels Algériens," *Revue Africaine*, 1947, p. 132.

14. *Ibid.*, p. 138.

15. Tailliart, *L'Algérie dans la litterature française*, (Paris: Librairie Ancienne Edourd Champion, 1925), p. 574.

16. Tailliart, p. 577.

17. Jacques Berque, *Le Maghreb entre deux guerres* (Paris: Seuil, 1962), p. 327. Although extreme, this statement captures the essence of the relationship between natives and colonists.

18. Lucienne Favre, *Orientale 1930*, quoted in Esquer, p. 58.

19. Général du Barail, *Mes souvenirs* (Paris: Plon, 1894), vol. 2, p. 38.

20. *Ibid.*

21. *Ibid.*, pp. 38–39.

22. *Ibid.*, p. 45.

23. Moulay Belhamissi, *L'Histoire de Mostaganem* (Alger: Société Nationale d'Edition et de Diffusion, 1982).

24. Charles-André Julien, *Histoire de l'Algérie contemporaine: La conquête et les débuts de la colonisation, 1827–1871* (Paris: Presses Universitaires de France, 1964), p. 297.

25. *Ibid.*

26. *Ibid.*

27. Léon Roches, *Trente deux ans à travers l'Islam* (Paris: Firmin Diderot et Cie., 1884), vol. 2, p. 271.

28. Général du Barail, *Mes souvenirs*, vol. 1, pp. 300–301.

29. J. Desparmet, "Les Réactions nationalitaires en Algérie," *Bulletin de la société de géographie d'Alger et de l'Afrique du nord*, No. 132, 1932, pp. 450–51. Note that while this account is consistent with those given by French military men, Desparmet dismisses it as the product of an "eternal and universal imagination spurred by patriotism." p. 451.

30. Jean Dejéux, *Femmes d'Algérie: Légendes, traditions, histoire, littérature* (Paris: La Boîte à Documents, 1987), pp. 170–172.

31. *Ibid.*, p. 153. See also pp. 152–156.

32. Hubertine Auclert, *Les femmes arabes en Algérie* (Paris: Société d'Editions Littéraires, 1900), pp. 25–26.

33. Arsène Berteuil, *L'Algérie française* (Paris: Dentu, 1856), vol. 1, pp. 312–314.

34. Bodichon, *Etudes sur l'Algérie et l'Afrique* (Alger; Chez l'Auteur, 1847), p. 231.

35. Yvonne Turin, *Affrontements culturels dans l'Algérie coloniale* (Alger: E.N.A.L., 1983), p. 52.

36. *Ibid.*, p. 63.

37. Allan Christelow, *Muslim Law Courts and the French Colonial State in Algeria* (Princeton: Princeton University Press, 1985), pp. 100–101.

38. *Ibid.*, p. 102.

39. For an analysis of changes in land tenure system and property laws see my *The Emergence of Classes in Algeria: A Study of Colonialism and Socio-Political Change* (Boulder, Colorado: Westview Press, 1976).

40. Allan Christelow, p. 93.

41. *Ibid.*, pp. 86–94.

42. *Ibid.*, p. 87.

43. Hubertine Auclert, *Les femmes arabes*, p. 3. The word *"moukère"* was a frenchification of the Spanish *mujer* used pejoratively to refer to any Algerian woman.

44. Charles-André Julien, *Histoire de l'Algérie*, pp. 409–10.

45. *Ibid.*, p. 439.

46. *Ibid.*

47. Hubertine Auclert, p. 1.

48. *Ibid.*, p. 2.

49. *Ibid.*, p. 3.

50. Charles-André Julien, p. 441.

51. *Ibid.*

52. *Ibid.*

53. *Ibid.*

54 . Allan Christelow, *Muslim Law Courts*, p. 123.

55. Hubertine Auclert, pp. 229–236.

56. Tailliart, *L'Algérie dans la littérature*, p. 139.

57. *Ibid.*, p. 73.

58. *Ibid.*, p. 73.

59. This number is provided by Tailliart for the year 1843.

60. Edouard de Tocqueville, quoted in Tailliart, pp. 71–72.

61. Charles-Robert Ageron, *Les Algériens Musulmans et la France 1871–1919* (Paris: Presses Universitaires de France, 1968), vol. 1, p. 288.

62. *Ibid.*

63. *Ibid.*, p. 289.

64. Hubertine Auclert, *Les femmes arabes*, p. 26.

65. Tailliart, p. 140.

66. Hubertine Auclert, p. 63.

Notes to Chapter 4

1. J. Desparmet, "L'entrée des Français à Alger vue par le Cheikh Abd-El-Kader," in *Revue Africaine*, 71, 1930, p. 228. The original text is also reprinted in Arabic.

2. Jean Mélia, *Le triste sort des indigènes Musulmans d'Algérie* (Paris: Mercure de France, 1935), p. 18.

3. J. Desparmet, "L'oeuvre de la France en Algérie jugée par les indigènes," *Bulletin de la Société de Géographie d'Algérie et de l'Afrique du Nord*, vol. XV, 1910, p. 182.

4. *Ibid.*

5. *Ibid.*, p. 177.

6. *Ibid.*, p. 174.

7. *Ibid.*, p. 178.

8. *Ibid.*, p. 183.

9. *Ibid.*, p. 174.

10. J. Desparmet, "Les reactions nationalitaires en Algérie," *Bulletin de la Société de Géographie d'Algérie et de l'Afrique du Nord*, 132, 1932, p. 438.

11. J. Desparmet, *op. cit.*, p. 176.

12. "Le problème de la prostitution et ses aspects particuliers," *Association Catholique de la Jeunesse Française*, Fédération D'Alger, 1947, p. 5.

13. F 80. 507, August 1850. Archives d'Outre-Mer, Aix-en-Provence, Bureaux Arabes Départementaux, Monthly Reports.

14. *Ibid.*

15. *Ibid.* It is possible that low birth rates reflected the fact that Algerians were obligated to report deaths but not births. However, the native population declined throughout the nineteenth century due to war, disease such as cholera and typhus, and famine.

16. *Ibid.*, 1849.

17. *Ibid.*

18. Gouvernement Général, Alger, Algérie, "Observations sur la prostitution," 1898, p. 7.

19. Association Catholique, pp. 5–6.

20. Maurice Lepoil, *Faut-il abolir la prostitution?* Alger: Ancienne Imprimerie V. Heintz, 1947), p. 53.

21. Association Catholique, p. 9.

22. Lepoil, p. 36.

23. Dr. H. Marchand, *La prostitution indigène à Alger* (Alger: Imprimerie Fontana, 1937. Extrait de l'Algérie Médicale), pp. 1–2.

24. *Ibid.*, p. 3.

25. Lepoil, p. 54.

26. Mahfoud Kaddache, *L'Emir Khaled* (Alger: Office des Publications Universitaires. Entreprise Algérienne de Presse, 1987), p. 154.

27. Saadia et Lakhdar, *L'Aliénation coloniale et resistance de la famille algérienne* (Lausanne: La Cité, 1961), pp. 116–128.

28. *Ibid.*, p. 112.

29. *Ibid.*, p. 111.

30. *Ibid.*

31. Augustin Berque, "Les Intellectuels Algériens," *Revue Africaine*, 1947, p. 136.

32. *Ibid.*, pp. 144, 145.

33. *Ibid.*, p. 141.

34. *Ibid.*, p. 144.

35. *Ibid.*, p. 138.

36. Quoted by Charles-Robert Ageron, "Le mouvement jeune algérien," in Charles-André Julien, ed., *Etudes maghrébines: mélanges* (Paris: Presses Universitaires de France, 1964), p. 219.

37. *Ibid.*, p. 226.

38. *Ibid.*, p. 219. Ageron mentions that the "Young Algerians" were so identified by Edmond Doutté and William Marçais.

39. Kaddache, *L'Emir Khaled*, p. 150. See also *L'Emir Khaled: la situation des Musulmans d'Algérie, (1924)*, Présentation: Nadya Bouzar Kasbadji (Office des Publications Universitaires, 1987), p. 27.

40. Kaddache, *L'Emir Khaled*, pp. 206–207.

11. Abdelkader Djeghloul, *Huit études sur L'Algérie* (Alger: Entreprise Nationale du Livre, 1986), pp. 33–72.

42. *Ibid.*, p. 39.

43. Kaddache, *L'Emir Khaled*, p. 161.

44. Maurice Borrmans, *Statut personnel et famille au Maghreb de 1940 à nos jours*, Dissertation, University of Paris IV, March 9, 1971. Service de Reproduction de Thèses, Université de Lille, III, 1972, p. 454.

45. Djeghloul, *Huit études*, p. 35.

46. F 80 507 1852. Archives d'Outre-Mer, Aix-en-Provence, Bureaux Arabes Départementaux.

47. Yvonne Turin, *Affrontements culturels dans L'Algérie coloniale: Écoles, médecine, religion, 1830–1880* (Alger: Entreprise Nationale du Livre, 1983), p. 54.

48. 22 S 2. Archives d'Outre-Mer, Aix-en-Provence, Bureaux Arabes Départementaux.

49. Turin, *op. cit.*, p. 55.

50. *Ibid.*, p. 54.

51. *Ibid.*, p. 55.

52. *Ibid.*

53. *Ibid.*, p. 181.

54. Report written by Berthe Fropo, Anna Gaepffel and Fanny Gadot, evaluators of the Muslim School for Girls. Archives d'Outre-Mer, Aix-en-Provence, Bureaux Arabes Départementaux, n.d.

55. *Ibid.*

56. 22 S 2. Archives d'Outre-Mer, Aix-en-Provence, Bureaux Arabes Départementaux, Education Correspondence.

57. Préfecture d'Alger, Report on Awards ceremony at the Arab-French School for Boys, October 15, 1852. Archives d'Outre-Mer, Aix-en-Provence, Bureaux Arabes Départementaux, Annual Reports.

58. Abdel Kader Djeghloul et al., *Lettrés, intellectuels, et militants en Algérie, 1880–1950* (Alger: Office des Publications Universitaires, Laboratoire d'Histoire et d'Anthropologie Culturelle, 1988), p. 6.

59. Préfecture d'Alger, Report on Awards Ceremony at the Muslim Girls School, November 10, 1851. Archives d'Outre-Mer, Aix-en-Provence, Bureaux Arabes Départementaux, Annual Reports.

60. Préfecture d'Alger, Report on Awards Ceremony at the Muslim School for Girls, October 20, 1852. Archives d'Outre-Mer, Aix-en-Provence, Bureaux Arabes Départementaux, Annual Reports.

61. Préfecture d'Alger, Report on Awards Ceremony at the Arab-French School for Boys, October 20, 1852.

62. 22 S 2. Archives d'Outre-Mer, Aix-en-Provence, Bureaux Arabes Départementaux, Education Correspondence.

63. Yvonne Turin, *Affrontements culturels*, p. 280.

64. Cubière, *Rapport au roi*, May 11, 1839. Archives d'Outre-Mer, Aix-en-Provence, Bureaux Arabes Départementaux.

65. Yvonne Turin, *op. cit.*, pp. 280–281.

66. *Ibid.*

67. Ali Mérad, *Le réformisme Musulman en Algérie de 1925 à 1940* (Paris: Mouton, 1967), p. 321.

Notes to Chapter 5

1. Ibn Badis was not the only religious leader to address the issue of the renovation of Algerian society. Muhammad Al Mili was another well-known leader based in the southern town of Tebessa. For studies of Ibn Badis's ideas, see Ali Mérad, *Le réformisme Musulman en Algérie de 1925 à 1940* (Paris: Mounton et Cie, 1967); and Ali Mérad, *Ibn Badis: Commentateur du Coran* (Paris: Librairie Orientaliste Paul Geuthner, 1971).

2. Charles-Robert Ageron, "Le Mouvement Jeune Algérien," in Charles-André Julien, ed., *Etudes Maghrébines-Mélanges* (Paris: Presses Universitaires de France, 1964), pp. 220–21.

3. Ali Mérad, *Ibn Badis: Commentateur du Coran* (Paris: Librairie Orientaliste Paul Geuthner, 1971), especially ch. XI.

4. *Ibid.*, p. 14.

5. *Ibid.*, p. 24.

6. Maurice Borrmans, *Document sur la famille au Maghreb de 1940 à nos jours* (I.P.O., 1979), Estrato da "Oriente Moderno," [n.p., n.d.] vol. LIX, 1–5, pp. 161 and 163.

7. Ali Mérad, *op. cit.*, p. 209.

8. Maurice Borrmans, *op. cit.*, p. 163.

9. Ali Mérad, *op. cit.*, pp. 201–202.

10. Clifford Geertz, *Islam Observed* (New Haven: Yale University Press, 1968), p. 65.

11. Ali Mérad, *Le réformisme algérien*, p. 287.

12. *Ibid.*, p. 319.

13. *Ibid.*, pp. 323–324.

14. *Ibid.*, p. 326.

15. *Ibid.*, p. 328.

16. *Ibid.*, p. 329.

17. *Ibid.*, pp. 29–30.

18. Maurice Borrmans, *Statut personnel et famille au Maghreb de 1940 à nos jours*, (Dissertation, University of Paris IV, March 9, 1971. Service de Reproduction des Thèses, III, 1972, p. 441.

19. Ali Mérad, *Ibn Badis: Commentateur du Coran*, p. 198.

20. Maurice Borrmans, *Statut Personnel*, p. 99.

21. *Ibid.*, p. 423. The Lamine-Geye Law of May 7, 1946 extended French citizenship to all native Algerians. However, it made the *shari'a* inapplicable to issues of inheritance, and allowed judges to ignore "customs

and practices used by the parties in matters of property and personal status." This meant, in effect, the nonapplication of the *shari'a*. Quoted in Borrmans.

22. For a good study of the process through which colonial authorities attempted to bring Algerian legal institutions under the control of French courts, see Allan Christelow, *Muslim Law Courts and the French Colonial State in Algeria* (Princeton: Princeton University Press, 1965).

23. Borrmans, *Status personnel et famille au Maghreb*, p. 443.

24. *Ibid.*, p. 115.

25. *Ibid.*, p. 105

26. *Ibid.*

27. *Ibid.*, p. 106.

28. *Ibid.*, p. 115.

29. *Ibid.*, p. 110.

30. *Ibid.*, p. 114.

31. *Ibid.*, p. 459.

32. *Ibid.*, pp. 463, 466, 468, and 469.

33. *Ibid.*, p. 478.

34. *Ibid.*

35. *Ibid.*, pp. 474 and 479.

36. *Ibid.*, p. 483.

37. *Ibid.*, pp. 445–450.

38. *La république algérienne*, No. 256, February 28, 1951.

39. *La république algérienne*, No. 257, March 2, 1951.

40. *La république algérienne*, No. 299, March 28, 1952.

41. *La république algérienne*, No. 266, May 12, 1951.

42. *La république algérienne*, No. 303, May 9, 1952.

43. *La république algérienne*, No. 272, September 21, 1951.

44. *La république algérienne*, No. 306, May 16, 1951.

45. Marie Bugéja, *Nos soeurs musulmanes* (Alger: Editions France Afrique, 1931), p. 12. For a critique of colonial women writers such as Bugéja, see Sakina Messaadi, Les romancières coloniales et la femme colonisée: Contribution à une étude de la littérature coloniale en Algérie (Alger: Entreprise Nationale du Livre, 1990).

46. *Ibid.*, p. 11.

47. *Ibid.*, p. 13.

48. *Ibid.*, pp. 187–88.

49. *Ibid.*, p. 81.

50. *Ibid.*, p. 157.

51. *Ibid.*, p. 123.

52. *Ibid.*, p. 149.

53. *Ibid.*, p. 9.

54. See Djamila Débèche, "Les Musulmans Algériens et la scolarisation." Lecture sponsored by the Schooling and Literacy Committee, Algiers, January 5, 1951, Archives d'Outre-Mer, Aix-en-Provence, B 4432.

55. Figure provided by Borrmans, *Statut personnel*, p. 441.

56. *Ibid.*, p. 455.

57. See Fatima Zohra Sai, *Mouvement national et question feminine des origines à la guerre de liberation* (C.R.I.D.S.S.H., University of Oran, Algeria, 1984), No. 11.

58. Jacques Berque, *Le Maghreb entre deux guerres* (Paris: Editions du Seuil, 1962), p. 293.

59. Andre Nouschi, "Le sens de certains chiffres: Croissance urbaine et vie politique en Algérie 1926–1936," in Charles-André Julien, ed., *Etudes Maghrébines-Mélanges*, Nouschi points out that in 1936 there were one thousand unionized Algerian workers in comparison with nine thousand unionized French workers in Algeria.

Notes to Chapter 6

1. The term "acculturated" is used here to avoid the problematic distinction usually made between "secularists" and religious "reformists." The issue at the time in the eyes of natives was not secularism as opposed to religion, but maintaining one's culture, which also included religion, or adopting French values. It so happened that the proponents of Algerian culture were also men of religion, opposed by acculturated men.

2. For a discussion of colonial laws that changed Algerians' land ownership see Marnia Lazreg, *The Emergence of Classes in Algeria: A Study of Colonialism and Socio-Political Change* (Boulder, Colorado: Westview Press, 1976). See, also, Abdellatif Benhachenhou, *Formation du sous-developpement en Algérie* (Alger: Office des Publications Nationales, 1976), ch. 2.

3. Jean Paul Charnay, *La vie Musulmane en Algérie d'après la jurisprudence du XXème siècle* (Paris: Presses Universitaires de France, 1965), p. 149.

4. *Ibid.*, p. 249

5. *Ibid.*, p. 153.

6. *Ibid.*, p. 85.

7. Jacques Berque, *Le Maghreb entre deux guerres* (Paris: Editions du Seuil, 1962), p. 208.

8. Pierre Bourdieu, *Outline of a Theory of Practice* (Cambridge: Cambridge University Press, 1977), p. 32.

9. I am using the term "traditional" not as the opposite of "modern" but

to refer to the age-old practices that individuals invoke at significant moments of their life cycles, such as birth, circumcision, marriage, and so on.

10. Charnay, *La vie musulmane*, pp. 22–23.
11. *Ibid.*, p. 41.
12. *Ibid.*, p. 105.
13. *Ibid.*, p. 21.
14. *Ibid.*, p. 290.
15. *Ibid.*, p. 44.
16. *Ibid.*, p. 47. The French government's circular of November 4, 1927 specified that native policemen will be used to take women back to their husbands.
17. *Ibid.*, pp. 42–43.
18. *Ibid.*, p. 47.
19. *Ibid.*, p. 26.
20. *Ibid.*, p. 37. Many Algerians preferred to emigrate to Syria or the Arabian Peninsula rather than live under French law.
21. *Ibid.*, p. 33.
22. *Ibid.*, pp. 35 and 36.
23. *Ibid.*, pp. 317 and 319.
24. *Ibid.*, p. 245.
25. *Ibid.*, p. 235.
26. *Ibid.*, p. 26.
27. J. Desparmet, *Coutumes, institutions, croyances des indigènes en Algérie*, vol. 1., L'Enfance, le mariage, et la famille (Alger: La Tipo-Litho et Jules Carbonel, 1939), p. 38.
28. *Ibid.*
29. Charnay, *La vie Musulmane*, p. 34.
30. Rabah Belamri, *Les graines de la douleur: Contes populaires* (Paris: Editions Publisud, 1982), p. 13.
31. *Ibid.*, p. 13.
32. Martine Bertrand, *Le jeu de la boqala* (Paris: Publisud, 1983), pp. 17–18.
33. *Ibid.*, pp. 19–20.
34. *Ibid.*, p. 24.
35. *Ibid.*, p. 29.
36. *Ibid.*
37. *Ibid.*, pp. 53–57.
38. *Ibid.*, pp. 82–87.

39. *Ibid.*, pp. 101–107.

40. *Ibid.*, p. 98.

41. See among others Mathéa Gaudry, *La femme chaouia de l'Aurès* (Librairie Orientaliste Paul Geuthner, 1929).

42. This discussion and the one that follows are based on an interview I had with Mrs. Fatima Ghrib, a seventy-five-year-old woman who grew up in a small rural town in Western Algeria, and moved to Algiers in 1962.

43. Charnay, *La vie Musulmane*, pp. 27–29.

Notes to Chapter 7

1. See among others, Juliette Minces, *The House of Obedience: Women in the Arab World* (London: Zed Press, 1980); and Sheila Rowbotham, *Women, Resistance, and Revolution* (New York: Vintage, 1974), ch. 8.

2. Djamila Amrane, "La femme algérienne et la guerre de liberation nationale," in *Combattantes de la lutte armée, les femmes aussi ecriront l'histoire* (Algiers: 1982), monograph issued by the the magazine *El Djazairiya* on the twentieth anniversary of independence, pp. 3–4.

3. *Ibid.*, p. 6.

4. *Ibid.*, p. 6.

5. Alistair Horne, *A Savage War of Peace, Algeria 1954–1962* (New York: Viking, 1977), pp. 221–2.

6. Interview with *Djamila Bouhired*, July 1983.

7. *Combattantes de la lutte armée*, p. 23.

8. *Ibid.*, p. 14.

9. *Ibid.*, p. 69.

10. *Ibid.*

11. *Ibid.*, pp. 62, 64, 22, 23. Fatima's account bears the wrong date, 1953, although the war started in 1954. She joined the F.L.N. in 1956. The incident she mentions must have taken place in 1956 or earlier.

12. *El Moudjahid* 46, July 20, 1959, p. 365.

13. *Combattantes de la lutte armée*, p. 7.

14. *Ibid.*

15. "Journal d'une Maquisarde," in *Ibid.*, pp. 29–30.

16. *Ibid.*, pp. 10–14.

17. *Ibid.*, p. 14.

18. *Ibid.*, p. 10.

19. Interview with a woman revolutionary who survived torture, summer 1983.

20. *Combattantes de la lutte armée*, p. 11.

21. *Ibid.*, p. 15.

22. *Ibid.*, pp. 5, 38, 54.

23. Djamila Amrane, "La Guerre de libération nationale, 1954–1962," *Cahiers du centre de documentation des sciences humaines*, 3, 1980, p. 223. See, also, Mériem Cadi-Mostéfai, "L'Image de la femme algérienne pendant la guerre (1954–1962) à partir des textes paralittéraires et littéraires," Diplôme d'Etudes Approfondies, 1978, University of Algiers, Institut des Langues Etrangères.

24. Frantz Fanon, *A Dying Colonialism* (New York: Grove Press, 1967), p. 48.

25. *Combattantes de la lutte armée*, p. 16.

26. Fanon, p. 48.

27. Alistair Horne, *A Savage War of Peace*, p. 407.

28. Fanon, pp. 49–50.

29. *Ibid.*, p. 58.

30. *Ibid.*, p. 66.

31. *Ibid.*, p. 52.

32. *Ibid.*, p. 54.

33. *Ibid.*, p. 66.

34. *El Moudjahid*, 47, August 3, 1959, p. 381.

35. Chérifa Benabdessadok, "Pour une analyse du discours sur la femme algérienne," Diplôme d'Etudes Avancées en Linguistique, University of Algiers, 1977, p. 206.

36. *El Moudjahid*, 42, May 25, 1959, p. 278.

37. *Ibid.*, p. 279. On women's participation in the war, see, also, Nora Benallègue, "La femme dans la lutte d'indépendance et la reconstruction nationale," *U.N.E.S.C.O.*, vol. XXXV, 4, 1983.

38. *El Moudjahid*, 44–49, June-August 1959. Also reprinted in *Combattantes*.

39. See Chérifa Benabdessadok, pp. 57–59; and Mériem Cadi-Mostefai, pp. 1–33.

40. *Combattantes de la lutte armée*, p. 29.

41. *Ibid.*

42. *El Moudjahid*, 2, 45, 1959, pp. 340–344.

43. Chérifa Benabdessadok, "Pour une analyse du discours," p. 207.

44. Chérifa Benabdessadok, "Synthèse des écrits sur la femme et la lutte armée, in *Combattantes de la lutte armée*, p. 60.

45. Maurice Borrmans, *Statut personnel et famille au Maghreb de 1940 à nos jours*, (Dissertation, Lille: Université de Lille III, Service de Reproduction des Thèses, 1972), pp. 491–2.

46. *Ibid.*, p. 491.

47. Alistair Horne, *A Savage War of Peace*, p. 403.

48. *Ibid.*, p. 223.

49. *Ibid.*, pp. 402–403.

50. *Ibid.*, p. 402.

51. *Plan de Constantine 1959–1961* (Alger: Délégation Générale du Gouvern-ment en Algérie, Direction du Plan et des Etudes, June 1960), p. 77.

52. *Ibid.*, p. 79.

53. Alistair Horne, p. 291. Note that Horne refers to Algerian women by a generic first name, Fatma, used by the colonists.

54. *Ibid.*

55. Chérifa Benabdessadok, "Pour une analyse du discours," p. 88.

56. Frantz Fanon, *A Dying Colonialism*, p. 64.

57. *Ibid.*

58. *Ibid.*, p. 63.

59. *Ibid.*, p. 45.

60. Statements made to the author by French women colleagues in 1961.

61. Fanon, p. 44.

62. Horne, p. 399.

63. For a discussion of women's associations in colonial Algeria, see Fatma-Zohra Sai, *Mouvement national et question feminine des origines à la veille de la guerre de libération nationale* (Oran: Centre de Documentation des sciences Humaines, 1984); and Mériem Cadi-Mostéfai, "L'image de la femme," pp. 58–61.

64. *El Moudjahid*, 2, 26, 1958, p. 525.

65. *El Moudjahid*, 3, 72, 1960, p. 270.

66. *El Moudjahid*, 2, 26, 1958, p. 525.

67. Sheila Rowbotham, *Women, Resistance, and Revolution*, pp. 244–5.

Notes to Chapter 8

1. Interview with four women during a focus group discussion in Algiers in November 1989.

2. *La Charte d'Alger*. Ensemble des Textes Adoptés par le Premier Congrès du parti du F.L.N. (Alger: F.L.N., Commission Centrale d'Orientation, 1964).

3. *Ibid.*, p. 63.

4. *Ibid.*, pp. 81–82.

5. *Ibid.*, p. 82.

6. *Ibid.*

7. *Ibid.*

8. *Ibid.*, p. 81.

9. *Ibid.*

10. *Ibid.*, pp. 44–45.

11. *Ibid.*, p. 150.

12. *Algérie, naissance d'une société nouvelle: Le texte intégral de la charte nationale adoptée par le peuple algérien* (Paris: Edition Sociale, 1976), p. 163.

13. *Ibid.*, p. 164.

14. *ISIS*, Bulletin du groupe de recherche sur les femmes algériennes (Oran: C.D.S.H., vol. 2, 1982), p. 4.

15. *Ibid.*

16. Marie-Victoire Louis, "Les algériennes, la lutte," *Les temps modernes*, July-August, 1982, p. 155.

17. *Ibid.*, pp. 455–56.

18. Jürgen Habermas, *Legitimation Crisis* (Boston: Beacon, 1975), part II.

19. *Algérie actualité*, No. 914, April 2–27, 1983.

20. Quoted in Hélène Vandevelde, *Machrek-Maghreb*, No. 97, July–August 1982, p. 31. For a discussion of the nature of family law up to 1984, see also: Ahmed Mahiou, "Rupture ou continuité du droit en algérie," *Revue algérienne juridique, économique, et politique* 1982; Ghaouti Benmelha, "La famille algérienne entre le droit des personnes et le droit public," *Ibid.*, pp. 29–74; Fatima-Zohra Sai, "Quelques remarques à propos de la codification du droit de la famille," C.R.I.D.S.S.H., No. 7, 1983.

21. The author was among the audience.

22. Hélène Vandevelde, "Où en est le problème du code de la famille en Algérie?" *Machrek-Maghreb*, 97, 1982.

23. Fatima-Zohra Sai, p. 12.

24. Marie-Victoire Louis, p. 153.

25. *Ibid.*, p. 159.

26. *Ministère de la Justice*, Avant-Projet de Code de la Famille, 1401H–1981, p. 10.

27. *Ibid.*, p. 8.

28. *Ibid.*, p. 13.

29. *Ibid.*, p. 14.

30. *Ibid.*, p. 10.

31. *Ibid.*, p. 15.

32. *Ibid.*

33. Quoted by Marie-Victoire Louis, "Les algériennes, la lutte." p. 163.

34. *Ibid.*, pp. 163–64.

35. *Ibid.*, p. 165.

36. *Ibid.*, p. 166.

37. *Ibid.*, p. 170.

38. *Ibid.*, pp. 172–78.

39. *Ibid.*, pp. 183–85.

40. *Ibid.*, pp. 188–91.

41. See *Code de la famille* (Centre National de Documentation de Presse et d'Information, Ministère de l'Information, 1988, Dossier Documentation 01). The text of the code was also reprinted in *El Moudjahid*, June 20 and 21, 1984.

42. *El Moudjahid*, June 20, 1984.

43. *Le code de la famille*, Articles 36, 38 and 39.

44. *El Moudjahid*, editorial, June 20, 1984.

45. See, among others, Marc Raffinot and Pierre Jacquemot, *Le capitalisme d'état algérien* (Paris: Maspéro, 1987).

46. See, among others, Irene Tinker, *Persistent Inequalities* (Oxford: Oxford University Press, 1990); and Noeleen Heyzer, *Working Women in South East Asia* (Milton Keynes: Open University Press, 1986).

47. *Statistiques: Situation de l'emploi 1986* (Alger: Office National des Statistiques, 1986, Collection des Statistiques, 5), pp. 16–18. The 1990 issue of this publication indicates that women's participation in the labor force is 8.38%. Yet it also points out that employment among women has remained stationary since 1987. These statistics are problematic given the nature of the census categories used (for example unemployed individuals are considered "active," a misleading term easily confused with employed), and the difficulty of ascertaining the extent of unpaid employment and unemployment among women.

48. *Ibid.* See the critique of census data on women's work by Fatiha Talahite, "Le travail féminin, emploi salarié et travail domestique," *Cahiers du Centre de Documentation des Sciences Humaines*, No. 3, 1980, pp. 35–105.

49. See Marnia Lazreg, "Women, Work, and Social Change in Algeria" in Sharon Stichter and Jane Parpart, eds., *Women, Work, the Family, and the International Division of Labor* (New York: MacMillan, 1990).

50. *Statistiques*, No. 27, Office National des Statistiques, 1990, p. 70.

51. Interviews with three women hired for executive positions in two state-owned enterprises in 1983.

52. Katherine McAfee, *Storm Signals* (New York: South End Press, 1991), especially Part I.

53. Moncer Rouissi, *Population et société au Maghreb* (Tunis: Office des Presses Universitaires, 1976), pp. 157–162.

54. Malika Ladjali, *L'espacement des naissances dans le tiers monde: L'expérience algérienne* (Alger: Office des Publications Universitaires, 1985), pp. 16–17.

55. *Ibid.*, pp. 111–126.

56. The fertility rate in Algeria was 6.9 up until 1990. In the last three years it has dropped to 6.6.

57. Leila Aslaoui, *Dérives de justice* (Alger: Bouchène, 1990), pp. 9–37.

58. Interview with two women, a pharmicist and a doctor in Algiers and Chéraga, 1984.

59. Communication by a senior psychiatrist practicing in Algiers.

60. See UNDP, *Human Development* (Oxford: Oxford University Press, 1990), ch. one. A new revised edition has been issued every year. The 1992 issue classifies Algeria as a country with a low Human Development index.

61. Various United Nations and other international agencies such as the World Bank have begun to address the issue of the marginalization of women in the development projects they sponsor.

62. *Human Development Report, 1990*, p. 152.

63. Interview with two female executives employed by two major state-owned enterprises in 1989.

64. See *Algérie Actualité*, Jan. 10–16, 1980. See also the critique of this paper's report in Claude Talahite, "L'enquête: Femmes à l'usine dans Algérie Actualité. Essai d'analyse des discours sur les femmes," in *Cahiers du C.D.S.H.*, Actes des journées d'étude et de réflexion sur les femmes algériennes, No. 3, 3–6 May 1980, pp. 352–386.

Notes to Chapter 9

1. As the Marxist approach has lost ground, if not relevance, cultural anthropology as well as cultural studies have emerged as areas of renewed interest in academic centers.

2. *Le programme de Tripoli, le F.L.N. et la constitution de l'Algérie socialiste*, edited by "La Tendance Révolutionnaire du Parti Communiste Français" (Paris, 1964), p. 25.

3. Ahmed Taleb Ibrahimi, *De la décolonisation à la révolution culturelle (1962–1972)* (Alger: Société Nationale d'Edition et de Diffusion, 1973), pp. 222–223.

4. See Marnia Lazreg, "The Kabyle-Berber Movement in Algeria," in Adamantia Pollis and Peter Schwab, eds., *Human Rights: Cultural and Ideological Perspectives* (New York: Praeger, 1979). See also Gilbert Grand-

guillaume, *Arabisation et politique linguistique au Maghreb* (Paris: Editions G.-P. Maisonneuve et Larose, 1983), ch. 5.

5. See Marnia Lazreg, "Media and Cultural Dependency in Algeria," *Studies of Broadcasting*, No. 26, 1990, pp. 43–45.

6. *Algérie actualité*, July 21–24, 1983.

7. *Les temps modernes*, July–August, 1982, No. 432–33, pp. 194–5.

8. See analysis of film in *Ibid.*, pp. 376–380.

9. Noureddine Toualbi, *Le sacré ambigu ou les avatars psychologiques du changement* (Alger: Entreprise Nationale du Livre, 1984), pp. 19–26.

10. Ali Ghalem, *Une femme pour mon fils* (Paris: Editions Syros, 1979). For an analysis of the Algerian film industry, see Abdelghani Megherbi, "Stratégies de cinéastes algériens et habitudes cinématographiques," in *Recueil des conférences: Aspects du changement socio-culturel algériens* (Paris: Centre Culturel Algérien, 1987), pp. 53–79.

11. Story communicated to me in 1985 by the subject's sister-in-law.

12. Mahfoud Boucebci, *Psychiatrie, société, et développement: Algérie 1978* (Alger: Société Nationale d'Edition et de Diffusion, 1982), p. 142.

13. Allan Christelow, *Muslim Law Courts and the French Colonial State in Algeria* (Princeton: Princeton University Press, 1985), 128–30.

14. Mahfoud Boucebci, *Psychiatrie*, pp. 148–9.

15. *Ibid.*, p. 146.

16. *Ibid.*, pp. 142–3.

17. *Ibid.*, pp. 153–4.

18. *Ibid.*, p. 157.

19. *Ibid.*, p. 158.

20. *Ibid.*

21. *Ibid.*, p. 159.

22. *Ibid.*, p. 144.

23. *Ibid.*, pp. 162–187.

24. Noureddine Toualbi, "Changement social et pratique du sacré en Algérie," in *Aspects du changement*, pp. 117–134.

25. A. Ouitis, *Les contradictions sociales et leur expression symbolique dans le sétifois* (Alger: Société Nationale d'Edition et de Diffusion, 1977), especially ch. 4, pp. 83–84.

26. *Ibid.*, pp. 97–98.

27. Noureddine Toualbi, *Le sacré ambigu*, p. 39.

28. Allan Christelow, *Muslim Law Courts*, p. 68.

29. Noureddine Toualbi, pp. 120–7.

30. *Ibid.*, p. 125.

31. *Ibid.*

32. Souad Khodja, *Les algériennes du quotidien* (Alger: Edition Nationale du Livre, 1985), p. 49.

33. Chafika Dib-Marouf, *Fonctions de la dot dans la cité algérienne: Le cas d'une ville moyenne: Tlemcen et son 'hawz'* (Alger: Office des Publications Universitaires, 1984), ch. one, especially pp. 44–45.

34. *Ibid.*, p. 92.

35. *Ibid.*, pp. 74–75.

36. *Code de la famille*, Article 16.

37. Chafika Dib-Marouf, p. 97.

38. *Ibid.*, p. 77.

39. *Ibid.*, p. 102.

40. *Ibid.*, p. 328.

41. Souad Khodja, *Les algériennes du quotidien*, pp. 50–51.

42. Algérie Actualité, April 21–24, 1983.

43. *Ibid.*

44. *Ibid.*

45. *Ibid.*

46. Chafika Dib-Marouf, *Fonctions de la dot*, p. 101.

47. *Ibid.*, p. 102.

48. *Ibid.* For the year 1983 *Algérie Actualité* reports illiteracy rates of 41.5 per cent and 82.6 per cent for women in the 9 to 13 and 18 to 59 age groups. The 1991 United Nations *World's Women* report indicates a total illiteracy rate of 40.5 per cent among women and 15.5 per cent among men (p. 50).

49. Chafika Dib-Marouf, *Fonctions de la dot*, pp. 74–75.

50. Leila Aslaoui, *Dérives de justice* (Alger: Editions Bouchène, 1990), pp. 40–73.

51. Chafika Dib-Marouf, *Fonctions de la dot*, p. 101.

52. See Azizah Al Hibri, "Islamic Herstory: Or How Did We Get Into This Mess?" in Al Hibri, ed., *Women and Islam* (New York: Pergamon Press, 1982), pp. 216–217.

53. *El Moudjahid.*, July 2, 1991.

54. *Ibid.*

55. *Ibid.*

56. *Ibid.*

57. *Ibid.*

58. Mohammed Ould Cheikh, *Myriem dans les palmes* (Alger: Office des Publications Universitaires, 1985) pp. 47, 19 and 26. See also Ahmed Lasnari,

'Myriem dans les Palmes', Roman de Mohammed Ould Cheikh," in C.R.I.D.D.S.H., 1983, No. 7, pp. 22–23; Christiane Achour, *Anthologie de la littérature algérienne de langue française* (Alger: Entreprise Algérienne de Presse, 1990), pp. 32–33.

59. The most interesting Dib's novel in this respect is his trilogy: *La grande maison* (Paris: Editions du Seuil, 1952); *L'Incendie* (Paris: Editions du Seuil, 1954): *Le Métier à tisser* (Paris: Editions du Seuil, 1957). Kateb Yacine's *Nedjma* (Paris: Editions du Seuil, 1956) is most useful in studying the symbolization of women.

60. Malek Haddad, *Le quai aux fleurs ne répond plus* (Paris: Julliard, 1961).

61. Rachid Boudjedra, *Le répudiation* (Paris: Denoël, 1969).

62. Rachid Boudjedra, *Journal d'une femme Insomniaque* (Alger: Dar El Idjtihad, 1989), pp. 10–14.

63. Rachid Boudjedra, *Le Démantèlement* (Paris: Denoël, 1982), p. 151.

64. *Ibid.*, pp. 145–6.

65. Malek Alloula, *The Colonial Harem* (Minneapolis: University of Minnesota Press, 1986), p. 5.

66. *Ibid.*, p. 64.

67. Mustapha Toumi, in *Promesses*, No. 92, n. d., p. 25. The original poem appeared in *El Moudjahid*, May 21, 1971.

68. See *Sunday New York Times*, Styles section, May 9, 1993.

69. *MAG* 7, July 28, 1991.

Notes to Chapter 10

1. Mériem Cadi-Mostefai, "L'image de la femme algérienne pendant la guerre (1954–1962) à partir de textes paralittéraires et littéraires." Diplôme D'Etudes Approfondies, University of Algiers, Institut des Langues Etrangères, 1978.

2. Chérifa Benabdessadok, "Pour une analyse du discours sur la femme algérienne." Diplôme d'Etudes Avancées En Linguistique," University of Algiers, Algiers, 1979.

3. Djamila Amrane, "La guerre de libération nationale, 1954–1962." *Cahiers du centre de documentation des sciences humaines*, No. 3, 1980, pp. 201–223.

4. Keltoum Lalmas and Amina Ouadjina, "Le hijab à la cité universitaire de jeunes filles d'Alger, 1981–1982." Mémoire de Fin de Licence, University of Algiers, Institut des Sciences Sociales.

5. See *Présences de femmes* (Algiers: Office des Publications Universitaires, 1984), see also 1986 edition.

6. [*Projet de réglement interieur*, document provided by the Association for Equality Before the Law Between Women and Men, n.d.

7. See *APEL*: Association Pour L'Egalité, No. 6, May 1990.

8. *L'Action*, No. 1, September 25, 1947.

9. Djamila Débèche, "L'enseignement de la langue arabe en algérie et le droit de vote aux femmes algériennes." Paper presented in Algiers, June 8, 1951. Archives d'Outre-Mer, Aix-en-Provence, B 345.

10. Djamila Débèche, "Les Musulmanes algériennes et la scolarisation," Talk sponsored by the Committee for Schooling and the Eradication of Illiteracy, January 15, 1950, p. 17. Archives d'Outre-Mer, Aix-en-Provence, 84432.

11. *Ibid.*, p. 19.

12. See *Leila, une jeune fille algérienne* (Alger: Imprimerie Charras, 1947); and *Aziza* (Alger: Imbert, 1955).

13. Assia Djebar, *Les alouettes naïves* (Paris: Julliard, 1967); and Rachid Boudjedra, *La Répudiation* (Paris: Denoël, 1969).

14. Assia Djebar, *Femmes d'Alger dans leur appartement* (Paris: Edition des Femmes, 1981).

15. Aicha Lemsine, *La chrysalide* (Paris: des Femmes, 1976), pp. 258–265.

16. *Ibid.*, pp. 130–142.

17. Christiane Achour, *Entre le roman rose et le roman exotique "La chrysalide" de A. Lemsine* (Alger: Entreprise Nationale de Presse, 1978).

18. Souad Khodja, *Les algériennes du quotidien* (Alger: Entreprise Nationale du Livre, 1985), pp. 1–113.

19. Yamina Méchakra, *La grotte éclatée* (Alger: Entreprise Nationale du Livre, 1986).

20. *Ibid.*, p. 96.

21. *Ibid.*, p. 100.

22. *Ibid.*, p. 51.

23. *Ibid.*, p. 98.

24. Leila Aslaoui, *Dérives de justice* (Alger: Bouchene, 1990).

25. Chérifa Benabdessadok, "Tradition et modernisme: Un faux débat?" in *Présences de femmes* (Alger: Office des Publications Universitaires, 1984), pp. 7–11.

26. Chafika Dib-Marouf, *Fonctions de la dot dans la cité algérienne: Le cas d'une ville moyenne: Tlemcen et son 'Hawz'* (Alger: Office Des Publications Universitaires, 1984), pp. 25–31.

27. Souad Khodja, *Les algériennes du quotidien*, pp. 21–22.

28. *Ibid.*, p. 44.

29. *Ibid.*, p. 106.

30. Chérifa Benabdessadok, "Tradition et Modernisme."

31. Khodja, p. 90.

32. Khodja, ch. 3.

33. Mostéfa Boutefnouchet, *La famille algérienne. Evolution et caracteris-tiques récentes* (Alger: Société Nationale d'Edition et de Diffusion, 1980), ch. 2, especially pp. 67–74.

34. On the media see Fatiha Talahite, "Lu dans la presse," in *Présences de femmes: Gestes acquis, gestes conquis* (Hiwar, n.p., 1986), pp. 175–181. In the same edition see entry by Christiane Achour, pp. 182–185. See, also, Zineb Benali and Christiane Achour, "Le discours culturel des manuels de langue française des enseignements primaire et moyen," in Collectif, *Balades dans la culture en Algérie en 1979* (Alger: Office des Publications Universitaires, 1984), pp. 7–48.

35. For an Analysis of Isabelle Eberhardt and Aurélie Picard's lives see Ursula Kingsmill Hart, *Two Ladies of Algeria: The Lives of Aurélie Picard and Isabelle Eberhardt* (Athens; Ohio University Center for International Studies, 1987).

36. Jean Déjeux, *Femmes d'Algérie: Légendes, traditions, histoire, littérature* (Paris: La Boîte à Document, 1987), p. 181. Ursula Hart gives a different account of *Picard*'s relation to Algerians.

37. Fanny Colonna, *Aurès/Algérie 1935–1936. Photographies de Thérèse Riviere* (Paris: Maison des Sciences de l'Homme, 1987).

Notes to Chapter 11

1. Kamel Hamdi, *Ali Benhadj, Abassi Madani, Mahfoud Nahnah, Abdellah Djaballah. Différents ou différends?* (Alger: Chihab, 1991), p. 56.

2. See Bruno Etienne, *L'Islamisme radical* (Paris: Hachette 1987) and Tuomo Melasuo, "How to understand Islamism in Algeria," Tampere Peace Research Institute, Nordic Society for Middle Eastern Studies, Copenhagen, October 22–25, 1992. Melasuo is wrong in seeing no continuity between the *'Ulema* movement and the religiose movement.

3. Bertrand Badie, Christian Coulon, Bernard Cubertafond, Paul Dumont, Robert Santucci, *Contestations en pays islamiques*, Collection Publiée par Le Centre des Hautes Etudes sur l'Afrique et l'Asie Modernes, Paris, 1984, p. 42.

4. Malek Bennabi, *Le phénomène coranique. Essai d'une theorie sur le Coran*, 2nd edition, n.p., n.d. First edition published in 1946.

5. Ahmed Aroua, *L'Islam et la science* (Alger: Entreprise Nationale du Livre, 1988), p. 87.

6. *Ibid.*, p. 82.

7. Kamel Hamdi, p. 31.

8. *Ibid.*

9. For an analysis of the social classes produced by the postcolonial state

see my *The Emergence of Classes in Algeria. A Study of Colonialism and Socio-Political Change* (Boulder, Colorado: Westview Press, 1976).

10. Like other people in the Middle East, Algerians saw the bombing of Iraq as an act of aggression against a Muslim country, not a retaliation for Iraq's invasion of Kuwait.

11. Kamel Hamdi, *Ali Benhadj*, p. 75.

12. *Ibid.*, p. 76.

13. *Ibid.*, pp. 76–77.

14. *Ibid.*, pp. 77–78.

15. *Ibid.*, p. 34.

16. *Ibid.*, p. 56.

17. *Ibid.*, p. 47.

18. *Ibid.*, p. 49.

19. *Ibid.*, p. 50.

20. *Ibid.*

21. *Ibid.*, p. 51.

22. *Ibid.*, p. 52.

23. *Ibid.*, p. 53.

24. *Ibid.*, p. 54.

25. Rachid Boudjedra accuses the F.I.S. of this murder in his *FIS de la haine* (Paris: Denoël, 1992).

26. Kamel Hamdi, p. 23.

27. Most books on Islam discuss these two traditions. See, for example, Fazlur Rahman, *Islam* (Chicago: University of Chicago).

28. Kamel Hamdi, p. 51.

29. *The New York Times*, August 18, 1993.

30. Kamel Hamdi, p. 51.

31. *Ibid.*, p. 54.

32. See Keltouma Lalmas and Amina Ouadjina, "Le hidjab a la cité universitaire de jeunes filles d'Alger 1981–1982." Mémoire de Fin de Licence, University of Algiers, Institut des Sciences Sociales, Département de Sociologie, esp. pp. 64–82.

33. The expression "political mosque" was used by the leader of the *Da'wa*, Mahfoud Nahnah, to refer to the political use of Islam. See Kamel Hamdi, p. 66.

34. See, for example, Noureddine Touaba, *Wajabat Al Mar'a Al Muslima Fi Al Kutab Wa Al Sunna*, 3d. edition (Constantine: Daar Al Baath, 1989),

and Abd Al Muna'am Qandil, *Fatnat Al Nissa* (Batna: Daar Al Shihab, n.d.).

35. See *The New York Times*, March 31 and April 4, 1994.

Notes to Conclusion

1. Gaston Bachelard, "La psychanalyse de la connaissance objective," in *Gaston Bachelard. Epistemologie, textes choisis par Dominique Lecourt* (Vendôme: Presses Universitaires de France, 1974), p. 160.

References Cited

Achour, Christiane, *Entre le roman rose et le roman exotique, la chrysalide de A. Lemsine*. Alger: Entreprise Nationale du Livre, 1978.

———, *Anthologie de la littérature algérienne de langue française*. Alger: Entreprise Algérienne de Presse, 1990.

Ageron, Charles-Robert, *Les algériens Musulmans et la France, 1871–1919*. Paris: Presses Universitaires de France, 1968.

———, "Le mouvement jeune algérien," in Charles-André Julien, editor, *Etudes Maghrébines. Mélanges*. Paris: Presses Universitaires de France, 1964.

Al Hibri, Azizah, "A Study of Islamic Herstory: Or How Did We Ever Get into this Mess?" in Al Hibri, ed., *Women and Islam*. New York: Pergamon, 1982.

Alloula Malek, *The Colonial Harem*. Minneapolis: University of Minnesota, 1986.

Amrane, Djamila, "La femme algérienne et la guerre de libération nationale," in *Combattantes de la lutte armée, les femmes aussi ecriront l'histoire*. Monograph published by the review *El Djazairiya* on the twentieth anniversary of independence.

Algérie, naissance d'une société nouvelle. Le texte intégral de la charte nationale adoptée par le peuple algérien. Paris: Edition Sociale, 1976.

Archives d'Outre-Mer, Aix-en-Provence, Bureaux Arabes Départmentaux. F 80 507 1849–1856 Monthly Reports. 22S 2 Education Reports. 1JJ11 1856–1862, 1JJ14 1863–1864 Reports on Marriage and Divorce for the cities of Oran, Mostaganem, Sidi Bel Abbès, and Tlemcen.

Aroua, Ahmed, *L'Islam et la science*. Alger: Entreprise Nationale du Livre, 1988.

Aslaoui, Leila, *Dérives de justice*. Alger: Bouchène, 1990.

Auclert, Hubertine, *Les femmes arabes en Algérie*. Paris: Société d'Editions Littéraires, 1900.

Avant-projet de code de la famille, Ministère de la Justice, 1401H–1981.

"Les aventures de Thédenat esclave et ministre d'un bey d'Afrique (XVIIIs.)," *Revue africaine*, 1948.

Bachelard, Gaston, *Gaston Bachelard. Epistémologie, textes choisis par Dominique Lecourt*. Vendôme: Presses Universitaires de France, 1974.

Badie, Bertrand, et al., *Contestations en pays Islamiques*. Paris: Centre des Hautes Etudes sur l'Afrique et l'Asie Modernes, 1984.

Général Du Barail, *Mes souvenirs*. Paris: Plon, 1894.

Belamri, Rabah, *Les graines de la douleur. Contes populaires*. Paris: Editions Publisud, 1982

Belhamissi, Moulay, *L'histoire de Mostaganem*. Alger: Société Nationale d'Edition et de Diffusion, 1982.

Benabdessadok, Chérifa, "Pour une analyse du disours sur la femme algérienne." Diplôme d'Etudes Avancées en Linguistique. Université d'Alger, 1977.

———, "Synthèse des écrits sur la femme et la lutte armée, in *Combattantes de la lutte armée, les femmes aussi ecriront l'histoire*. Monograph edited by *El Djazairiya*, 1982.

———, "Tradition et modernisme: Un faux débat?" *Présences de femmes*. Alger: Office des Publications Universitaires, 1984.

Benachenhou, Abdellatif, *Formation du sous-développement en Algérie*. Alger: Office des Publications Universitaires, 1976.

Benali Zineb and Achour, Christiane, "Le Discours culturel des manuels de langue française des enseignements primaire et moyen." *Balades dans la culture en Algérie en 1979*. Alger: Office des Publications Universitaires, 1984.

Benallègue, Nora, "La femme dans la lutte d'indépendance et la reconstruction nationale," *U.N.E.S.C.O.* Vol. XXXV, 4, 1983.

Benhadouga, Abdelhamid, *La mise à nu*. Translated from Arabic by Marcel Bois. Alger: Société Nationale d'Edition et de Diffusion, 1981.

Benmelha, Ghaouti, "La famille algérienne entre le droit des personnes et le droit public." *Revue algérienne juridique, economique, et politique*. Special issue, 1982.

Bennabi, Malek, *Le phenomène coranique: Essai d'une théorie sur le Coran*. Second edition, n.p., n.d. First edition published in 1946.

Berque, Augustin, "Les intellectuels algériens," *Revue africaine*, 1947.

Berque, Jacques, *Le Maghreb entre deux guerres*. Paris: Editions du Seuil, 1962.

Berteuil, Arsène, *L'Algérie française*. Vol. 1. Paris: Dentu, 1856.

Bertrand, Martine, *Le jeu de la boqala*. Paris: Editions Publisud, 1983.

Bodichon, *Etudes sur l'Algérie et l'Afrique.* Alger: Chez l'Auteur, 1847.

Borrmans, Maurice, *Statut personnel et famille au Maghreb de 1940 à nos jours.* Dissertation, University of Paris IV, March 9, 1971. Service de Reproduction des Thèses, Université de Lille, III, 1972.

———, *Document sur la famille au Maghreb de 1940 à nos jours.* (I.P.O, 1979) Estrao da "Oriente Moderno", Vol. LIX, n.p., n.d.

Boucebci, Mahfoud, *Psychiatrie, société, et développement.* Alger: Société Nationale d'Edition et de Diffusion, 1982.

Boudjedra, Rachid, *La répudiation.* Paris: Denoël, 1969.

———, *Journal d'une femme insomniaque.* Alger: Dar El Idjtihad, 1989.

———, *Le démantèlement.* Paris: Denoël, 1982.

———, *Le FIS de la haine.* Paris: Denoël, 1992.

Bourdieu, Pierre, *Outline of a Theory of Practice.* Cambridge: Cambridge University Press, 1977.

Boutefnouchet, Mostéfa, *La famille algérienne. Evolution et caractéristiques récentes.* Alger: Société Nationale d'Edition et de Diffusion, 1980.

Boyer, Pierre, *La vie quotidienne à Alger à la veille de l'intervention française.* Paris: Hachette, 1963.

Bruno, Etienne, *l'Islamisme radical.* Paris: Hachette, 1987.

Bugéja, Marie, *Nos soeurs Musulmanes.* Alger: Editions de France, 1931.

Bulkin, Elly, et al., *Yours in Struggle.* New York: Long Haul Press, 1984.

Cadi-Mostefai, Mériem, "L'image de la femme algérienne pendant la guerre (1954–1962) à partir de textes paralittéraires et littéraires." Diplôme d'Etudes Approfondies. Université d'Alger, 1978.

Chaillou, Lucien, *L'Algérie en 1871. Mémoire du consul C-Ph. Vallière.* Toulon: Chez l'Auteur, Villa "Beau Site", 1974.

Charnay, Jean-Paul, *La vie Musulmane en Algérie d'après la jurisprudence du XXème siecle.* Paris: Presses Universitaires de France, 1965.

La Charte d'Alger. Ensemble des textes adoptés par le premier congrès du parti du F.l.N. Alger: F.L.N., Commission Centrale d'Orientation, 1964.

Christelow, Allan, *Muslim Law Courts and the French Colonial State in Algeria.* Princeton: Princeton University Press, 1985.

Code de la famille. Alger: Ministère de l'Information, 1988.

Collins, Patricia Hill, *Black Feminist Thought. Knowledge, Consciousness, and the Politics of Empowerment.* New York: Routledge, 1991.

Colonna, Fanny, *Aurès/Algérie 1935–1936. Photographies de Thérèse Rivière.* Paris: Maison des Sciences de l'Homme, 1987.

Débèche, Djamila, "Les Musulmans algériens et la scolarisation," Lecture sponsored by the Comité de Scolarisation et de Lutte Contre l'Analphabétisme, Alger, Jan. 5, 1951. Archives d'Outre Mer, Aix-en-Provence, B4432.

————, "L'enseignement de la lange arabe en Algérie et le droit de vote aux femmes algériennes." June 8, 1951. Archives d'Outre Mer, Aix-en-Provence, B345.

————, *Leila, une jeune fille algérienne*. Alger: Imprimerie Charras, 1947.

————, *Aziza*. Alger: Imbert, 1955.

Dejeux, Jean, *Femmes d'Algérie. Légendes, traditions, histoire, littérature*. Paris: La Boîte à Documents, 1987

Djebar, Assia, *Femmes d'Alger dans leur appartement*. Paris: Edition des Femmes, 1981.

Djeghloul, Abdelkader, *Huit études sur l'Algérie*. Alger: Entreprise Nationale du Livre, 1986.

————, *Lettrés, intellectuels, et militants en Algérie, 1880–1950*. Alger: Office des Publications Universitaires, 1988.

Deloncle, Pierre, *La caravane aux éperons verts. Mission Alger-Niger*. Paris: Plon, 1927.

Dermenghem, Emile, *Le pays d'Abel*. Paris: Gallimard, 1960.

Desparmet, J., "Les Réactions Nationalitaires en Algérie," *Bulletin de la Société de Géographie d'Alger et de l'Afrique du Nord*. No. 132, 1987.

————, "L'entrée des Français à Alger vue par le Cheikh Abd-El-Kader," in *Revue Africaine*, 1930.

————, "L'oeuvre de la France en Algérie jugée par les indigènes," *Bulletin de la Société de Géographie d'Algérie et de l'Afrique du Nord*, Vol. XV, 1910.

————, *Coutumes, institutions, croyances des indigènes en Algérie*, Vol. 1, *L'Enfance, le mariage et la famille (Alger: "La Typo-litho et Jules Carbonal*, 1939.

Dib, Mohammed, *La grande maison*. Paris: Editions du Seuil, 1952.

————, *L'incendie*. Paris: Editions du Seuil, 1954.

————, *Le métier à tisser*. Paris: Editions du Seuil, 1957.

Dib-Marouf, Chafika, *Fonctions de la dot dans la cité algérienne: Tlemcen et son "hawz"*. Alger: Office des Publications Universitaires, 1984.

Dinet, Etienne and Ben Brahim, Sliman, *Khadra la danseuse des Ouled Nail*. Paris: Piazza, n.d.

Eberhardt, Isabelle, *Notes de route*. Paris: Eugène Fasquelle, 1923.

Esquer, Gabriel, "L'Algérie vue par les ecrivains," *Simoun*, 1925.

Fanon, Frantz, *A Dying Colonialism*. New York: Grove Press, 1967.

Foucault, Michel, *Language, Counter-Memory, Practice*. D.F. Bouchard, ed. Ithaca: Cornell University, 1977.

Fromentin, Eugène, *Une année dans le Sahel*. Paris: Plon, 1884.

Ghalem, Ali, *Une femme pour mon fils*. Paris: Editions Syros, 1979.

Gaudry, Mathéa, *La femme Chaouia de l'Aurès. Etude de sociologie Berbère.* Paris: Librairie Orientaliste Paul Geuthner, 1929.

Geertz, Clifford, *Islam Observed.* New Haven: Yale University Press, 1968.

————, *Local Knowledge: Further Essays in Interpretive Anthropology.* New York: Basic Books, 1983.

Goldmann, Lucien, *The Hidden God. A Study of the Tragic Vision in the Pensées of Pascal and the Tragédies of Racine.* New York: Routledge and Kegan Paul, 1964.

————, *Marxisme et sciences humaines.* Paris: Gallimard, 1970.

Grandguillaume, Gilbert, *Arabisation et politique linguistique au Maghreb.* Paris: Editions G.-P. Maisonneuve et Larose, 1983.

Guha, Ranajit, ed., *Subaltern Studies VI: Writings on South Asian History and Society.* Delhi, Oxford, New York: Oxford University Press, 1989.

Habermas, Jürgen, *Legitimation Crisis.* Boston: Beacon, 1975.

Hadj-Sadok, Mohammed, "A Travers la Berbérie Orientale avec le Voyageur Al Warthilani," *Revue Africaine,* 1951.

Hamdi, Kamel, *Ali Benhadj, Abassi Madani, Mahfoud Nahnah, Abdellah Djaballah. Différents ou différends?* Alger: Chihab, 1991.

Hart, Ursula Kingsmill, *Two Ladies of Algeria. The Lives and Times of Aurélie Picard and Isabelle Eberhardt.* Athens: Ohio University Center for International Studies, 1987.

Horne, Alistair, *A Savage War of Peace, Algeria 1954–1962.* New York: Viking, 1977.

Human Development 1990. Published for the United Nations Development Program, New York: Oxford University Press, 1990.

Kadra-Hadjaji, Houaria, "La Kahina, personnage littéraire." *Présences de femmes.* Alger: Office des Publications Universitaires, 1984.

Kateb, Yacine, *Nedjma.* Paris: Editions du Seuil, 1956.

Khodja, Souad, *Les Algériennes du quotidien.* Alger: Entreprise Nationale du Livre, 1985.

ISIS, Bulletin du Groupe de Recherche sur les Femmes Algériennes. Vol. 2. Oran: C.D.S.H., 1982.

Julien, Charles-André, *Histoire de l'Algérie contemporaine. La conquête et les débuts de la colonisation, 1827–1871.* Paris: Presses Universitaires de France, 1964.

Kaddache, Mahfoud, *L'Emir Khaled.* Alger: Office des Publications Universitaires, 1987.

Ladjali, Malika, *L'espacement des naissances dans le tiers monde. L'expérience algérienne.* Alger: Office des Publications Algériennes, 1985.

Lalmas, Keltoum et Ouadjina, Amina, "Le hidjab à la cité universitaire de jeunes filles d'Alger, 1981–1982." Mémoire de Fin de Licence, Université d'Alger, Institut des Sciences Sociales, 1982.

Lambing, Clement. *The French in Algeria*. New York: Wiley Putnam, 1845.

Lasnari, Ahmed, "Myriem dans les palmes, roman de Mohammed Ould Cheikh." *C.R.I.D.S.S.H.* No. 7, 1983.

Lazreg, Marnia, *The Emergence of Classes in Algeria. A Study of Colonialism and Socio-Political Change*. Boulder: Westview Press, 1976.

————, "The Kabyle-Berber Movement in Algeria," in Adamantia Pollis and Peter Schwab, eds., *Human Rights: Cultural and Ideological Perspectives*. New York: Praeger, 1979.

————, "Media and Cultural Dependency in Algeria." *Studies of Broadcasting* #26, 1990.

————, "Feminism and Difference: The Perils of Writing as a Woman on Women in Algeria." *Feminist Studies*, vol. 14, No. 1, 1988.

————, "Women, Work and Social Change in Algeria," in Sharon Stichter and Jane Parpart, eds., *Women, Employment and the Family in the International Division of Labor*. London: Macmillan, 1990.

Lehuraux, Léon, *Musulmans 1938. Un mariage arabe dans le sud Algérien*. Alger: Editions Baconnier, 1938.

Levy, Reuben, *The Social Structure of Islam*. Cambridge: Cambridge University Press, 1959.

Lemsine, Aicha, *La chrysalide*. Paris: Des Femmes, 1976.

Lepoil, Maurice, *Faut-il abolir la prostitution?* Alger: Imprimerie Ancienne V. Heintz, 1947.

Louis, Marie-Victoire, "Les algériennes, la lutte." *Les Temps Modernes*, July–August, 1982.

Mahiou, Ahmed, "Rupture ou continuité du droit en Algérie?" *Revue algérienne juridique, economique, et politique*. Special issue. 1982.

Marchand, Dr. H., *La prostitution indigène à Alger*. Alger: Imprimerie Fontana, 1937.

McAfee, Katherine, *Storm Signals*. New York: South End Press, 1991.

Méchakra, Yamina, *La grotte eclatée*. Alger: Entreprise Nationale du Livre, 1986.

Megherbi, Abdelghani, "Stratégies de cinéastes algériens et habitudes cinématographiques," in *Recueil des conférences. Aspects du changement socio-culturel algérien*. Paris: Centre Culturel Algérien, 1987.

Mélia, Jean, *Le triste sort des indigènes Musulmans d'Algérie*. Paris: Mercure de France, 1935.

Melasuo, Tuomo, "How to Understand Islamism in Algeria." *Tampere Peace Research Institute*, Nordic Society for Middle Eastern Studies, Copenhagen, October 22–25, 1992.

Merad, Ali, *Le réformisme Musulman en Algérie de 1925 à 1940*. Paris: Mouton, 1967.

———, *Ibn Badis commentateur du Coran*. Paris: Librairie Orientaliste Paul Geuthner, 1971.

Mernissi, Fatima, *Beyond the Veil: Male-Female Dynamics in a Modern Muslim Society*. Cambridge: Schenkman, 1975.

Messaadi, Sakina, *Les romancières coloniales et la femme colonisée. Contribution à une étude de la littérature coloniale en Algérie*. Alger: Entreprise Nationale du Livre, 1990.

Minces, Juliette, *The House of Obedience. Women in the Arab World*. London: Zed Press, 1980.

Moore, Barrington, *Injustice: The Social Bases of Obedience and Revolt*. New York: M.E. Sharpe, 1978.

Morelet, M., *Les maures de Constantine en 1840*. Dijon: Imprimerie Darantière, 1876.

Noushi, André, "Le sens de certains chiffres: Croissance urbaine et vie politique en Algérie," in Charles-André Julien, ed., *Etudes Maghrébines. Mélanges*. Paris: Presses Universitaires de France, 1964.

"Observations sur la prostitution," *Gouvernement Général d'Alger*. 1898.

Ouitis, A., *Les contradictions sociales et leur expression symbolique dans le sétifois*. Alger: Société Nationale d'Edition et de Diffusion, 1977.

Ould-Cheikh, Mohammed, *Myriem dans les Palmes*. Reprinted. Alger: Office des Publications Universitaires, 1985.

Plan de Constantine 1959–1961. Alger: Délégation Générale du Gouvernement en Algérie, Direction du Plan et des Etudes, 1960.

Le Problème de la prostitution et ses aspects particuliers," *Association Catholique de la Jeunesse Française*. Alger: 1947.

Le programme de Tripoli, le F.L.N. et la constitution de l'Algérie socialiste. ed. la Tendance Révolutionnaire du Parti Communiste Français. Paris: 1964.

Promesses, No. 92 n.d.

Qandil, Abd Al Muna'am, *Fatnat Al Nissa*. Batna: Daar Al Shihab, n.d.

Raffinot, Marc et Jacquemot, Pierre, *Le capitalisme d'état algérien*. Paris: Maspéro, 1987.

Rahman, Fazlur, *Islam*. Chicago: Chicago University Press, 1979.

Roches, Léon, *Trente deux ans à travers l'Islam*. Vol. 1. Paris: Firmin Diderot, 1884.

Rouissi, Moncer, *Population et société au Maghreb*. Tunis: Office des Presses Universitaires, 1976.

Rowbotham, Sheila, *Women, Resistance, and Revolution*. New York: Vintage, 1974.

Saadawi, Nawal, *The Hidden Face of Eve*. Boston: Beacon Press, 1980.

Saadia et Lakhdar, *L'aliénation coloniale et la résistance de famille algérienne*. Lausanne: La Cité, 1961.

Sai, Fatima Zohra, *Mouvement national et question feminine des origines à la guerre de libération*. C.R.I.D.S.S.H., University of Oran, 1984.

———, "Quelques remarques à propos de la codification du droit de la famille. *C.R.I.D.S.S.H.*, No. 7, 1983.

Sartre, Jean-Paul, *Search for a Method*. New York: Vintage, 1963.

Smith, Margaret, *Rabi'a the Mystic and her Fellow Saints in Islam*. Amsterdam: Pluto Press, 1974.

Spivak, Gayatry Chakravorty, " 'Draupadi' by Mahasveta Devi," Elizabeth Abel, ed., *Writing and Sexual Difference*. Chicago: University of Chicago Press, 1982.

Statistiques. Situation de l'emploi 1986. Alger: Office National des Statistiques.

Tailliart, Charles, *L'Algérie dans la littératire française*. Paris: Librairie Ancienne Edouard Champion, 1925.

———, "Le travail feminin, emploi salarié, et travail domestique." *Cahiers du Centre de Documentation des Sciences Humaines*. 33, 1980.

Talahite, Fatiha, "Lu dans la presse." *Présences de femmes. Gestes acquis, gestes conquis*. Hiwar, n.p., 1986.

Taleb Ibrahimi, Ahmed, *De la décolonisation à la révolution culturelle (1962– 1972)*. Alger: Société Nationale d'Edition et de Diffusion, 1973.

Tinker, Irene, *Persistent Inequalities*. Oxford: Oxford University Press, 1990.

Touaba, Noureddine, *Wajabat Al Mar'a Al Muslima Fi Al Kutab Wa Al Sunna*. Constantine: Daar Al Baath, 1989.

Toualbi, Noureddine, *Le sacré ambigu ou les avatars psychologiques du changement*. Alger: Entreprise Nationale du Livre, 1984.

Turin, Yvonne, *Affrontements culturels dans l'Algérie coloniale*. Alger: Edition National Algérienne du Livre, 1983.

Vandevelde-Daillière, Hélène, "Ou en est le problème du code de la famille en Algérie?" *Machrek/Maghreb*. No. 97, 1982.

Newspapers Cited

El Moudjahed
El Moudjahid
Algérie actualité
Mag 7
The Sunday New York Times
La République algérienne

Glossary

'ada: old custom

Armée de Libération Nationale: Army that waged the struggle against the French, 1954–1962

'Azriya (pl. Azriyat): Women of the Aurès Mountains reputed for their libertine ways

Bey: Provincial governor during the Ottoman period

Beylik: Domain under a Bey's jurisdiction. Also used to refer to the Ottoman state.

Boqala: Divination game played by women

Dey: Head of the Regency of Algiers

Front Islamique du Salut (F.I.S.): Front of Islamic Salvation. Leading religiose opposition party banned in 1992

Front de Libération Nationale (F.L.N.): Political association that led the movement of decolonization in 1954–1962. Since 1962, it has been the party in power.

Gourbi: Modest rural dwelling. Also, a shack.

Guwal or Maddah: A man who alternately sang and spoke in verse at regular public meetings throughout the nineteenth century and the first half of the twentieth century, about political and social issues

Habous: Designation of a religious institution as the ultimate owner of property willed to relatives thus preventing its sale. The term also refers to property donated to a mosque

Hammam: Turkish bath

Janissary: Ottoman military corps

Jdib: Cathartic dance practiced by women to the beat of drums and castanets played originally by Black men

Keshf: Exposure or discovery

Médersa: School. During the colonial era this term referred specifically to specialized schools where students were taught in both Arabic and French

Moudjahid (masc.) Moudjahida (fem.): Fighter

Nailiya (pl. Nailiyat): Women of the Ouled Nail tribe reputed for their dances and freedom to choose their husbands

ser: Secret or charm

Taleb (pl. Tolba): Student. It also refers to a man who engages in magical practices involving written materials such as talismans

Qadi: Judge practicing Islamic law

'Ulama (pl. of 'Alim): Scholars (usually of Islamic law)

Union Nationale des Femmes Algériennes (U.N.F.A.): Association of women created by the F.L.N. party in 1962

Wa'da: Ritual of exorcism

Waqt: Time, especially historical time or period

Wilaya: District. Also used during the war of decolonization as military zone

Zawiya: Usually seat of a Sufi order comprised of a mosque, a school and other social services

Index